Some comments from our readers...

"I have to praise you and your company on the fine products you turn out. I have twelve of the *Teach Yourself VISUALLY* and *Simplified* books in my house. They were instrumental in helping me pass a difficult computer course. Thank you for creating books that are easy to follow."

–*Gordon Justin (Brielle, NJ)*

"I commend your efforts and your success. I teach in an outreach program for the Dr. Eugene Clark Library in Lockhart, TX. Your *Teach Yourself VISUALLY* books are incredible and I use them in my computer classes. All my students love them!"

–*Michele Schalin (Lockhart, TX)*

"Thank you so much for helping people like me learn about computers. The Maran family is just what the doctor ordered. Thank you, thank you, thank you."

–*Carol Moten (New Kensington, PA)*

"I would like to take this time to compliment maranGraphics on creating such great books. Thank you for making it clear. Keep up the good work."

–*Kirk Santoro (Burbank, CA)*

"I write to extend my thanks and appreciation for your books. They are clear, easy to follow, and straight to the point. Keep up the good work!"

–*Seward Kollie (Dakar, Senegal)*

"What fantastic teaching books you have produced! Congratulations to you and your staff. You deserve the Nobel prize in Education in the Software category. Thanks for helping me to understand computers."

–*Bruno Tonon (Melbourne, Australia)*

"Over time, I have bought a number of your 'Read Less-Learn More' books. For me, they are THE way to learn anything easily."

–*José A. Mazón (Cuba, NY)*

"I was introduced to maranGraphics about four years ago and YOU ARE THE GREATEST THING THAT EVER HAPPENED TO INTRODUCTORY COMPUTER BOOKS!"

–*Glenn Nettleton (Huntsville, AL)*

"Compliments To The Chef!! Your books are extraordinary! Or, simply put, Extra-Ordinary, meaning way above the rest! THANK YOU THANK YOU THANK YOU! for creating these."

–*Christine J. Manfrin (Castle Rock, CO)*

"I'm a grandma who was pushed by an 11-year-old grandson to join the computer age. I found myself hopelessly confused and frustrated until I discovered the Visual series. I'm no expert by any means now, but I'm a lot further along than I would have been otherwise. Thank you!"

–*Carol Louthain (Logansport, IN)*

"Thank you, thank you, thank you....for making it so easy for me to break into this high-tech world. I now own four of your books. I recommend them to anyone who is a beginner like myself. Now....if you could just do one for programming VCR's, it would make my day!"

–*Gay O'Donnell (Calgary, Alberta, Canada)*

"You're marvelous! I am greatly in your debt."

–*Patrick Baird (Lacey, WA)*

**maranGraphics is a family-run business
located near Toronto, Canada.**

At **maranGraphics**, we believe in producing great computer books — one book at a time.

maranGraphics has been producing high-technology products for over 25 years, which enables us to offer the computer book community a unique communication process.

Our computer books use an integrated communication process, which is very different from the approach used in other computer books. Each spread is, in essence, a flow chart — the text and screen shots are totally incorporated into the layout of the spread.

Introductory text and helpful tips complete the learning experience.

maranGraphics' approach encourages the left and right sides of the brain to work together — resulting in faster orientation and greater memory retention.

Above all, we are very proud of the handcrafted nature of our books. Our carefully-chosen writers are experts in their fields, and spend countless hours researching and organizing the content for each topic. Our artists rebuild every screen shot to provide the best clarity possible, making our

screen shots the most precise and easiest to read in the industry. We strive for perfection, and believe that the time spent handcrafting each element results in the best computer books money can buy.

Thank you for purchasing this book. We hope you enjoy it!

Sincerely,

Robert Maran
President
maranGraphics
Rob@maran.com
www.maran.com

CREDITS

Acquisitions, Editorial, and Media Development

Project Editor
Sarah Hellert

Acquisitions Editor
Jen Dorsey

Product Development Supervisor
Lindsay Sandman

Copy Editor
Jill Mazurczyk

Technical Editor
Yanier Gonzalez

Editorial Manager
Rev Mengle

Permissions Editor
Laura Moss

Special Help
Timothy J. Borek, Yanier Gonzalez

Manufacturing
Allan Conley, Linda Cook,
Paul Gilchrist, Jennifer Guynn

Production

Book Design
maranGraphics®

Production Coordinator
Dale White

Layout
Melanie DesJardins, LeAndra Johnson
Kristin McMullan

Screen Artists
Mark Harris, Jill A. Proll

Illustrators
Ronda David-Burroughs, David E. Gregory

Proofreaders
Christine Pingleton

Quality Control
John Bitter, Carl Pierce, Charles Spencer

Indexer
Anne Leach

ACKNOWLEDGMENTS

General and Administrative

Wiley Technology Publishing Group: Richard Swadley, Vice President and Executive Group Publisher; Bob Ipsen, Vice President and Executive Publisher; Barry Pruett, Vice President and Publisher; Joseph Wikert, Vice President and Publisher; Mary Bednarek, Editorial Director; Mary C. Corder, Editorial Director; Andy Cummings, Editorial Director.

Wiley Production for Branded Press: Debbie Stailey, Production Director

ABOUT THE AUTHORS

Janine Warner is the author of several books about the Internet including *Dreamweaver For Dummies* and *Managing Web Projects For Dummies*. She is also a part-time faculty member at the University of Miami, where she teaches a Dreamweaver Web Design course for the School of Communication.

From 1998 to 2000, she worked for *The Miami Herald*, first as their Online Managing Editor, and later as Director of New Media, managing a team of designers, programmers, journalists, and marketing staff for *The Miami Herald*, *El Nuevo Herald*, and Miami.com. She also served as Director of Latin American Operations for CNET Networks, an international technology media company.

From 1994 to 1998, Janine ran Visiontec Communications, a Web design business in Northern California, where she worked on such diverse projects as the corporate intranet for Levi Strauss & Co., an extranet sales site for AirTouch International, and e-commerce solutions for many small- and medium-size businesses.

A syndicated newspaper columnist, Janine's Web Strategies business column appears online and off, including in *The Miami Herald*. An award-winning former reporter, she earned a degree in journalism and Spanish from the University of Massachusetts, Amherst, and worked for several years in Northern California as a reporter and editor. She speaks fluent Spanish.

To learn more, visit www.janinewarner.com.

Ivonne Berkowitz is the co-author of *Dreamweaver MX For Dummies* and is the Web Designer for PBS&J, a top-ranking engineering firm in South Florida.

She also consults for ModernMethod, a Web design firm that has worked on projects for numerous clients, including Metabolic Nutrition, the University of Miami, and the Orange Bowl Committee.

Ivonne's strengths include graphic design for the Web, Web site planning, Flash animation, and logo design. Ivonne's Web design talents have also landed her consultancy positions with major corporations, such as Knight-Ridder.

Her experience, design talent, and almost-unhealthy attention to detail have also ushered a flurry of freelance clients her way, including such names as *The New York Post* Online Store, Florida Counseling Association, photographer Robin Hill, photographer/illustrator Philip Brooker, forensic psychologist Dr. Charles Winick, and the popular South Florida cult horror store, Oh! The Horror.

Ivonne lives in Miami Springs, Florida, where she spends her free time (if she gets any!) working out, vegging in front of the TV, working obsessively on home improvement projects, and writing "the big novel" in the form of an e-journal.

AUTHORS' ACKNOWLEDGMENTS

Janine Warner:

I've always thanked many people in my books — former teachers, mentors, friends — but I have been graced by so many wonderful people now that no publisher will give me enough pages to thank them all. So I focus here on the people who made *this* book possible.

Above all others, I have to thank my incredible co-author Ivonne Berkowitz for never missing a deadline and adding her beautiful design work to bring this book to life in many of the Web site examples. Thanks also to Yanier Gonzales, who was not only a detail-oriented Tech Editor: he also deserves credit for writing and revising the two most complex chapters in this book. I have no doubt they could both write their own books and any publisher would be lucky to have them. Thanks also to Adam Cohen for his quick abilities in figuring out how to help redo screen shots at the last minute and to Jenna Papakalos for all her effort and support.

Thanks to Sarah Hellert, our ever-understanding editor for keeping the rest of us on track. Thanks to Jen Dorsey for helping me recruit the best team I could and to Bob Woerner for letting her "borrow" us. Thanks to Margot, my awesome agent. And, of course, thanks to my four fabulous parents Malinda, Janice, Helen, and Robin.

And finally, let me thank the beautiful stars that this book is finally done. Complete. Finished. This is it. (And don't even tell me those aren't complete sentences.)

Ivonne Berkowitz:

Wow. Second book in one year. When it rains it really does pour. I'm so thankful to everyone I've come in contact with during the process of putting together this revision. Family, friends, editors, co-workers — everyone has been so supportive of my work, and so patient and understanding about all the adjustments I've had to make at home and at the office in order to get this book finished.

This one's for you guys ... Janine Warner, my talented co-author; Yanier Gonzalez, the love of my life and the best tech editor in the world (I'll put money on that); Sarah Hellert and Jen Dorsey, two of the most pleasant editors I've been lucky to work with; Jenna Mandic-Papakalos, a talented technical writer with a very large collection of "hats"; my families, Mom, Dad, Emilio, George, Heri, Mari, and the rest of y'all; the gang at ModernMethod; my co-workers and bosses at PBS&J; my friends new and old, distant and close.

Lastly, I'd like to dedicate this book (and don't laugh!) to my cat, Cat Berkowitz, who almost died recently. He hung in there and made it through. Without this boy in my life, I don't know what I'd do. He kept me company and kept my feet warm while I slaved away into the wee hours taking screenshots for this book. I love you Cat!

TABLE OF CONTENTS

Chapter 1

GETTING STARTED WITH DREAMWEAVER

Chapter 2

SETTING UP YOUR WEB SITE

Chapter 3

EXPLORING THE DREAMWEAVER INTERFACE

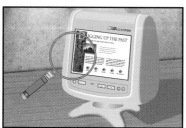

Chapter 4

UNDERSTANDING HTML CODE

Chapter 5

FORMATTING AND STYLING TEXT

Chapter 6

WORKING WITH IMAGES AND MULTIMEDIA

TABLE OF CONTENTS

Chapter 7

CREATING HYPERLINKS

Chapter 8

USING TABLES TO DESIGN A WEB PAGE

Chapter 9

CREATING PAGES WITH FRAMES

Chapter 10

CREATING WEB-BASED FORMS

Chapter 11

USING LIBRARY ITEMS AND TEMPLATES

TABLE OF CONTENTS

Chapter 12

CREATING AND APPLYING STYLE SHEETS

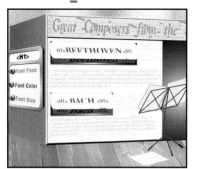

Chapter 13

USING DYNAMIC HTML

Chapter 14

PUBLISHING A WEB SITE

Chapter 15

Chapter 16

System DSN   User DSN   File DSN

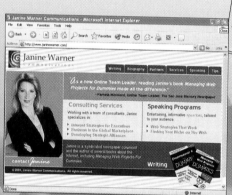

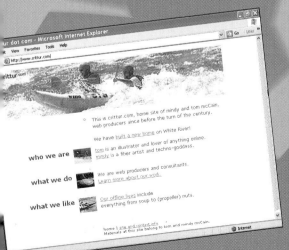
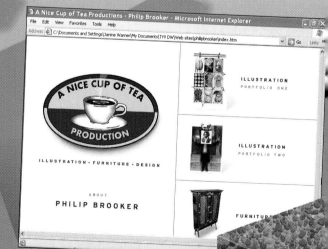

CHAPTER 1

Getting Started with Dreamweaver

This chapter describes the World Wide Web, introduces the different types of information you can put on a Web site, and tells you how to start Dreamweaver.

INTRODUCTION TO THE WORLD WIDE WEB

You can use Dreamweaver to create and publish pages on the World Wide Web.

World Wide Web

The *World Wide Web (Web)* is a global collection of documents located on Internet-connected computers that you can access by using a Web browser. Web pages are connected to one another through clickable hyperlinks.

Web Site

A *Web site* is a collection of linked Web pages stored on a Web server. Most Web sites have a *home page* that describes the information located on the Web site and provides a place where people can start their exploration of the site. The pages of a good Web site are intuitively organized and have a common theme.

Dreamweaver

Dreamweaver is a program that enables you to create Web pages with links, text, images, and multimedia. You create your Web pages on your computer and then use Dreamweaver to transfer the finished files to a Web server where others can view them on the Web.

HTML

Hypertext Markup Language (HTML) is the formatting language used to create Web pages. You can use Dreamweaver to create Web pages without knowing HTML because Dreamweaver writes the HTML for you behind the scenes.

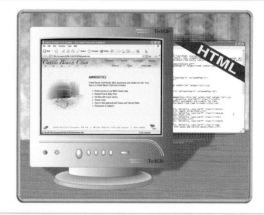

Web Server

A *Web server* is a computer that is connected to the Internet and has software that "serves" Web pages to visitors. Each Web page that you view in a browser on the World Wide Web resides on a Web server somewhere on the Internet. When you are ready to publish your pages on the Web, you can use Dreamweaver to transfer your files to a Web server.

Web Browser

A *Web browser* is a program that can download Web documents from the Internet, interpret their HTML, and then display the Web page text and any associated images and multimedia as a Web page. Two popular Web browsers are Microsoft Internet Explorer and Netscape Navigator.

PARTS OF A WEB PAGE

You can communicate your message on the Web in a variety of ways. The following are some of the common elements found on Web pages.

Text

Text is the simplest type of content you can publish on the Web. Dreamweaver enables you to change the size, color, and font of Web-page text and organize it into paragraphs, headings, and lists. Perhaps the best thing about text is that practically everyone can view it, no matter what type of browser or Internet connection a person may have, and it downloads very quickly.

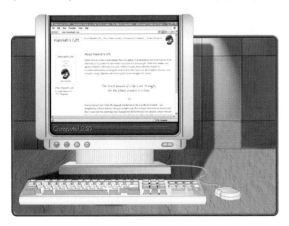

Images

You can take photos for your Web site with a digital camera and you can scan drawings, logos, or other images for the Web by using a scanner. Images must be created or edited in a graphics program, such as Adobe Photoshop or Macromedia Fireworks, and then placed on Web pages with Dreamweaver.

Links

Usually called simply a *link*, a *hyperlink* is text or an image that has been associated with another file. You can access the other file by clicking the hyperlink. Hyperlinks usually link to other Web pages or other Web sites, but they can also link to other locations on the same page or to other types of files.

Tables

Tables organize information in columns and rows on your Web page, and they are used for much more than just organizing financial data. Tables provide one of the best ways to create complex Web designs. By turning off a table's borders and setting it to span an entire page, you can use a table to organize the entire layout of a page. See Chapter 8 for more about tables.

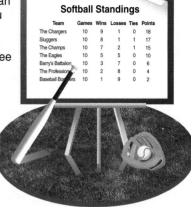

Forms

Forms reverse the information flow on Web sites — they enable your site's visitors to send information back to you. With Dreamweaver, you can create forms that include text fields, drop-down menus, radio buttons, and other elements.

Frames

In a framed Web site, the browser window is divided into several rectangular frames, and a different Web page is loaded into each frame. Users can scroll through content in each frame, independently of the content in the other frames. Dreamweaver offers visual tools for building frame-based Web sites.

PLAN YOUR WEB SITE

Carefully planning your pages before you build them can help ensure that your finished Web site looks great and is well organized. Before you start building your site, take a little time to organize your ideas and gather the materials you will need.

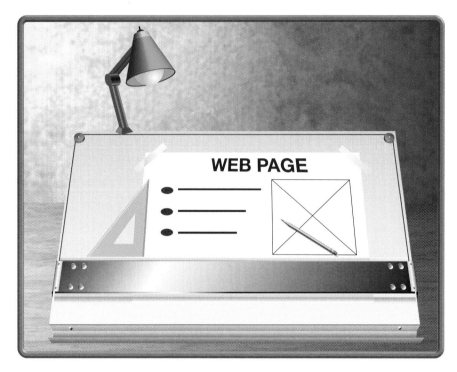

Organize Your Ideas

Build your site on paper before you start building it in Dreamweaver. Sketching out a site map, with rectangles representing Web pages and arrows representing links, can help you visualize the size and scope of your project. Use sticky notes if you want to be able to move pages around as you plan your site.

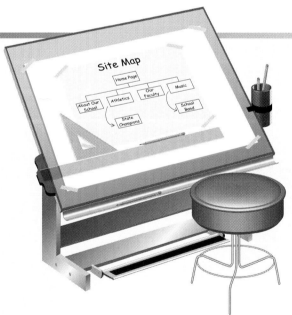

Gather Your Content

Before you start building your Web site, gather all the elements you want on your Web site. This process may require writing text, taking photos, and designing graphics. It can also involve producing multimedia content such as audio and video files. Gathering all your material together in the beginning makes it easier to organize your Web site.

Define Your Audience

Identifying your target audience can help you decide what kind of content to offer on your Web site. For example, you might create a very different design for small children than for older adults. It is also important to know if visitors are using the latest browser technology and how fast they connect to the Internet, because this affects how well they can view more advanced features, such as multimedia.

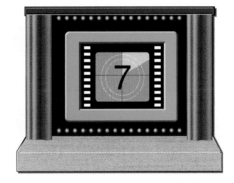

Host Your Finished Web Site

For your finished site to be accessible on the Web, you need to have it stored, or *hosted*, on a Web server. Many people have their Web sites hosted on a Web server at a commercial *Internet service provider (ISP)* or at their company or university.

You can start Dreamweaver on a PC and begin building pages that you can publish on the Web.

START DREAMWEAVER ON A PC

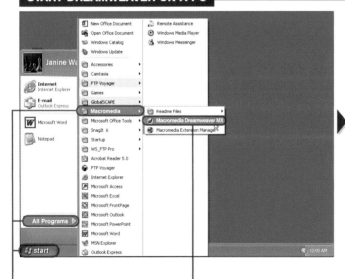

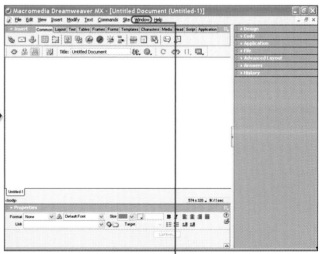

1 Click **Start**.

2 Click **All Programs**.

3 Click **Macromedia**.

4 Click **Macromedia Dreamweaver MX**.

Note: Your path to the Dreamweaver application may be different, depending on how you installed your software and your operating system.

■ An untitled Web page appears in a Document window.

■ If the Advanced Layout and History panels are not visible when you start Dreamweaver, click **Window**, **Other**, and then **Layers**, or **History**, to add them.

START DREAMWEAVER ON A MACINTOSH

You can start
Dreamweaver on a
Macintosh and begin
building pages that you
can publish on the Web.

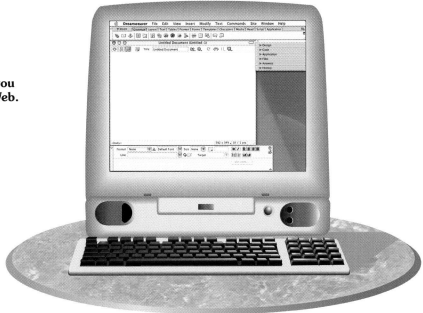

START DREAMWEAVER ON A MACINTOSH

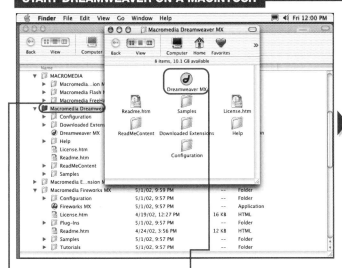

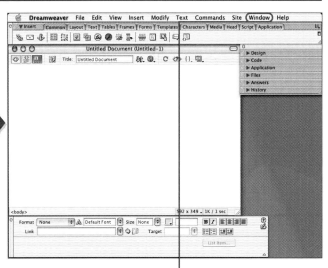

1 Double-click your hard
drive.

2 Double-click the
Macromedia Dreamweaver
MX folder ( ).

3 Double-click the
Dreamweaver MX icon ( ).

*Note: The exact location of the
Dreamweaver folder will depend on
how you installed your software.*

■ An untitled Web page
appears in a Document
window.

■ If the History panel is not
visible when you start
Dreamweaver, click
Window, **Other**, and then
History to add it.

Dreamweaver MX on a PC features a variety of windows, panels, and inspectors.

Document Window

The main workspace where you insert and arrange the text, images, and other elements of your Web page.

Property Inspector

This window is used to edit attributes. It changes to feature the attributes of any element selected in the Document window.

Panels

Provides access to the Design, Code, Application, Files, Advanced Layout, Answers, and History panels.

Toolbar

Contains shortcuts to preview and display features and a text field where you can specify a page's title.

Menus

Contains the commands for using Dreamweaver. Many of these commands are duplicated in Dreamweaver's windows, panels, and inspectors.

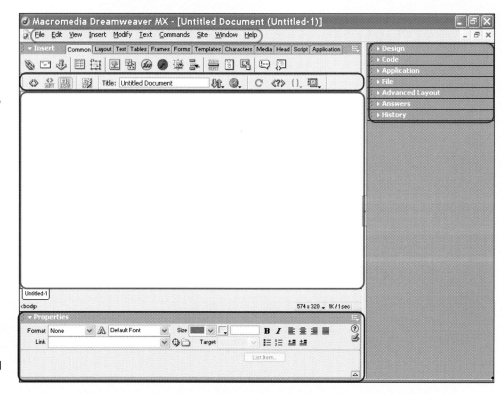

TOUR THE DREAMWEAVER INTERFACE ON A MACINTOSH

Dreamweaver MX on a Macintosh features a variety of windows, panels, and inspectors.

Document Window

The main workspace where you insert and arrange the text, images, and other elements of your Web page.

Property Inspector

This window is used to edit attributes. It changes to feature the attributes of any element selected in the Document window.

Panels

Provides access to the Design, Code, Application, Files, Answers, and History panels.

Toolbar

Contains shortcuts to preview and display features and a text field where you can specify a page's title.

Menus

Contains the commands for using Dreamweaver. Many of these commands are duplicated in Dreamweaver's windows, panels, and inspectors.

Note: Most of the screen shots you see in this book were taken on a PC. Except for minor differences, the icons, menus, and commands are the same on a Macintosh. When PC and Macintosh commands are different, the Macintosh commands are in parentheses. For example: Press Enter *(* Return *).*

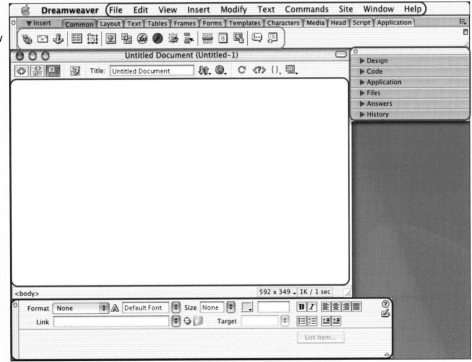

SHOW OR HIDE A WINDOW

You can show or hide accessory windows, also called panels and inspectors, by using commands in the Window menu.

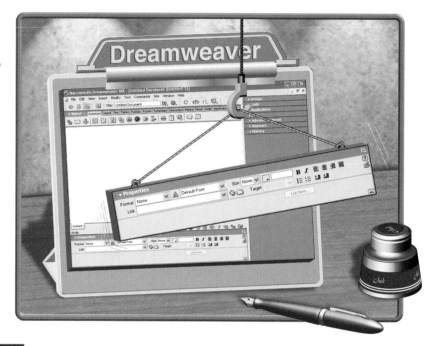

SHOW OR HIDE A WINDOW

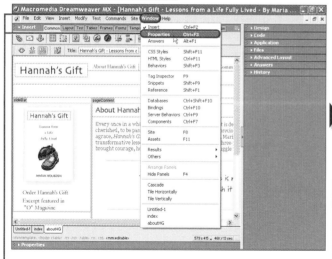

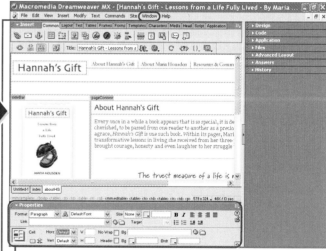

1 Click **Window**.

2 Click an unchecked window name.

■ A ✔ denotes windows that are already open.

■ Dreamweaver shows the window.

■ To hide a window, click **Window** and then the checked window name.

■ You can click **Window** and then **Hide Panels** to hide everything except the Document window.

14

EXIT DREAMWEAVER

You can exit Dreamweaver to close the program.

You should always exit Dreamweaver and all other programs before turning off your computer.

EXIT DREAMWEAVER

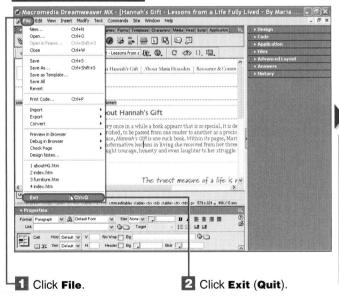

1 Click **File**.

2 Click **Exit** (**Quit**).

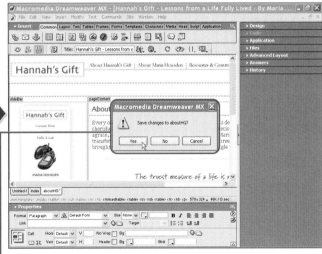

■ Before exiting, Dreamweaver alerts you to any open documents that have unsaved changes, allowing you to save them.

■ Dreamweaver exits.

You can use the help tools built into Dreamweaver to get answers to your questions.

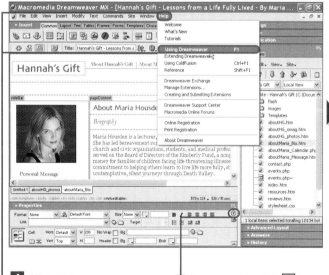

1 Click **Help**.

2 Click **Using Dreamweaver**.

■ You can also click ? in the Property inspector.

■ The Using Dreamweaver MX help page opens.

■ A clickable table of contents appears.

■ You can click the **Index** tab for access to an index of topics.

Are there different ways of getting the same thing done in Dreamweaver?

Very often, yes. For example, you may be able to access a command one way through a Dreamweaver menu, another way through the Insert panel or Property inspector, and yet another way by right-clicking (Control + clicking) an object with the mouse.

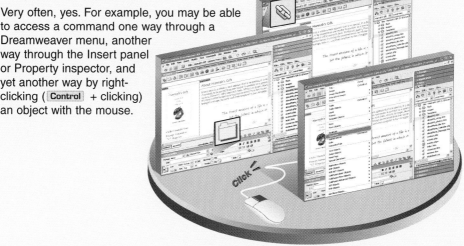

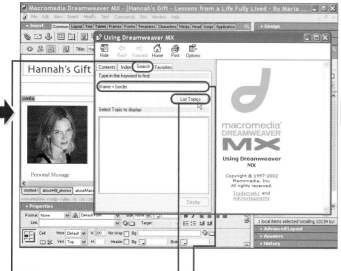

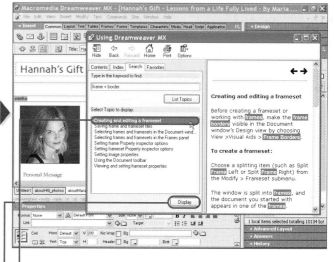

3 Click the **Search** tab to search for a keyword.

■ The Search window appears.

4 Type one or more keywords, separating multiple keywords with a + (frame + border, in this example).

5 Click **List Topics**.

6 Click a topic from the search result list.

7 Click **Display**.

■ Information on your topic appears.

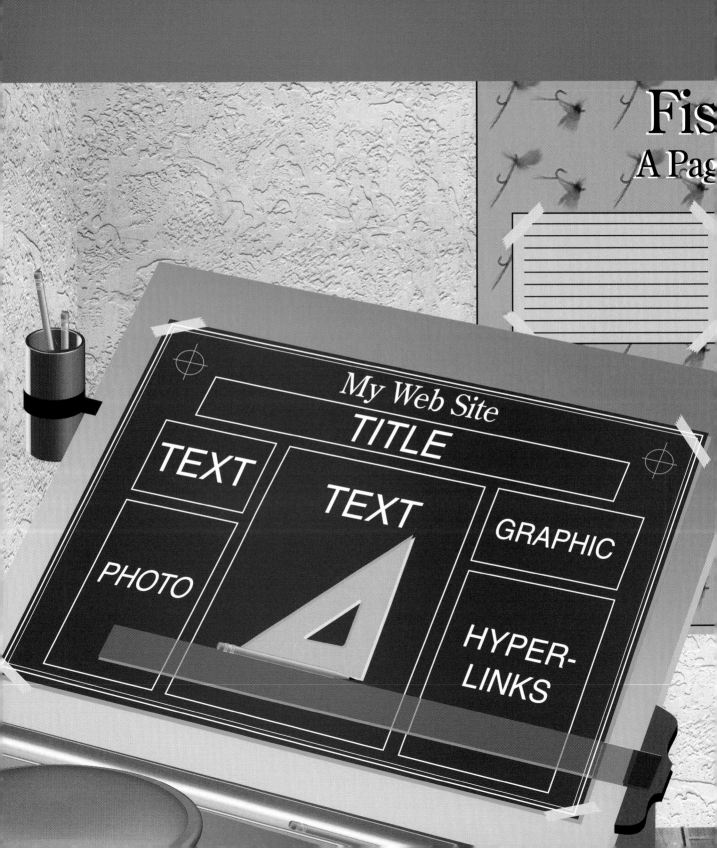

n' Buddies

or Fishing Friends

Setting Up Your Web Site

You start a project in Dreamweaver by setting up a local site on your computer and then creating the first Web page of the site. This chapter shows you how.

Graphics

Photos

Text

SET UP A NEW WEB SITE

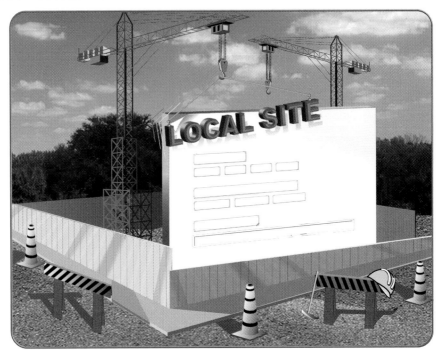

Before creating your Web pages, you need to define a local site for storing the information in your site, such as your HTML documents and image files. Defining a local site allows you to manage your Web-page files in the Site window. See Chapter 14 for more information on the Site window.

SET UP A NEW WEB SITE

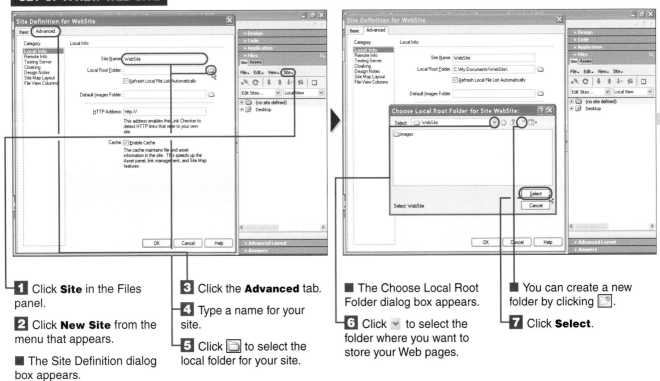

1 Click **Site** in the Files panel.

2 Click **New Site** from the menu that appears.

■ The Site Definition dialog box appears.

3 Click the **Advanced** tab.

4 Type a name for your site.

5 Click 📁 to select the local folder for your site.

■ The Choose Local Root Folder dialog box appears.

6 Click ⌄ to select the folder where you want to store your Web pages.

■ You can create a new folder by clicking 📁.

7 Click **Select**.

Why is it important to keep all my Web site files in a main folder on my computer?

Keeping everything in the same folder enables you to easily transfer your site files to a Web server without changing the organization of the files. If you do not organize your site files on the Web server the same as they are organized on your local computer, hyperlinks may not work, and images may not display properly. See Chapter 14 for more about working with Web site files.

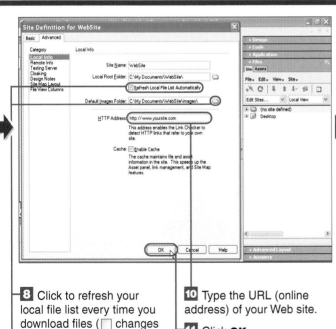

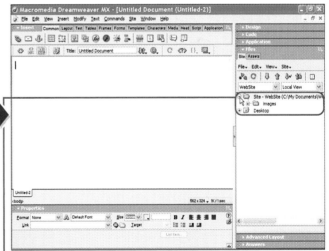

8 Click to refresh your local file list every time you download files (☐ changes to ☑).

9 Click 📁 to select the folder where you want to store the images for your Web site.

10 Type the URL (online address) of your Web site.

11 Click **OK**.

■ A window appears asking if you want to create a site cache.

12 Click **Create** to create one.

■ The Site panel shows the root of your new site. Any files or folders already in your site's root folder appear in the Site panel. You can now start adding pages, folders, and images to your site.

CREATE A NEW WEB PAGE

When you open Dreamweaver, a new blank page appears by default. You can use this page, or create a new page yourself and then add text, images, and other elements to create a new Web page design.

CREATE A NEW WEB PAGE

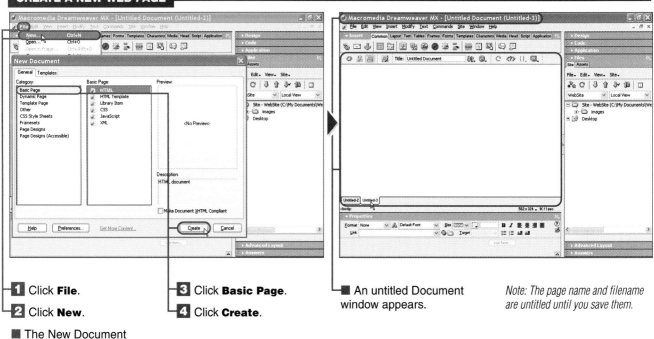

1 Click **File**.

2 Click **New**.

■ The New Document dialog box appears.

3 Click **Basic Page**.

4 Click **Create**.

■ An untitled Document window appears.

Note: The page name and filename are untitled until you save them.

Adding a title to a Web page tells viewers what page they are on and what they will find on the page, plus it helps search engines index pages with more accuracy. A Web page title appears in the title bar when the page opens in a Web browser.

ADD A TITLE TO A WEB PAGE

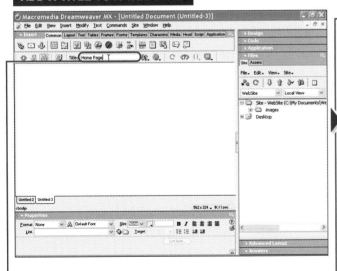

1 Type a name for your Web page.

2 Press Enter (Return).

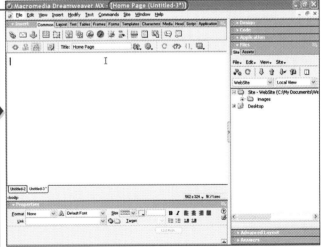

■ The title appears in the title bar of the Document window.

SAVE A WEB PAGE

You should save your Web page before closing the program or transferring the page to a remote site. It is also a good idea to save all your files frequently to prevent work from being lost due to power outages or system failures. For more information on connecting to remote sites, see Chapter 14.

SAVE A WEB PAGE

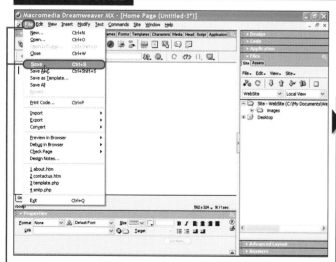

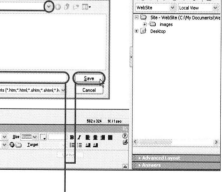

SAVE YOUR DOCUMENT

1 Click **File**.

2 Click **Save**.

■ You can click **Save As** to save an existing file with a new filename.

■ If you are saving a new file for the first time, the Save As dialog box appears.

3 Click ☑ to select your local site folder.

■ Your local site folder is where you want to save the pages and other files for your Web site.

4 Type a name for your Web page.

Note: Web pages are HTML files and usually end with the `.htm` or `.html` filename extensions.

5 Click **Save**.

Where should I store the files for my Web site on my computer?

You should save all the files for your Web site in the folder that you defined as the local root folder. See "Set Up a New Web Site," earlier in this chapter, for more about this. Keeping all the files of the site in this folder, or in subfolders inside this folder, makes it easier to hyperlink between local files, and to transfer files to a remote Web server.

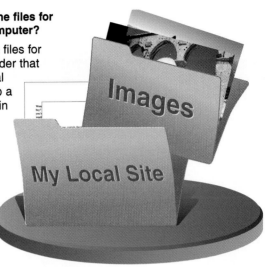

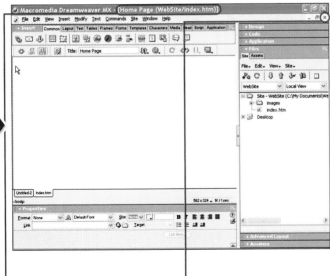

■ The Web page saves, and the filename and path appear in the title bar.

■ You can click × to close the page.

REVERT A PAGE

-1 Click **File**.

-2 Click **Revert**.

■ The page reverts to the previously saved version. All the changes made since last saving are lost.

PREVIEW A WEB PAGE IN A BROWSER

You can see how your page will appear online by previewing it in a Web browser. The Preview in Browser command works with the Web browsers installed on your computer. Keep in mind that Dreamweaver does not come with browser software.

PREVIEW A WEB PAGE IN A BROWSER

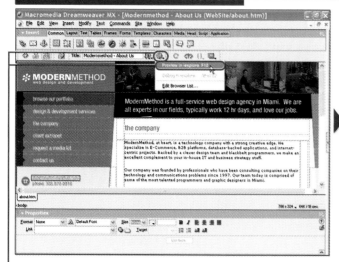

1 Click 🔍.

2 Click a Web Browser from the menu that appears.

■ You can also preview the page in your primary browser by pressing **F12**.

■ Your Web browser launches and opens the current page.

■ The file has a temporary filename for viewing in the browser.

Why does Dreamweaver create a temporary file when I preview my page?

Dreamweaver creates a temporary file when you preview your page so you do not have to save the document to see what it would look like in the browser. That way, you do not have to commit to changes every time or save separate versions for brief tests. The "Temp" files also allow you to compare multiple versions of pages onscreen in various browser windows and on different browsers. If you do not want Dreamweaver to create temporary files, you can disable this feature by clicking **Edit**, **Preferences**, **Preview in Browser**, and then unchecking **Preview Using Temporary File**.

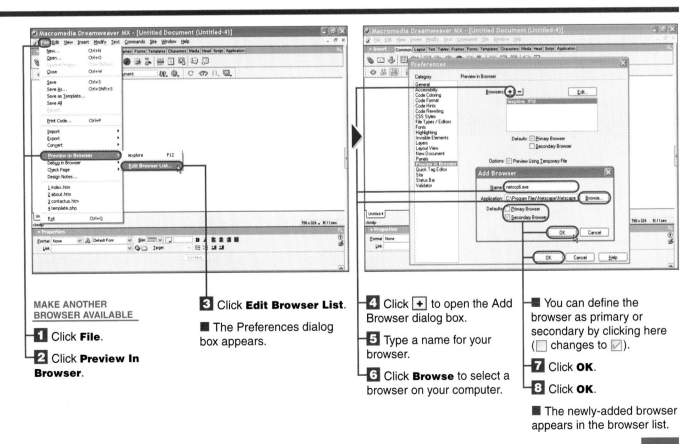

MAKE ANOTHER BROWSER AVAILABLE

1 Click **File**.

2 Click **Preview In Browser**.

3 Click **Edit Browser List**.

■ The Preferences dialog box appears.

4 Click **+** to open the Add Browser dialog box.

5 Type a name for your browser.

6 Click **Browse** to select a browser on your computer.

■ You can define the browser as primary or secondary by clicking here (□ changes to ☑).

7 Click **OK**.

8 Click **OK**.

■ The newly-added browser appears in the browser list.

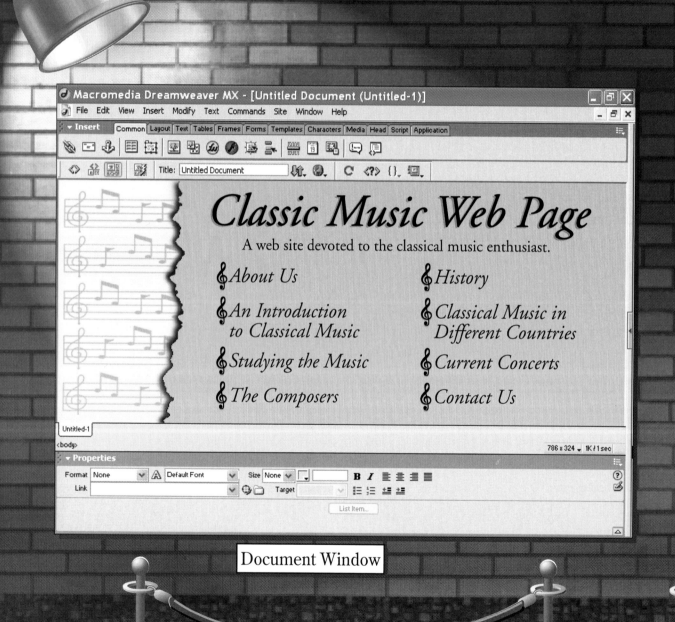

Document Window

CHAPTER 3

Save Web Page

RETURN TO: Resize Image ◁

Apply Font

Apply Bold

Set Alignment

Font Color

Apply Italic

History Panel

Leisure Vacations, Inc.

Custom Command

Custom
Command

ormat Heading

ange Font
ange Size
ke Text Red
nter Text

lace Graphics

size Image
ce Image
d Border
ve for Web

Exploring the Dreamweaver Interface

*Take a tour of the panels and windows
that make up Dreamweaver's interface
and discover all the handy tools
and features that make this an
award-winning Web design program.*

CUSTOMIZE THE DOCUMENT WINDOW

The Document window is the main workspace in Dreamweaver, where you create Web pages, and enter and format text, images, and other elements. Customizable panels now lock into position to keep the workspace clear and make it more intuitive to use.

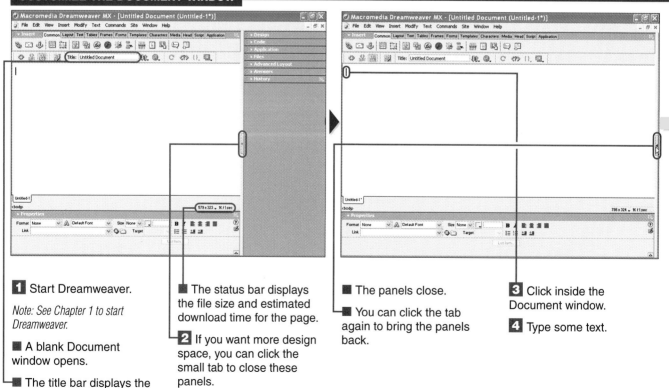

1 Start Dreamweaver.

Note: See Chapter 1 to start Dreamweaver.

■ A blank Document window opens.

■ The title bar displays the document title and filename.

■ The status bar displays the file size and estimated download time for the page.

2 If you want more design space, you can click the small tab to close these panels.

■ The panels close.

■ You can click the tab again to bring the panels back.

3 Click inside the Document window.

4 Type some text.

What is WYSIWYG?

WYSIWYG, pronounced "wizzy-wig," stands for **W**hat **Y**ou **S**ee **I**s **W**hat **Y**ou **G**et. Dreamweaver is a WYSIWYG Web editor because it provides a visual interface. You build Web pages visually in the Document window, and you see the content as it should appear in a Web browser. With text-based Web editors, you can only create Web pages by writing HTML code. In Dreamweaver, you can see the underlying HTML tags by clicking the Code View button ([<>]).

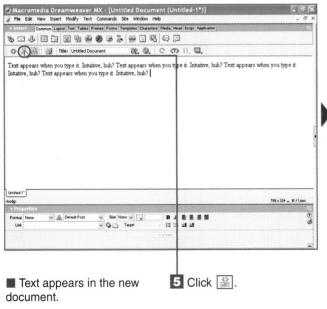

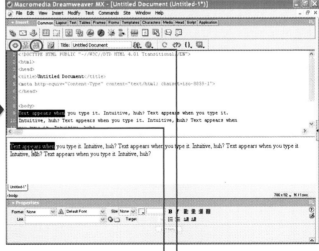

■ Text appears in the new document.

5 Click [🔲].

■ The Document window splits to display the code and design views.

■ When you select text in one view, it is highlighted in the other, making it easy to find formatting tags.

■ You can return to the purely WYSIWYG view by clicking [🔲].

■ You can click [<>] to view just the code.

FORMAT CONTENT WITH THE PROPERTY INSPECTOR

The Property inspector enables you to view the properties associated with the object or text currently selected in the Document window. Text fields, drop-down menus, buttons, and other form elements in the Property inspector allow you to modify these properties.

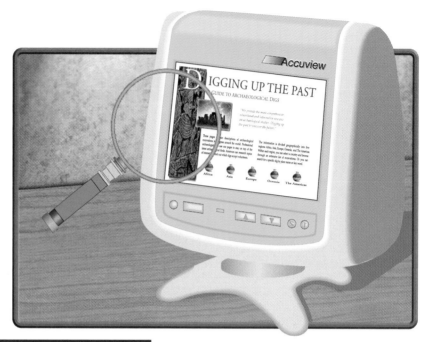

FORMAT CONTENT WITH THE PROPERTY INSPECTOR

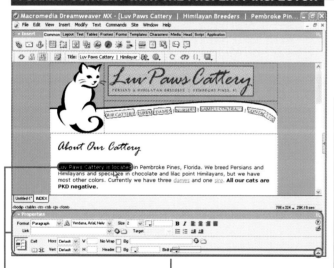

FORMAT TEXT

1 Open an existing Web page or enter new text on a page.

2 Click and drag to select some text.

■ Text properties appear.

■ You can change many text properties in the Property inspector, such as format, size, and alignment.

■ You can click △ to switch between standard and expanded modes of the inspector.

FORMAT AN IMAGE

1 Click an image.

■ Image properties appear.

■ You can change many image properties in the Property inspector, such as dimensions, filename, and alignment.

ADD ELEMENTS WITH THE INSERT PANEL

You can insert elements such as images, tables, and layers into the Document windows with the Insert panel. The panel, located at the top of the window, features tabs with options such as Tables, Forms, and Characters.

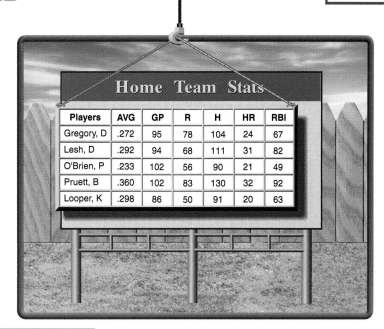

Players	AVG	GP	R	H	HR	RBI
Gregory, D	.272	95	78	104	24	67
Lesh, D	.292	94	68	111	31	82
O'Brien, P	.233	102	56	90	21	49
Pruett, B	.360	102	83	130	32	92
Looper, K	.298	86	50	91	20	63

ADD ELEMENTS WITH THE INSERT PANEL

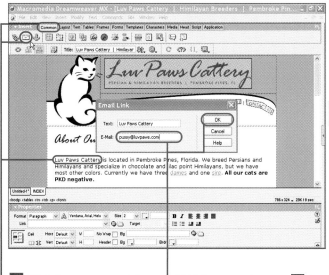

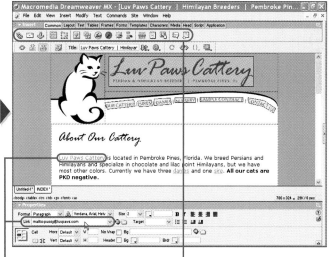

■1 Click the **Common** tab.

■2 Click and drag to select some text.

■3 Click a button in the Insert panel.

■ This example uses 📧 to insert an e-mail link.

■ A dialog box appears.

■4 Type your information to define your object.

■5 Click **OK**.

■ In the example shown, the text is now an e-mail link.

■ The link information appears in the Property inspector.

■ You can click any object button in the Insert panel to add that element to your document.

CORRECT ERRORS WITH THE HISTORY PANEL

The History panel keeps track of the commands you perform in Dreamweaver. You can return your page to a previous state by backtracking through those commands. This is a convenient way to correct errors.

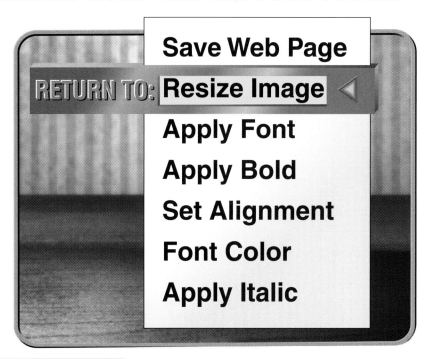

RETURN TO:

Save Web Page

Resize Image ◁

Apply Font

Apply Bold

Set Alignment

Font Color

Apply Italic

CORRECT ERRORS WITH THE HISTORY PANEL

1 Click **Window**.

2 Click **Others**.

3 Click **History**.

■ The History panel appears.

■ The History panel, when open, records any commands you perform in Dreamweaver.

■ To undo one or more commands, click and drag the slider (🡒) upward.

■ The page reverts to its previous state.

■ To redo the commands, click and drag the slider (🡒) downward.

Note: You can only add steps to the end of the sequence. If you move the slider up and then add a step, the steps below the slider are deleted.

Dreamweaver MX features an uncluttered workspace with windows that lock into place and can expand or collapse. You can also rearrange panels and move them around the screen to create the best interface for you.

VIEW PANELS

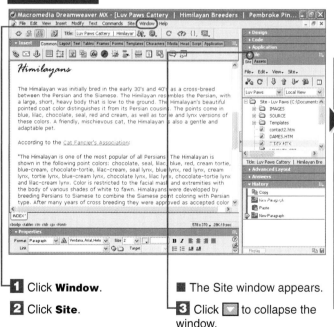

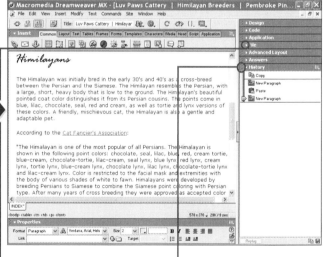

1 Click **Window**.

2 Click **Site**.

■ The Site window appears.

3 Click ![down] to collapse the window.

■ The window collapses.

■ You can click ![right] to expand a window.

■ When you collapse a panel, such as the Files panel, others become more visible, such as the History panel, shown here.

■ You can rearrange the stacking order of the panels by clicking the dotted edge on the left side of the panel. You can then move the panel up or down over the other panels.

CREATE AND APPLY A CUSTOM COMMAND

You can select a sequence of commands that has been recorded in the History panel and save the sequence as a custom command. The new command will appear under the Commands menu. You can apply it to other elements on the page to automate repetitive tasks.

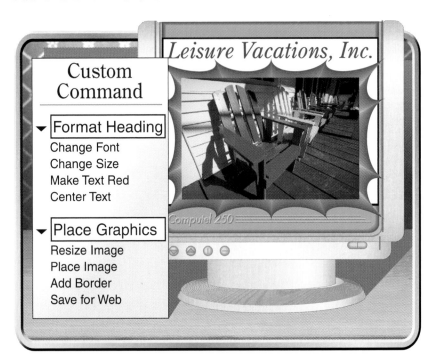

Custom Command

▼ Format Heading
Change Font
Change Size
Make Text Red
Center Text

▼ Place Graphics
Resize Image
Place Image
Add Border
Save for Web

Leisure Vacations, Inc.

Compufel 250

CREATE AND APPLY A CUSTOM COMMAND

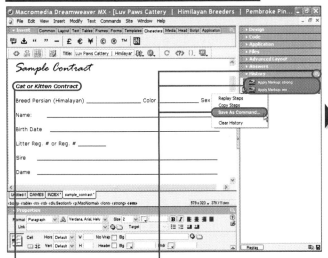

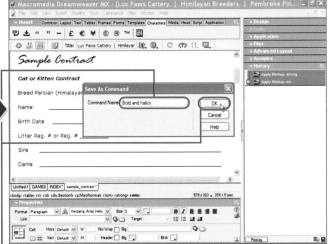

1 Select an element and perform a sequence of commands.

■ In this example, text is formatted in bold and italicized.

2 In the History panel, `Ctrl` + click (`Shift` + click) to select the steps you want to save as a single command.

3 Right-click or click ▦.

4 Click **Save As Command**.

■ The Save As Command dialog box appears.

5 Type a name for the command.

6 Click **OK**.

■ Dreamweaver saves the command.

Note: You cannot use this feature with all commands. For example, clicking and dragging an element cannot be included in the command.

How do I change the name of a custom command?

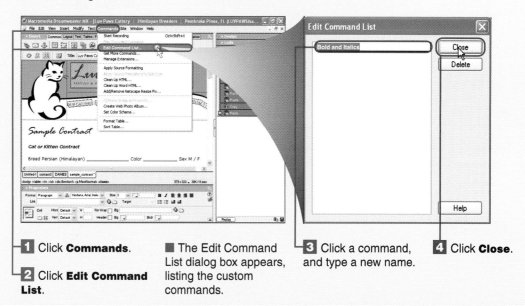

1 Click **Commands**.

2 Click **Edit Command List**.

■ The Edit Command List dialog box appears, listing the custom commands.

3 Click a command, and type a new name.

4 Click **Close**.

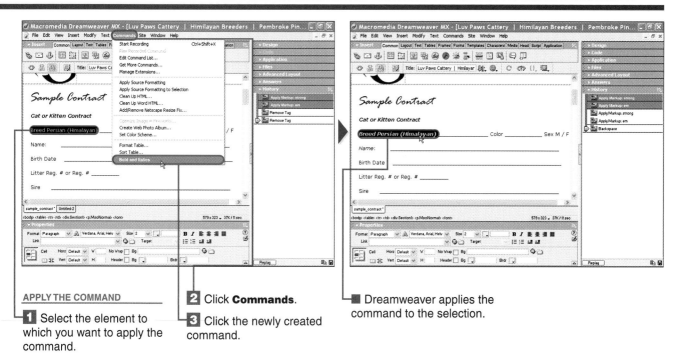

APPLY THE COMMAND

1 Select the element to which you want to apply the command.

2 Click **Commands**.

3 Click the newly created command.

■ Dreamweaver applies the command to the selection.

SET PREFERENCES

You can easily change the default appearance and behavior of Dreamweaver by specifying settings in the Preferences dialog box. You can modify the user interface of Dreamweaver to better suit how you like to work.

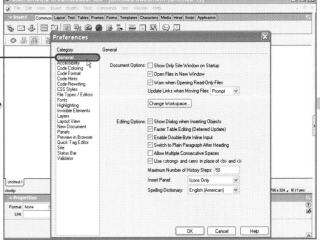

SET PREFERENCES

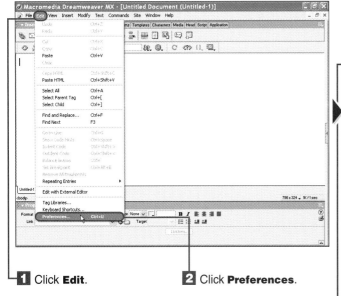

-**1** Click **Edit**.

-**2** Click **Preferences**.

■ The Preferences dialog box appears.

-**3** Click a Preferences category.

■ Options for the category appear.

38

**How do I ensure that
Dreamweaver does not change
my HTML or other code?**

You can select options under the
Code Rewriting category in the
Preferences dialog box to ensure
that Dreamweaver does not
automatically correct or modify
your code. You can turn off its
error-correcting functions, specify
files that it should not rewrite
based on file extension, and
disable its character encoding
features.

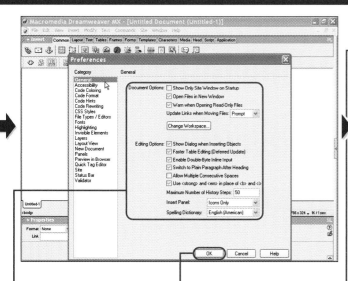

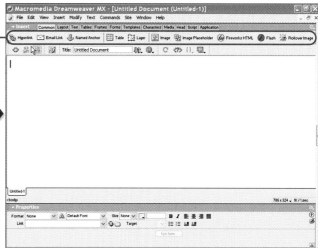

4 Make changes to the
options. You can make
multiple changes.

■ In this example, the Insert
Panel ⌄ and then **Icons
and Text** are clicked to
display both icons and text
descriptions in the Insert
panel.

5 Click **OK**.

■ The preference changes
take effect.

■ In this example, the icons
in the Insert panel now
display with text
descriptions.

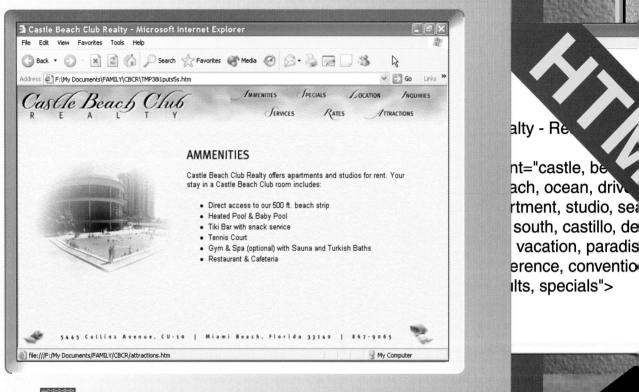

```
<HTML>
<HEAD>
      Fruit and Flowers Inc</TITLE>
</HEAD>
<BODY>

<H2> <CENTER>Fruit and Flowers, Inc.</CENTER> </H2>
<P> <B> <CENTER>No garden? No problem!</CENTER> </B> </P>
<P>Our special, patented fertilizer lets you grow lush flowers and
healthy fruit INDOORS!</P>
<BR>Grow beautiful, exotic flowers and impress your friends!
<BR>Grow your own fruit and save on your grocery bills!

</BODY>
</HTML>
```

ules

HTML Tags

JAVASCRIPT CODE

CHAPTER 4

Understanding HTML Code

Dreamweaver helps you build your Web pages by writing HTML. This chapter introduces the important features of this language and the tools in Dreamweaver that enable you to edit HTML.

Dreamweaver creates your Web pages by writing HTML. This saves you time by not having to write the code yourself.

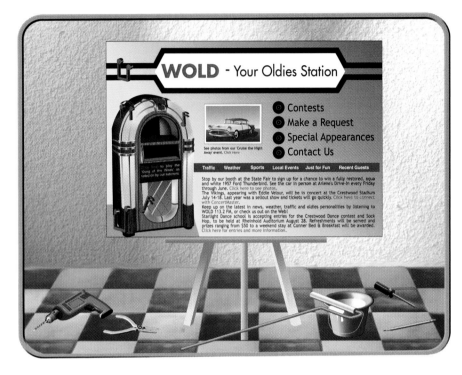

HTML

Hypertext Markup Language (HTML) is the formatting language that you use to create Web pages. When you open a Web page in a browser, it is HTML code telling the browser how to display the text, images, and other content on the page. At its most basic level, Dreamweaver is an HTML-writing application, although it can do many other things as well.

HTML Tags

The basic unit of HTML is a *tag*. You can recognize HTML tags by their angle brackets:

```
<p>Today the weather was
<b>nice</b>.<br>Tomorrow it may
<i>rain</i>.</p>
```

You can format text and other elements on your page by placing it inside the HTML tags.

How Tags Work

Some HTML tags work in twos: Opening and closing tags surround content in a document and control the formatting of the content. For example: <b> tags cause text to be bold. Closing tags are distinguished by a forward slash (/). Other tags can stand alone. For example, the <br> tag adds a line break. HTML tags are not case-sensitive; they can be uppercase, lowercase, or mixed case.

HTML Documents

Because HTML documents are plain text files, you can open and edit them with any text editor. In fact, in the early days of the Web, most people created their pages with simple editors such as Notepad (Windows) and SimpleText (Macintosh). But writing HTML by hand can be a slow, tedious process, especially when creating advanced HTML elements such as tables, forms, and frames.

Create Web Pages Without Knowing Code

Dreamweaver streamlines the process of creating Web pages by giving you an easy-to-use, visual interface with which to generate HTML. You specify formatting with menu commands and button clicks, and Dreamweaver takes care of writing the underlying HTML code. When you build a Web page in the Document window, you see your page as it will eventually appear in a Web browser, instead of as HTML.

Direct Access to the Code

Dreamweaver gives you direct access to the raw HTML code if you want it. This can be an advantage for people who know HTML and want to do some formatting of their page by typing tags. The Code View mode, Code inspector, and Quick Tag Editor in Dreamweaver enable you to edit your page by adding HTML information manually. Access to the code also means you can add HTML features that Dreamweaver might not yet support.

VIEW AND EDIT THE SOURCE CODE

You can switch to Code View in the Document window to inspect and edit the HTML and other code of a Web page.

Code View

```
<HTML>
<HEAD>
<TITLE>Into the Wild</TITLE>
</HEAD>
<BODY>

<H1> <I>Into the Wild!</I>
<IMG SRC-"cougar.jpg"
<P><B>Would you like
the Wild's adventure
...Whether ye
```

You will probably do most of your work in Design View, which displays your page approximately as it will be viewed in a Web browser.

VIEW AND EDIT THE SOURCE CODE

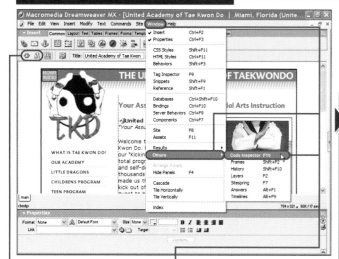

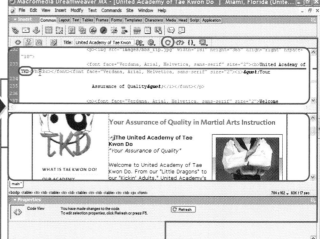

1 With your page open in the Document window, click a code-viewing option.

■ Clicking the Code and Design Views button ( ) splits the window and displays both your source code and the design in the Document window.

■ Clicking the Code View button ( ) displays only the source code of your page in the Document window.

■ Clicking **Window**, **Others**, and then **Code Inspector** displays the code in a separate window.

■ The Code and Design Views appear in the Document window.

■ The HTML and other code appear in one pane.

■ The Design View appears in the other pane.

2 Click in the code to edit the text, or to add or modify the HTML.

3 Click the Refresh button ( ).

How do I turn on line numbers in Code View or make code wrap at the right edge of the window?

Both of these options, as well as others, are available by clicking the Options button (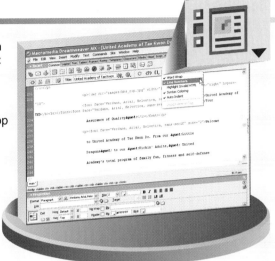) at the top of the Document window when you are in Code View.

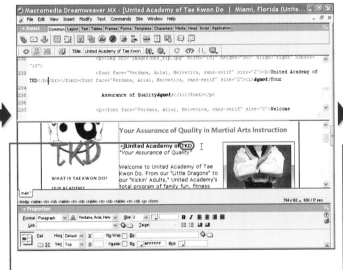

■ The content in Design View updates to reflect the code changes.

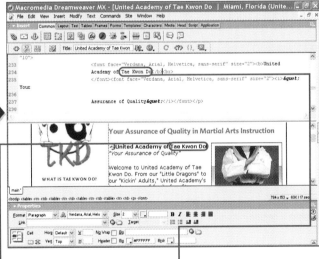

4 Click in the Design View window and type to make changes.

■ The content in the Code View updates dynamically as you make your changes.

EXPLORE STRUCTURAL TAGS

You define the basic structure of every HTML document with several basic tags. To view the HTML of a Web page, click a Code View icon in the Document window, or click Window, Other, then Code Inspector.

<body> Tags

Opening and closing <body> tags surround content that appears inside the Web browser window. The bgcolor attribute of the <body> tag defines the background color, and the text attribute of the <body> tag defines the text color.

<head> Tags

Opening and closing <head> tags surround descriptive and accessory information for a page. This includes <title> and <meta> tag content.

Page Title

The content inside the opening and closing <title> tags is displayed in the Document window title bar.

<html> Tags

Opening and closing <html> tags begin and end every HTML document.

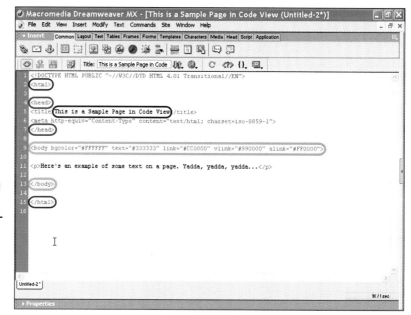

You can organize information in your Web page with block-formatting tags. To view the HTML of a Web page, click a Code View button in the Document window, or click Window, Other, then Code Inspector.

CODE VIEW

`<p>` Tag

The `<p>` tag organizes information into a paragraph.

`<ul>` and `<li>` Tags

The `<ul>` tag defines an unordered list. Each list item is defined with an `<li>` tag.

DESIGN VIEW

This page features a heading, a paragraph, and an unordered list.

Heading

Paragraph

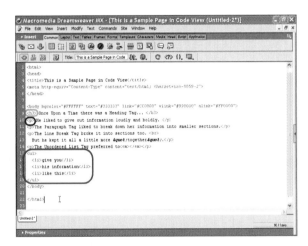

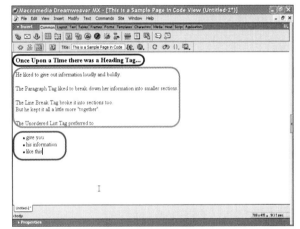

`<h>` Tag

An `<h>` tag organizes information into a heading. There are six levels of headings, `<h1>` (the largest) through `<h6>` (the smallest).

`<br>`, `<ol>`, and `<pre>` Tags

Other block-formatting tags include `<br>` (line break), `<ol>` (ordered list), and `<pre>` (preformatted text).

Unordered List

EXPLORE TEXT-FORMATTING TAGS

You can format the style of sentences, words, and characters with text-formatting tags. To view the HTML of a Web page, click a Code View button in the Document window or click Window, Other, then Code Inspector.

CODE VIEW

<font> Tag

The <font> tag controls various characteristics of text on a Web page.

<size> Attribute

The <size> attribute goes inside the <font> tag and specifies the size of text.

DESIGN VIEW

This page features text with a different font size, as well as bold and italic text.

Font Size　　**Italic Text**　　**Bold Text**

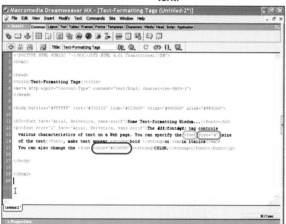

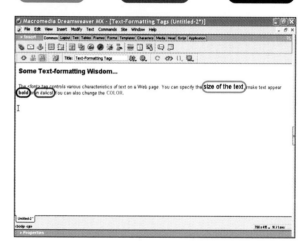

<b> Tag

The <b> tag defines text as bold.

<i> Tag

The <i> tag defines text as italic.

<color> Attribute

The <color> attribute also goes inside the <font> tag and specifies the color of text.

EXPLORE IMAGE AND HYPERLINK TAGS

You can add an image to your page with the <img> tag, and with the <a> tag you can create a hyperlink. To view the HTML of a Web page, click the Code View button in the Document window or click Window, Other, then Code Inspector.

CODE VIEW

<img> Tag

The <img> tag inserts an image into a page.

<src> Attribute

The <src> attribute specifies an image file to insert.

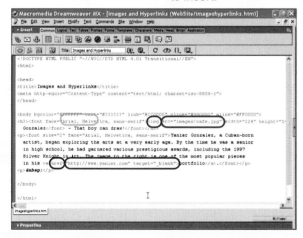

<align> Attribute

The <align> attribute specifies the alignment of an image.

<a> Tag

The <a> tag specifies the content that will serve as a hyperlink.

<href> Attribute

The <href> attribute specifies the hyperlink destination.

DESIGN VIEW

This page features a heading, a paragraph, and an unordered list.

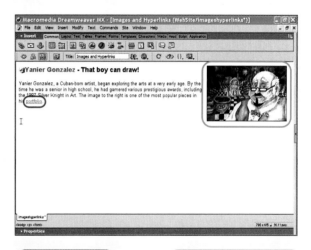

Text Hyperlink

Right-Aligned Image

49

CLEAN UP HTML CODE

Dreamweaver can optimize the HTML in your Web page by deleting redundant or non-functional tags. This can decrease a page's file size and make the source code easier to read in Code View.

It is a good idea to run the Clean Up HTML command when editing documents originally created in other HTML editors, such as FrontPage.

CLEAN UP HTML CODE

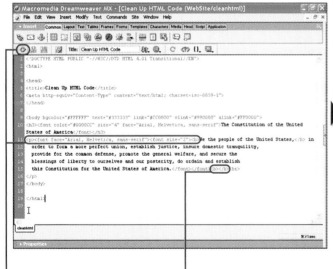

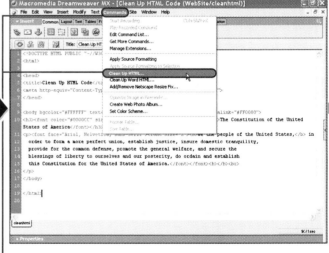

1 Click 🕸 to view the HTML in Code View.

■ In this example, multiple `<font>` tags appear in the code, adding unnecessary bulk.

■ This example also includes an empty `<b>` tag. This tag serves no purpose and can be deleted.

2 Click **Commands**.

3 Click **Clean Up HTML**.

■ The Clean Up HTML/XHTML dialog box appears.

How do empty tags end up appearing in Dreamweaver's HTML?

Sometimes if you heavily edit Web-page text in the Document window — cutting and pasting sentences, reformatting words, and so on — Dreamweaver will inadvertently remove text from inside tags without removing the tags themselves.

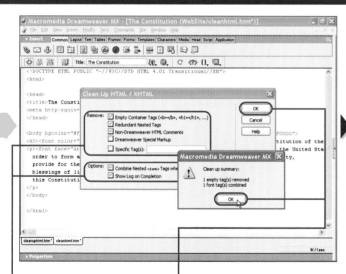

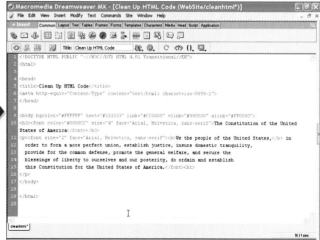

4 Click the check boxes to define the information that you want to remove (☐ changes to ☑).

5 Click the check boxes to select other options (☐ changes to ☑).

6 Click **OK**.

■ Dreamweaver parses the HTML and displays the results, including a summary of what was removed.

7 Click **OK**.

■ The cleaned up HTML appears in the Document window.

51

VIEW AND EDIT HEAD CONTENT

Dreamweaver gives you various ways to view, add to, and edit a Web page's head content, where special descriptive information about the page is stored.

Head Info.
Description: This travel site will help you book a vacation.
Keywords: travel, vacations, airlines, hotels.

VIEW AND EDIT HEAD CONTENT

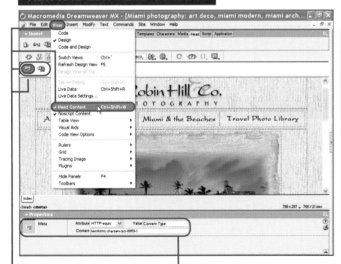

-**1** Click **View**.

-**2** Click **Head Content**.

-■ Buttons indicating head content appear.

-**3** Click a button in the Head Content panel.

-■ Information on the head content appears in the Property inspector.

■ In the example, clicking gives you information on meta head content.

INSERT HEAD CONTENT

-**1** Click the **Head** tab from the Insert panel.

-**2** Click a content button.

■ In this example, the Keywords button (⌨) is selected.

How can I influence how my pages are ranked by search engines?

Search engines work by organizing the important information found in Web pages into a searchable database. Many search engines give greater importance to the description and keyword information that can be added to the head content of HTML documents. Short of paying for high-ranking placement, you can influence how search engines rank your pages by making sure you add concise descriptions and relevant keywords to the head content of each page you create.

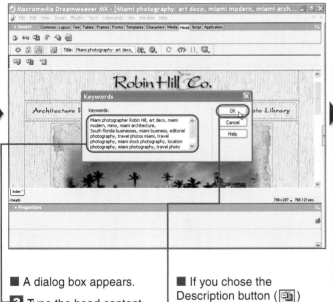

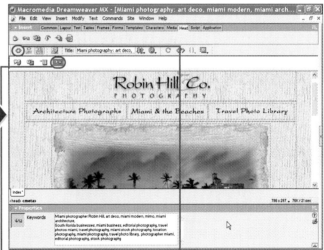

■ A dialog box appears.

3 Type the head content for the page, separating keywords with a comma.

■ If you chose the Description button (🖾) in step **2**, type a sentence description for the page.

4 Click **OK**.

■ The new head content appears as a button in the head section of the Document window.

■ To view the HTML code for the new head content, click the Code View button (⟨⟩).

USING THE REFERENCE PANEL

You can get quick access to reference information about HTML tags and their attributes via the Reference tab in the Code panel.

USING THE REFERENCE PANEL

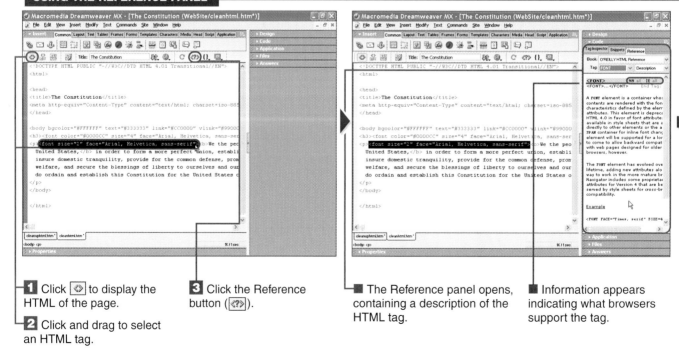

1 Click to display the HTML of the page.

2 Click and drag to select an HTML tag.

3 Click the Reference button (<?>).

■ The Reference panel opens, containing a description of the HTML tag.

■ Information appears indicating what browsers support the tag.

Does Dreamweaver have commands for creating all the tags listed in the Reference panel?

With Dreamweaver's commands you create *most* of the tags listed in the Reference panel, in particular, frequently-used tags. But there are tags listed for which Dreamweaver does not offer commands. For example, you cannot insert the `<thead>` tag with any of Dreamweaver's table commands. Tags that Dreamweaver does not support with commands can be inserted by hand in Code View.

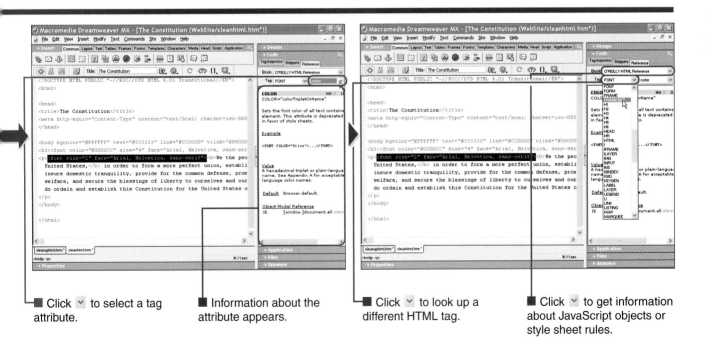

■ Click to select a tag attribute.

■ Information about the attribute appears.

■ Click to look up a different HTML tag.

■ Click to get information about JavaScript objects or style sheet rules.

CHAPTER 5

Formatting and Styling Text

Text is the easiest type of information to add to a Web page using Dreamweaver. This chapter shows you how to create paragraphs, bulleted lists, stylized text, and more.

CREATE A HEADING

You can add headings to structure the text on your Web page hierarchically with titles and subtitles. You can also align your heading text.

x

x

CREATE A HEADING

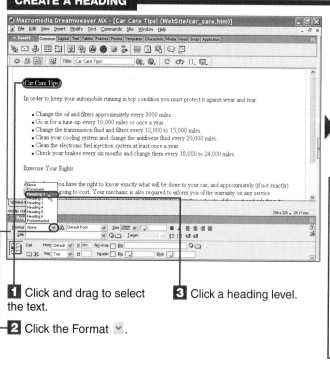

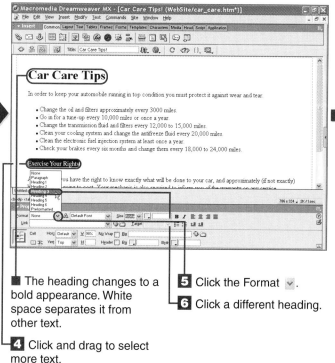

1 Click and drag to select the text.

2 Click the Format 🔽.

3 Click a heading level.

■ The heading changes to a bold appearance. White space separates it from other text.

4 Click and drag to select more text.

5 Click the Format 🔽.

6 Click a different heading.

58

What heading levels should I use to format my text?

Headings 1, 2, and 3 are often used for titles and subtitles. Heading 4 is similar to a bold version of default text. Headings 5 and 6 are often used for copyright and disclaimer information in page footers.

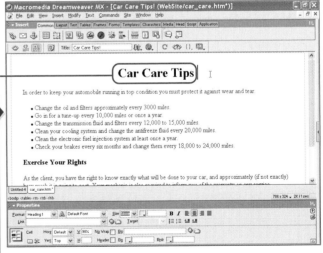

International Pastries Online

We've supplied the Midwest with the finest pastries in the world for over 20 years. Now our international taste delights are available online for delivery across the United States and Canada!

Gift Boxes

An elegant card containing a message you supply is included with each gift box you order.

Gift Boxes for Every Occasion

Happy Anniversary!
Delivered with a single long-stemmed rose.

Happy Birthday!
Delivered with three helium-filled balloons.

Thank You!
Delivered with five carnations in the colors of your choice.

Valentine's Day
Receive a 10% discount if you order before January 20.

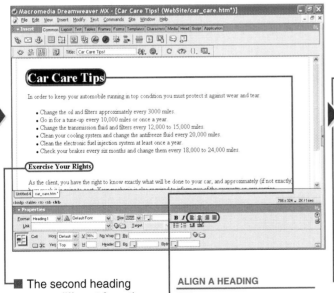

■ The second heading appears different from the first.

Note: The greater the heading level, the smaller the text formatting.

ALIGN A HEADING

7 Click and drag to select some heading text.

8 Click 🗐, 🗐, 🗐, or 🗐 to align.

■ The heading text is aligned on the page.

CREATE PARAGRAPHS

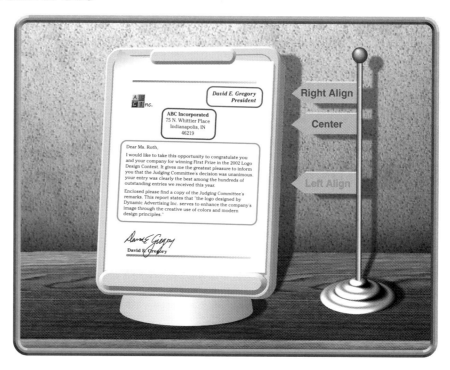

You can organize text on your Web page by creating and aligning paragraphs.

CREATE PARAGRAPHS

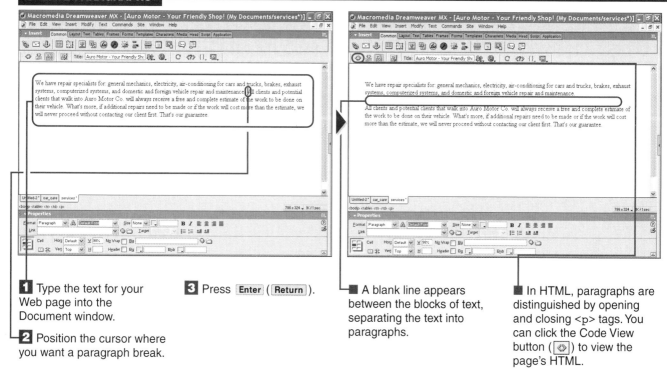

1 Type the text for your Web page into the Document window.

2 Position the cursor where you want a paragraph break.

3 Press Enter (Return).

■ A blank line appears between the blocks of text, separating the text into paragraphs.

■ In HTML, paragraphs are distinguished by opening and closing <p> tags. You can click the Code View button (◇) to view the page's HTML.

What controls the width of the paragraphs on my Web page?

The width of your paragraphs depends on the width of the Web browser window. When a user changes the size of the browser window, the widths of the paragraphs also change. That way the user always sees all the text of the paragraph. You can also use tables to further control the width of your paragraphs. See Chapter 8 for more about tables.

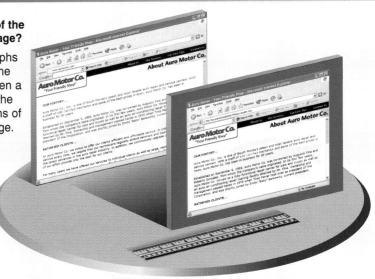

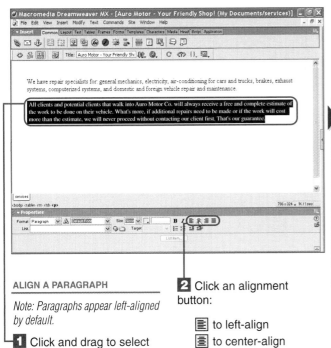

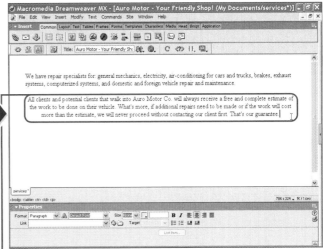

ALIGN A PARAGRAPH

Note: Paragraphs appear left-aligned by default.

1 Click and drag to select the text of a paragraph.

2 Click an alignment button:

≣ to left-align
≣ to center-align
≣ to right-align
≣ to justify

■ The paragraph is aligned on the page.

CREATE LINE BREAKS

By adding line breaks to your page, you can keep adjacent lines of related text close together without creating a new paragraph.

CREATE LINE BREAKS

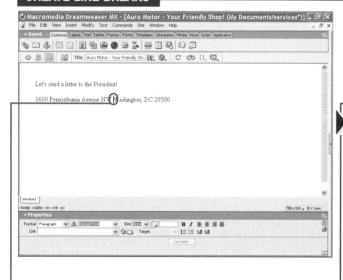

1 Click where you want the line of text to break.

2 Press Shift + Enter (Shift + Return).

■ A line break is added.

Note: You can insert multiple line breaks to add more space between lines of text.

INDENT PARAGRAPHS

You can make selected paragraphs stand out from the rest of the text on your Web page by indenting them. Indents are often used for displaying quotations.

INDENT PARAGRAPHS

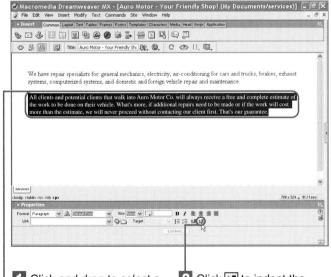

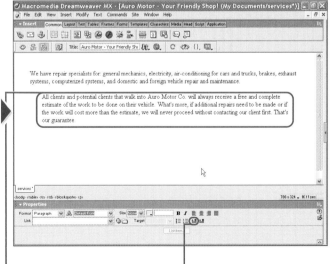

1 Click and drag to select a paragraph.

2 Click 🔲 to indent the text.

■ Additional space appears in both the left and right margins of the paragraph.

■ You can repeat steps **1** and **2** to indent a paragraph further.

■ You can outdent an indented paragraph by clicking 🔲.

CREATE LISTS

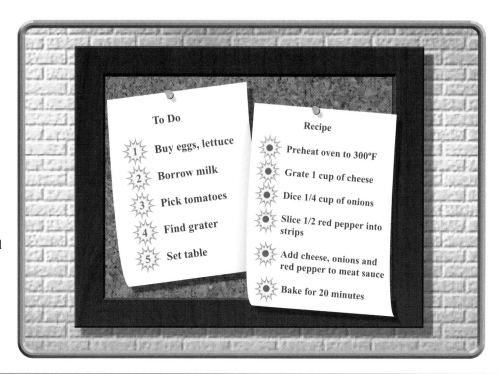

You can organize text items on your Web page into lists. Ordered lists have items that are indented and numbered. You can display step-by-step instructions with an ordered list. Unordered lists have items that are indented and bulleted but are not listed in order by number or letter.

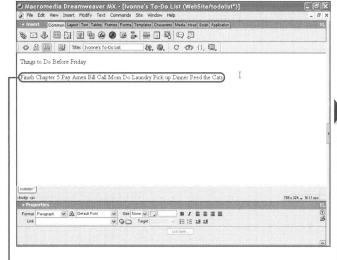

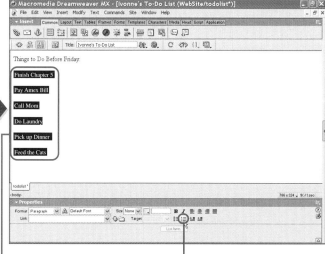

CREATE AN ORDERED LIST

1 Type your list items into the Document window.

2 Click between the items and press **Enter** (**Return**) to place each item in a separate paragraph.

3 Click and drag to select all the list items.

4 Click the Ordered List button (⊞) in the Property inspector.

**Can I modify the appearance
of my lists?**

You can modify the style of
ordered or unordered lists by
highlighting an item in the list
and clicking **Text**, **List**, and then
Properties. The dialog box that
appears enables you to select
different numbering schemes for
your ordered list, or different
bullet styles for your
unordered list.

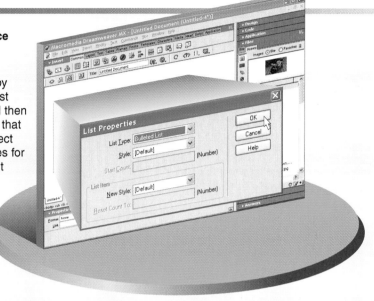

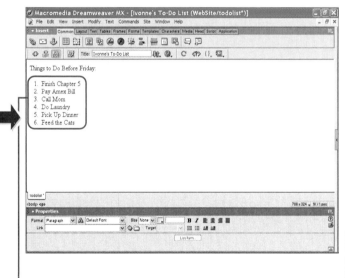

■ The list items appear
indented and numbered.

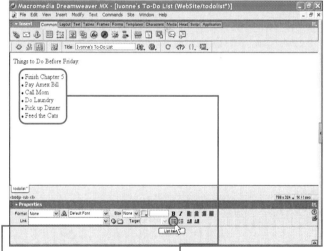

CREATE AN UNORDERED LIST

1 Repeat steps **1** to **3** from
the previous page.

2 Click the Unordered List
button ( ) in the Property
inspector.

■ The list items appear
indented and bulleted.

INSERT SPECIAL CHARACTERS

You can insert special characters into your Web page that do not commonly appear on your keyboard.

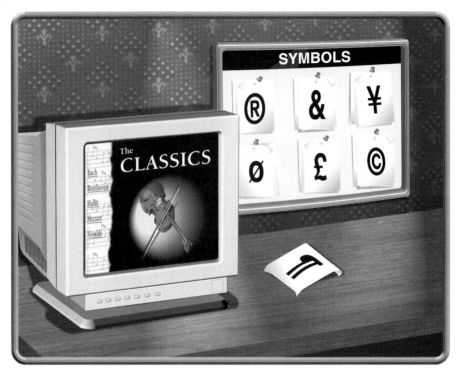

INSERT SPECIAL CHARACTERS

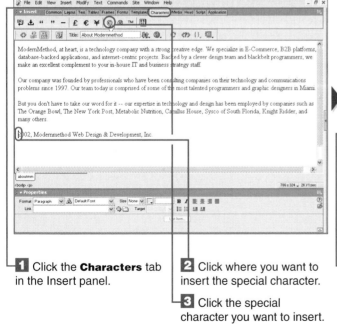

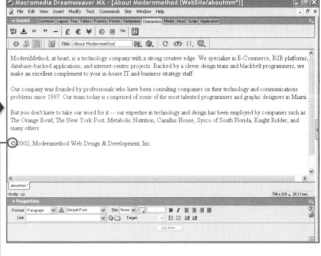

1 Click the **Characters** tab in the Insert panel.

2 Click where you want to insert the special character.

3 Click the special character you want to insert.

■ The special character appears in your Web page text.

**How do I include non-English
language text on my Web page?**

Many European languages feature
accented characters that do not
appear on standard keyboards.
You can insert many of these
characters using the special
characters tools described in
this section.

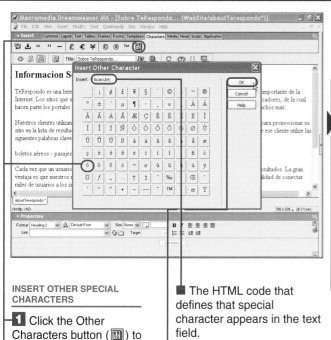

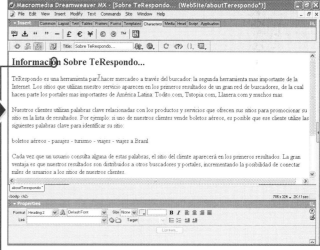

**INSERT OTHER SPECIAL
CHARACTERS**

1 Click the Other
Characters button (▥) to
access a wider variety of
special characters.

2 Click a special character.

■ The HTML code that
defines that special
character appears in the text
field.

3 Click **OK**.

■ The special character
appears in your Web page
text.

CHANGE THE FONT FACE

For aesthetic purposes or to emphasize certain elements on your Web page, you can change the font style of your text.

You can also customize the fonts on your Web pages by using Style Sheets. See Chapter 12 for more about Style Sheets.

CHANGE THE FONT FACE

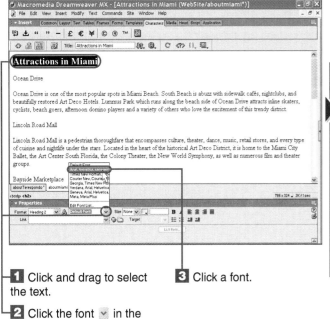

1 Click and drag to select the text.

2 Click the font ⊠ in the Property inspector.

3 Click a font.

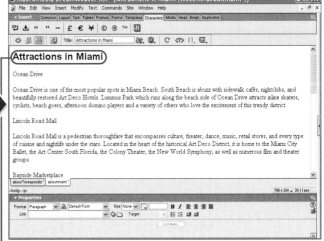

■ The text changes to the new font.

Note: A font must be installed on the user's computer to display in the browser. Dreamweaver's default list of fonts specifies common typefaces and alternate styles if the user does not have certain fonts installed.

How are fonts classified?

The two most common categories of fonts are *serif* and *sans-serif* fonts. Serif fonts are distinguished by the decorations, or serifs, on the ends of their lines. Common serif fonts include Times New Roman, Palatino, and Garamond. Sans-serif fonts lack these decorations. Common sans-serif fonts include Arial, Verdana, and Helvetica.

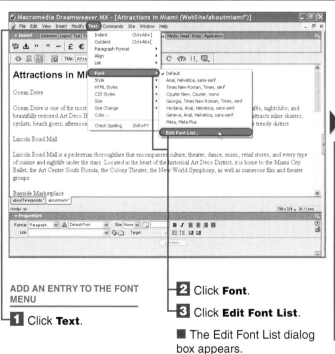

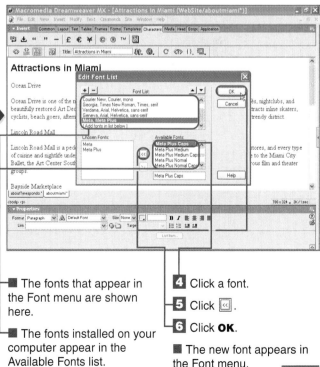

ADD AN ENTRY TO THE FONT MENU

1 Click **Text**.

2 Click **Font**.

3 Click **Edit Font List**.

■ The Edit Font List dialog box appears.

■ The fonts that appear in the Font menu are shown here.

■ The fonts installed on your computer appear in the Available Fonts list.

4 Click a font.

5 Click 〈〈.

6 Click **OK**.

■ The new font appears in the Font menu.

CHANGE THE FONT SIZE

You can emphasize or de-emphasize sections of text by changing the font size. Absolute font sizes on a Web page range from 1, the smallest, to 7, the largest.

CHANGE THE ABSOLUTE TEXT SIZE

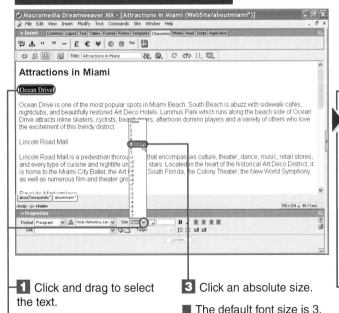

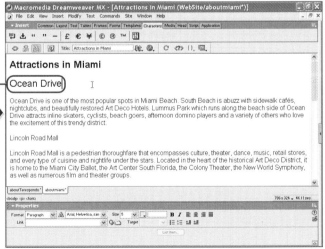

1 Click and drag to select the text.

2 Click the Size ⌄.

3 Click an absolute size.

■ The default font size is 3.

■ The text changes size.

How can changing the size of text enhance my Web page?

You can experiment with the size of words to produce interesting headlines on your Web pages. You can change the size of individual characters at the beginning of text passages for a traditional effect. You can create even more text effects using style sheets. See Chapter 12 for more about style sheets.

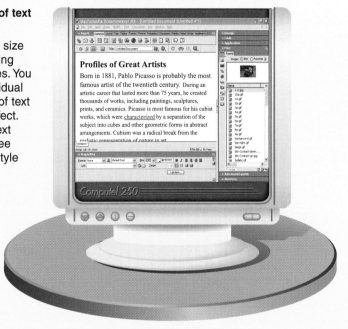

CHANGE THE RELATIVE TEXT SIZE

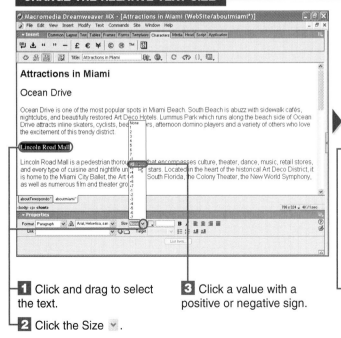

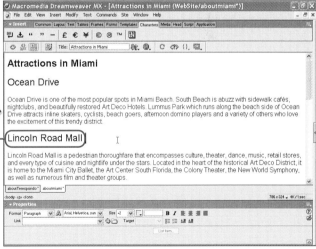

1 Click and drag to select the text.

2 Click the Size ⍙.

3 Click a value with a positive or negative sign.

■ The text changes size relative to the default size, which is 3.

Note: To adjust text size by creating a heading, see "Create a Heading."

CHANGE THE FONT COLOR

You can change the color of text on all or part of your Web page so that it complements the background and other page elements.

CHANGE THE COLOR OF ALL TEXT

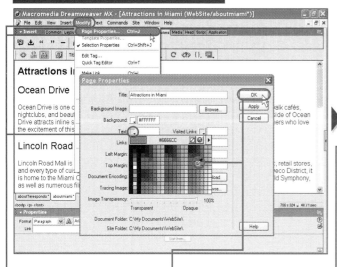

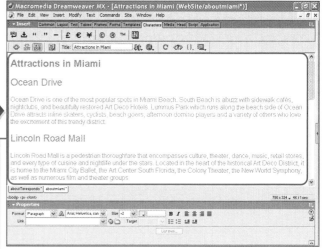

■ Click **Modify**.

■ Click **Page Properties**.

■ The Page Properties dialog box appears.

■ Click the Text □ (□ changes to ◢).

■ Click a color.

■ Click **OK**.

Note: The default color of text on a Web page is black.

■ Your text appears in a new color on your Web page.

What are the letter and number combinations that appear in the color fields of Dreamweaver?

HTML represents colors using six-digit codes called *hexadecimal codes*, which represent the amount of red, green, and blue used to create a particular color. Hex codes are preceded by a pound sign (#). Instead of ranging from 0 to 9, hex-code digits range from 0 to F with A equal to 10, B equal to 11, and so on through F, which is equal to 15. The first two digits in the hex code specify the amount of red in the selected color. The second two digits specify the amount of green, and the third two digits specify the amount of blue.

Color	Hex code
Aqua	#00FFFF
Black	#000000
Blue	#0000FF
Fuchsia	#FF00FF
Gray	#808080
Green	#008000
Lime	#008000
Maroon	#800000
Navy	#000080
Olive	#808000
Purple	#800080
Red	#FF0000
Silver	#C0C0C0
Teal	#008080
White	#FFFFFF
Yellow	#FFFF00

CHANGE THE COLOR OF SELECTED TEXT

1 Click and drag to select the text.

2 Click the ⬜ in the Property inspector (⬚ changes to 🖊).

3 Click a color.

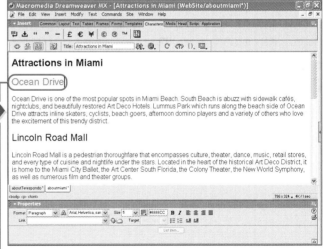

■ The selected text appears in the new color.

ADD A HORIZONTAL RULE

You can add a horizontal rule to your Web page to separate the page into sections.

ADD A HORIZONTAL RULE

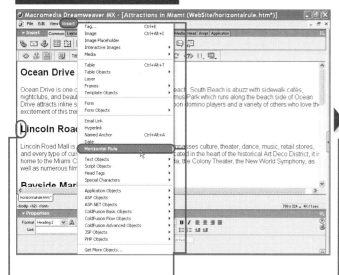

1 Position the cursor where you want to insert the horizontal rule.

2 Click **Insert**.

3 Click **Horizontal Rule**.

■ You can also use the 🖿 button.

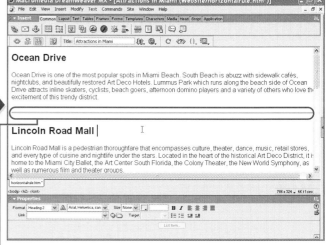

■ A thin horizontal line spans the entire width of the Web page.

Can I customize the color of my horizontal rule?

You can define the shading, but not the color of your horizontal rule. If you want your rules to have a particular color, you can create them as custom graphics in programs such as Macromedia Fireworks or Adobe Photoshop.

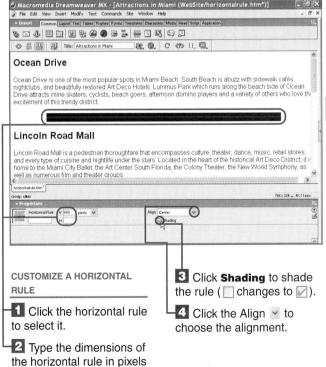

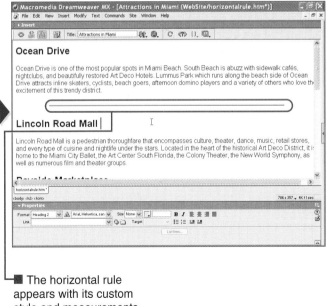

CUSTOMIZE A HORIZONTAL RULE

1 Click the horizontal rule to select it.

2 Type the dimensions of the horizontal rule in pixels in the W (width) and H (height) fields.

3 Click **Shading** to shade the rule (☐ changes to ☑).

4 Click the Align ⊻ to choose the alignment.

■ The horizontal rule appears with its custom style and measurements.

IMPORT TEXT FROM ANOTHER DOCUMENT

You can save time by importing text from an existing document, instead of typing it all over again. This is particularly convenient when you have tabular data that needs to appear in a table. By importing a comma- or tab-delimited text file, you do not have to re-create the entire table in HTML. Dreamweaver creates it automatically.

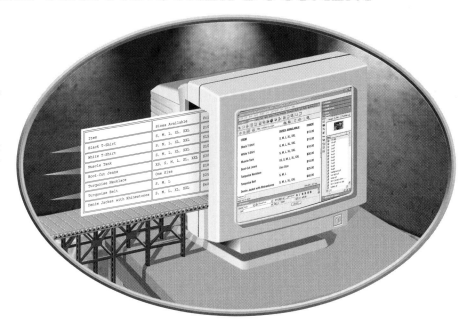

IMPORT TABULAR DATA FROM ANOTHER DOCUMENT

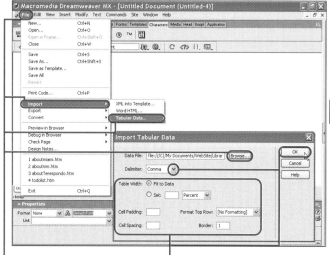

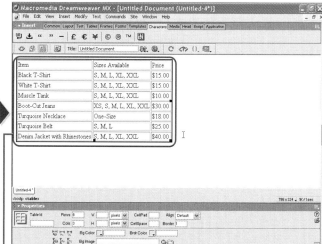

-1 Click **File**.

-2 Click **Import**.

-3 Click **Tabular Data**.

■ The Import Tabular Data dialog box appears.

-4 Click **Browse** to find the file you want to import.

-5 Click ✓ to select the appropriate delimiter.

■ You can specify the properties of the table. For more about formatting tables, see Chapter 8.

-6 Click **OK**.

■ The imported data appears in the Document window.

Note: When importing tabular data, make sure it has been converted into a comma-delimited or tab-delimited file.

When is importing text a good idea?

Unless you type at speeds of over 100 words per minute, typing large amounts of text can be very time-consuming. If your original text file was created using a word processing program such as Microsoft Word, you can speed up the process by saving the Word document as an HTML file, and then importing it into Dreamweaver. Then, just format the font, size, and color of the text.

IMPORT HTML TEXT FROM ANOTHER DOCUMENT

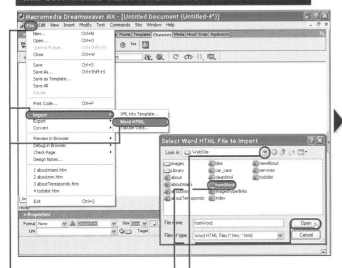

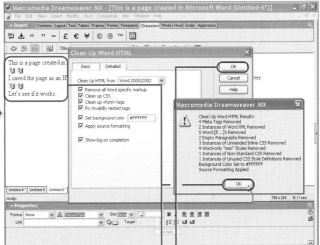

1 Click **File**.

2 Click **Import**.

3 Click **Word HTML**.

■ The Select Word HTML File to Import dialog box appears.

4 Click ⬇ to select the folder containing the HTML file.

5 Select the HTML file you want to import.

6 Click **Open**.

■ The Clean Up Word HTML dialog box appears.

■ If the HTML file you imported was not created with Microsoft Word, Dreamweaver warns you that it cannot determine the version of Word used to generate the file. Click **OK** to continue.

7 Click **OK**.

■ Dreamweaver cleans up the Word HTML file and lists the results.

8 Click **OK**.

■ The imported HTML appears in the Document window.

77

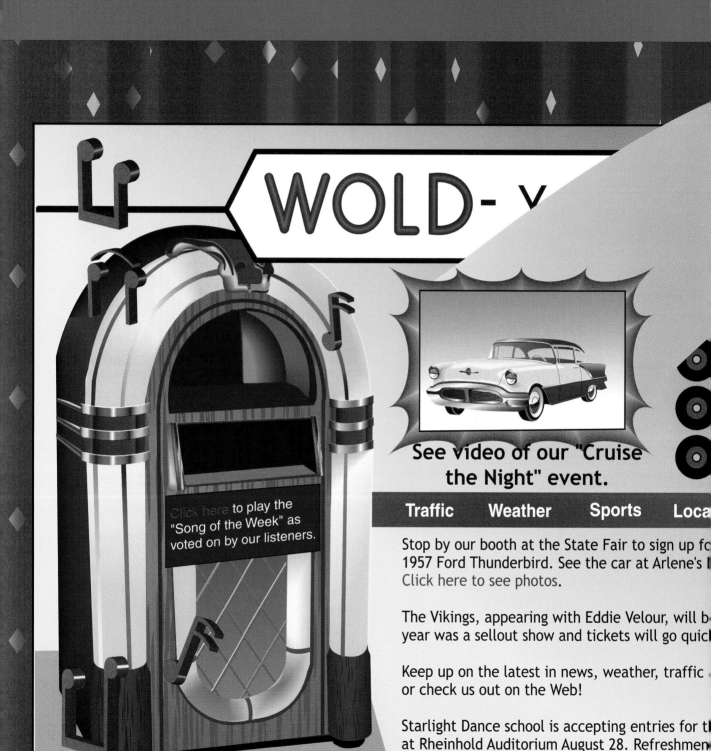

WOLD- V

See video of our "Cruise the Night" event.

Click here to play the "Song of the Week" as voted on by our listeners.

Traffic   **Weather**   **Sports**   **Loca**

Stop by our booth at the State Fair to sign up fo
1957 Ford Thunderbird. See the car at Arlene's I
Click here to see photos.

The Vikings, appearing with Eddie Velour, will b
year was a sellout show and tickets will go quic

Keep up on the latest in news, weather, traffic
or check us out on the Web!

Starlight Dance school is accepting entries for t
at Rheinhold Auditorium August 28. Refreshmen
weekend stay at Conner Bed & Breakfast will be

CHAPTER 6

Working with Images and Multimedia

You can make your Web page much more interesting by adding digital photos, scanned art, animation, and other types of visual elements. This chapter shows you how to insert and format them.

on

ntests

ke a Request

ecial Appearances

ntact Us

| ts | Just for Fun | Recent Guests |

nce to win a fully-restored, aqua-and-white
every Friday through June.

ncert at the Crestwood Stadium July 14-18. Last
ck here to connect with ConcertMaster.

ies personalities by listening to WOLD 113.2 FM,

twood Dance contest and Sock Hop, to be held
be served and prizes ranging from $50 to a
ed. Click here for entries and more information.

INSERT AN IMAGE INTO A WEB PAGE

Different types of images, including clip art, digital camera images, and scanned photos, can be inserted into your Web page.

INSERT AN IMAGE INTO A WEB PAGE

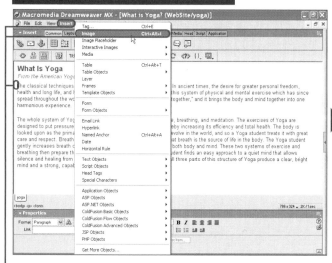

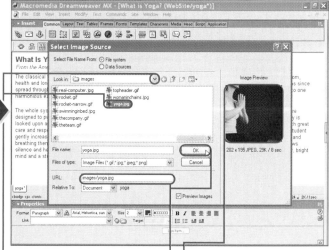

1 Click to position the cursor where you want to insert the image.

2 Click **Insert**.

3 Click **Image**.

■ You can also click the **Common** tab in the Insert menu, and then click the Insert Image button (🖼).

■ The Select Image Source dialog box appears.

4 Click ☑ to select the folder containing the image.

5 Click the image file that you want to insert into your Web page.

Note: Most Web image files end in .gif, *for GIF files, or* .jpg, *for JPEG files.*

■ A preview of the image appears.

■ You can insert an image that exists in an external Web address by typing the address into the URL field.

6 Click **OK**.

What are the file formats for Web images?

The majority of the images you see on Web pages are GIF or JPEG files. Both GIF and JPEG are compressed file formats, which means they store image information in a small amount of space. GIF is best for images that use flat colors and for other images that contain a limited number of colors — it only supports a maximum of 256 colors. JPEG is great for storing photographic information — it supports millions of colors. You can insert GIF and JPEG files into your Web page by using the steps described in this section.

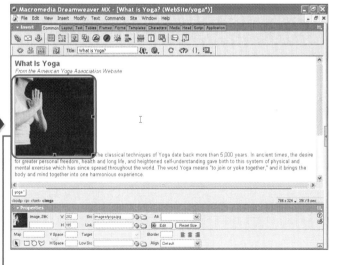

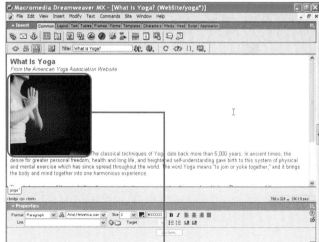

■ The image appears where you positioned your cursor in the Web page.

■ To delete an image, click the image and press **Delete**.

ADD A BORDER TO AN IMAGE

1 Click the image to select it.

2 Type the width, in this example in pixels, into the Border field.

3 Press **Enter** (**Return**).

■ A border appears around the image in the same color as the text.

WRAP TEXT AROUND AN IMAGE

Aligning the image to one side of a Web page allows you to wrap text around it. Wrapping text around images enables you to fit more information onto the screen and gives your Web pages a more finished, professional look.

WRAP TEXT AROUND AN IMAGE

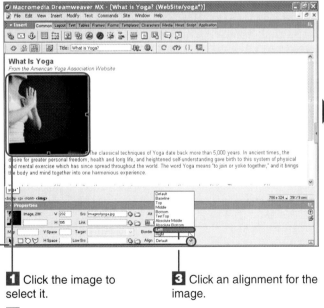

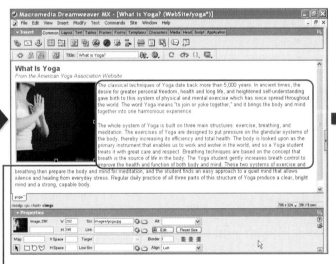

1 Click the image to select it.

2 Click the Align ▾.

3 Click an alignment for the image.

■ The text flows around the image according to the alignment you selected.

■ In this example, the text flows to the right of the left-aligned image.

How can I tell how much file space my images and text are taking up on my Web page?

The total size of your page appears in kilobytes (K) on the status bar. The total size includes the size of your HTML file, the size of your images, and the size of anything else on the page. Next to the size is the estimated download time for the page. You can specify how Dreamweaver estimates the download speed in the Preferences dialog box. See Chapter 3 to set preferences.

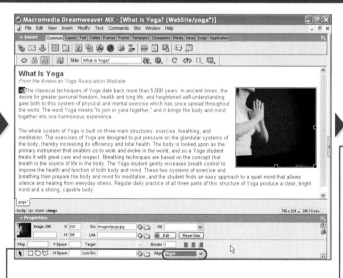

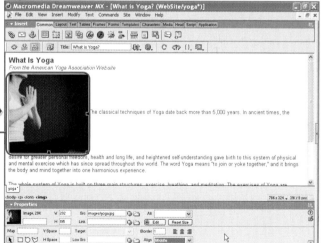

■ You can select other options from the Align ▾ for different wrapping effects such as right or middle.

■ In this example, the text flows to the left of the right-aligned image.

■ In this example, the text is aligned to the vertical middle of the image.

ALIGN AN IMAGE

The alignment of an image can give a photo or banner prominence on your page. You can center it or align it left or right, depending on the layout of your Web page.

ALIGN AN IMAGE

1 Click to place the cursor to the immediate right of the image.

2 Press `Enter` (`Return`) to place the image on its own line.

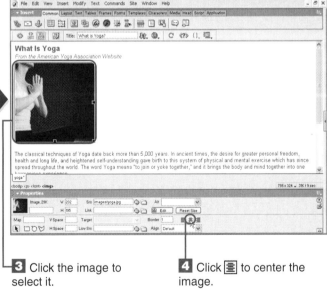

3 Click the image to select it.

4 Click 📰 to center the image.

How can I use centered images to enhance my text?

You can create custom graphics or icons in a graphics-editing program and use these as visual elements on your page. Center small icons to divide main sections of text in your Web page. These icons serve the same purpose as horizontal rules, but add a more sophisticated look to your pages. See Chapter 5 for more about horizontal rules.

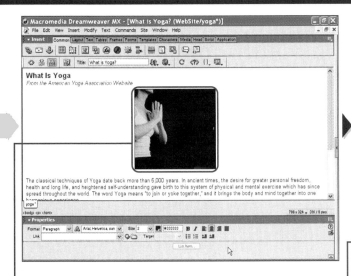

■ The image appears in the center of the page.

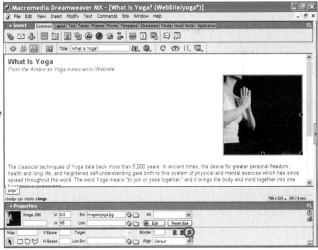

■ You can also align the image to the right side of the page by clicking 🖼.

■ You can toggle the alignment selection on or off by clicking it again.

RESIZE AN IMAGE

You can change the size of an image by changing the pixel dimensions, making the image a percentage of the browser window, or clicking and dragging the corner of the image.

Pixels, tiny, solid-color squares, make up a digital image.

RESIZE AN IMAGE

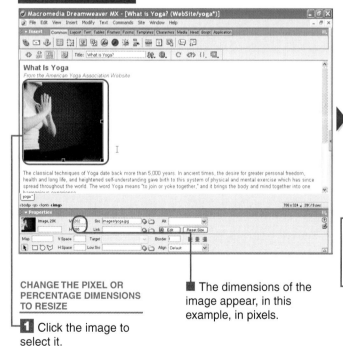

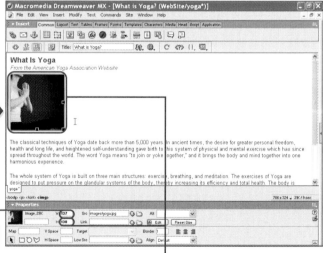

CHANGE THE PIXEL OR PERCENTAGE DIMENSIONS TO RESIZE

1 Click the image to select it.

■ The dimensions of the image appear, in this example, in pixels.

2 Type the desired width in pixels.

■ Instead of pixels, you can type a percentage of the window or table cell for the width and height. For example, type **50%** and **50%**.

3 Press **Enter** (**Return**).

4 Type the desired height, in pixels or percentage, of the image.

5 Press **Enter** (**Return**).

■ The image displays with its new pixel dimensions.

**What is the best way to change the
dimensions of an image on a Web page?**

Changing the dimensions of an image in
Dreamweaver stretches or shrinks the
presentation of an image on the Web page,
but does not actually resize the graphic's
true dimensions. The best way to change
the dimensions of an image used on a Web
page is with a graphics editor, such as
Macromedia Fireworks. This enables you to
adjust the image's real height and width
and save it as a new file. This maximizes
the quality of the image. If you have
Fireworks installed, you can open it
to edit a graphic directly from the
Dreamweaver Property inspector by
clicking the Edit/Fireworks Logo
button (Edit).

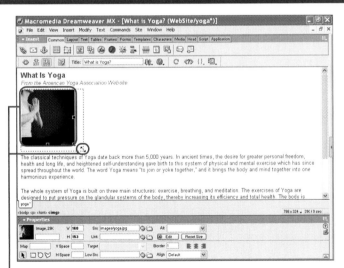

CLICK AND DRAG TO RESIZE

1 Click the image to
select it.

2 Drag the handle at the
edge of the image.

■ To resize an image
proportionally, press and
hold Shift as you drag a
corner.

■ The image expands or
contracts to its new
dimensions.

**RESET THE IMAGE TO ORIGINAL
SIZE**

■ If you change your mind
after resizing an image, you
can reset the image to its
original size.

1 Right-click the image.

2 From the menu that
appears, click **Reset Size**.

■ The image returns to its
original size in pixels.

ADD SPACE AROUND AN IMAGE

You can add space around an image to distinguish it from the text and other images on your Web page. This creates a cleaner page layout.

ADD SPACE AROUND AN IMAGE

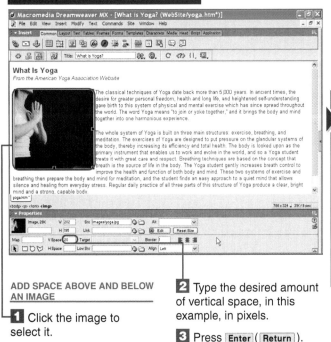

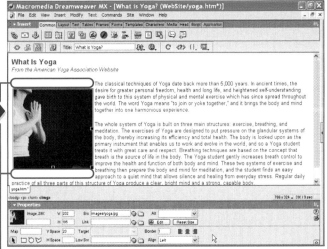

ADD SPACE ABOVE AND BELOW AN IMAGE

1 Click the image to select it.

2 Type the desired amount of vertical space, in this example, in pixels.

3 Press `Enter` (`Return`).

■ Extra space appears above and below the images.

Why should I add space around my image?

In many cases, adding space around your images enhances the appearance of your Web page. The extra space makes text easier to read and keeps adjacent images from appearing as a single image.

ADD SPACE TO THE LEFT AND
RIGHT OF AN IMAGE

1 Click the image to select it.

2 Type the desired amount of horizontal space, in this example, in pixels.

3 Press **Enter** (**Return**).

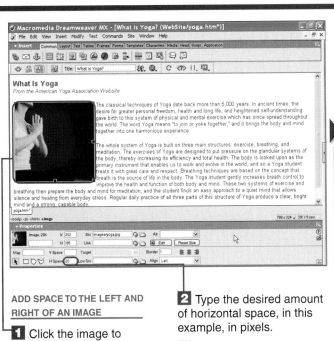

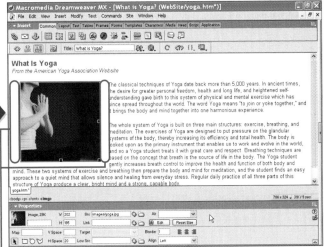

■ Extra space appears to the left and right of the image.

ADD A BACKGROUND IMAGE

You can incorporate a background image to add texture to your Web page. Background images appear beneath any text or images on your page.

ADD A BACKGROUND IMAGE

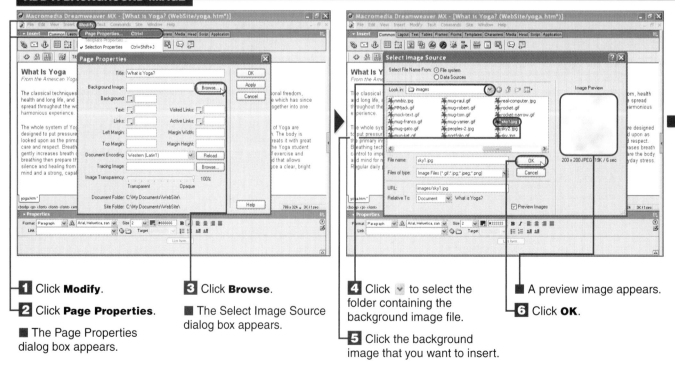

1 Click **Modify**.

2 Click **Page Properties**.

■ The Page Properties dialog box appears.

3 Click **Browse**.

■ The Select Image Source dialog box appears.

4 Click ⌄ to select the folder containing the background image file.

5 Click the background image that you want to insert.

■ A preview image appears.

6 Click **OK**.

What types of images make good backgrounds?

Typically, images that do not clash with the text and other content in the foreground make good background images. You do not want your background images to overwhelm the rest of the page. Using an image that tiles seamlessly is also a good idea so that your background appears to be one large image that covers the entire page. An example of a seamless tile can be seen in the section below.

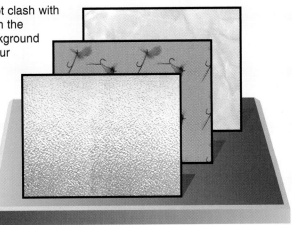

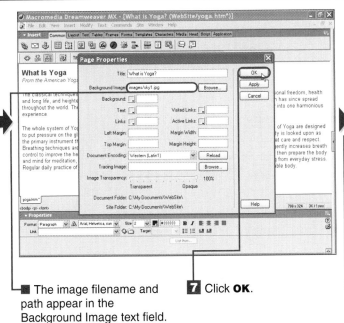

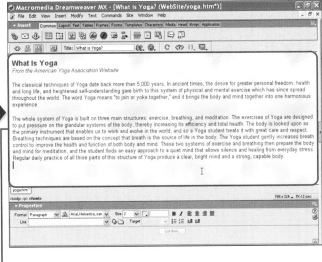

■ The image filename and path appear in the Background Image text field.

7 Click **OK**.

■ The image appears as a background on the Web page.

Note: If necessary, the image tiles horizontally and vertically to fill the entire window.

CHANGE THE BACKGROUND COLOR

For variety, you can change the background color of your Web page.

White is the default background color of Web pages created in Dreamweaver.

CHANGE THE BACKGROUND COLOR

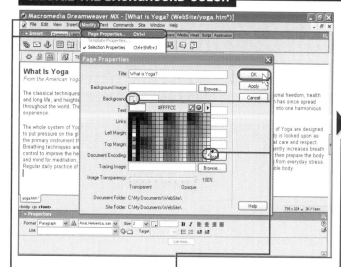

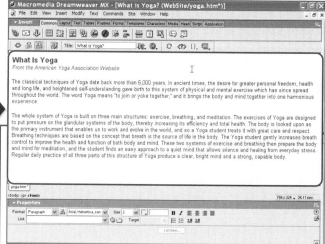

■1 Click **Modify**.

■2 Click **Page Properties**.

■ The Page Properties dialog box appears.

■3 Click the Background to open the color menu (⬚ changes to ✐).

■4 Click a color from the menu using the eyedropper tool (✐).

■5 Click **OK**.

■ The background of your Web page displays in the color you selected.

Note: See page 73 for additional information about Web color.

Note: A background image will appear over any background color. See "Add a Background Image" for more information.

ADD ALTERNATE TEXT

You can add alternate text for users to read when they place their mouse over an image, or if an image does not appear on their page.

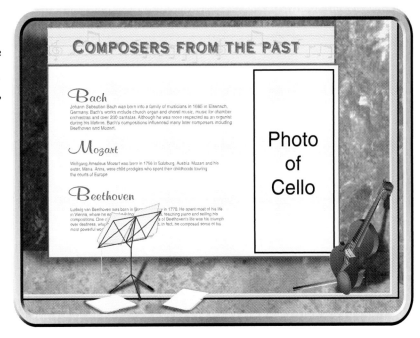

Some Web browsers cannot display images, and some users view Web pages with images turned off.

ADD ALTERNATE TEXT

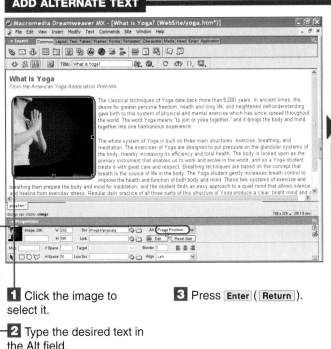

1 Click the image to select it.

2 Type the desired text in the Alt field.

3 Press Enter (Return).

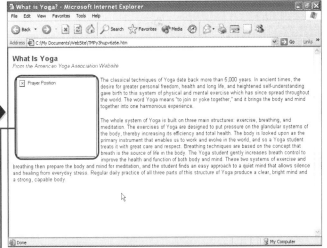

■ The alternate text appears when the image does not display in the browser window.

Note: Some browsers briefly display alternate text when you hold your mouse over an image.

INSERT A FLASH FILE

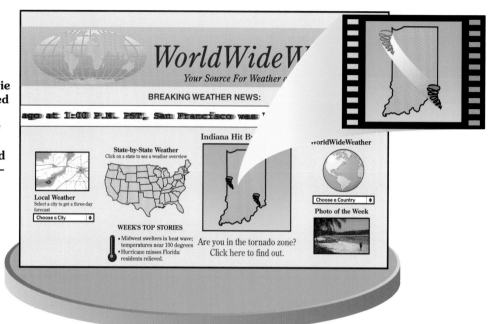

You can add life to your Web page by inserting a Flash movie. A Flash movie is a multimedia file created with Macromedia Flash software. There are many uses for Flash movies — both for informational and entertainment purposes — animated banner ads, cartoons, e-learning content, interactive animations, site navigation, and so on.

INSERT A FLASH FILE

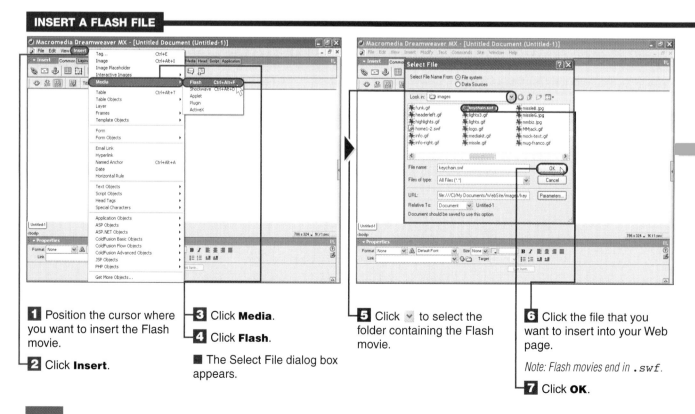

1 Position the cursor where you want to insert the Flash movie.

2 Click **Insert**.

3 Click **Media**.

4 Click **Flash**.

■ The Select File dialog box appears.

5 Click ⌄ to select the folder containing the Flash movie.

6 Click the file that you want to insert into your Web page.

Note: Flash movies end in .swf.

7 Click **OK**.

What HTML tags does Flash insert into the HTML document?

When you insert a Flash movie into a Dreamweaver document, Dreamweaver automatically inserts the tags necessary for playing the Flash movie in the browser window. Dreamweaver inserts the `object` tag needed for Microsoft's Internet Explorer browser and the `embed` tag needed for Netscape's Navigator browser. The `object` and `embed` tags create the movie display window used to play the Flash movie. Dreamweaver also adds a path to the plug-in on the Macromedia site so that the Web browser can install it if it is not present. It also writes `param` tags, which instruct the Flash movie what quality to play in (high is default), and what the name of the file is. You can create additional `param` tags easily by clicking the Flash movie and then clicking **Parameters** in the Property inspector. A very useful one is `wmode`, which lets you define the transparency of the Flash movie background as transparent or opaque.

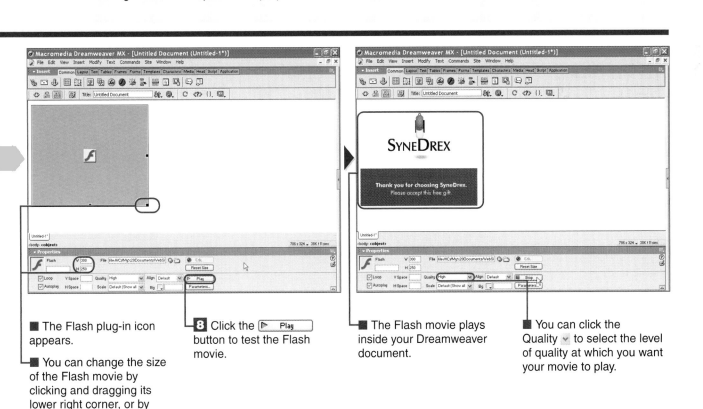

■ The Flash plug-in icon appears.

■ You can change the size of the Flash movie by clicking and dragging its lower right corner, or by entering a width and height in the Property inspector.

8 Click the **Play** button to test the Flash movie.

■ The Flash movie plays inside your Dreamweaver document.

■ You can click the Quality to select the level of quality at which you want your movie to play.

INSERT OTHER MULTIMEDIA FILES

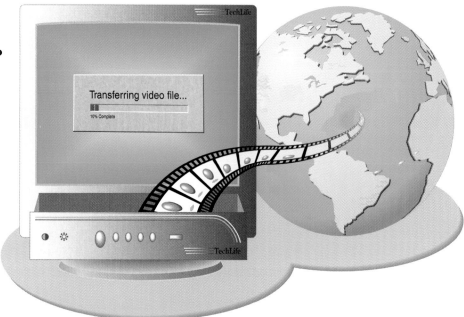

You can insert video clips and other multimedia to add variety to your Web page.

INSERT OTHER MULTIMEDIA FILES

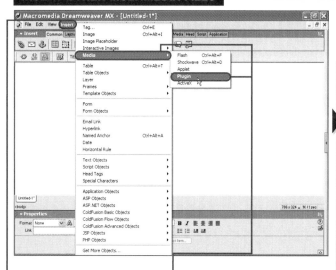

1 Position the cursor where you want to insert the multimedia in the Document window.

2 Click **Insert**.

3 Click **Media**.

4 Click **Plugin** to add a video or sound clip.

■ Many multimedia features in Web browsers are handled by special add-ons called plug-ins.

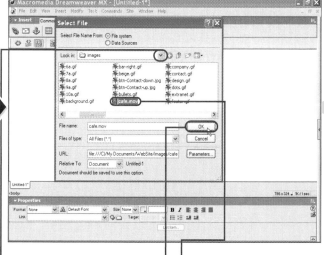

■ The Select File dialog box appears.

5 Click ⌄ to select the folder containing the multimedia file.

6 Click the multimedia file that you want to insert into your Web page.

7 Click **OK**.

■ A plug-in icon appears.

What should I consider when adding multimedia content to my site?

You can add Flash movies, video clips, sounds, and interactive features to jazz up a Web site. But remember that some users cannot view the content because their browsers do not support it. Size should also be a consideration. Many multimedia files are large and may take a while to download. Know your audience before you add a 3-megabyte file to your Web page. If they are mainly using dial-up connections, most will not wait for the download. In addition, some users are unwilling to spend the time to download and install the plug-in. From a legal perspective, if you add music or other copyrighted material to your multimedia files, make sure you have the proper permissions and are not in violation of any copyright laws.

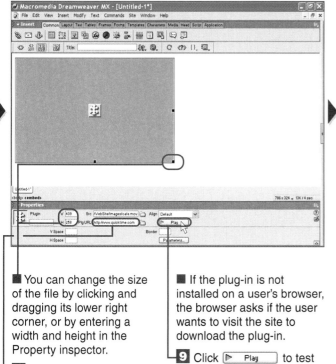

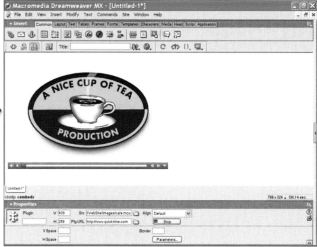

■ You can change the size of the file by clicking and dragging its lower right corner, or by entering a width and height in the Property inspector.

8 Type the URL of the site where the user can download the plug-in.

■ If the plug-in is not installed on a user's browser, the browser asks if the user wants to visit the site to download the plug-in.

9 Click ▶ Play to test the multimedia file.

■ You can use this feature to test multimedia files, such as QuickTime movies, in the Dreamweaver Document window.

THE BEST

Reviews of Golf Courses Here and Abroad

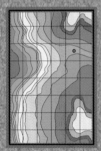

Discover how the professionals rate golf courses in nine countries around the world. Each course has a rating, course schematics, aerial and ground photos, along with the professionals' notes and tips for playing each hole. Historical background and course designers are listed, as well as resorts and hotels in the immediate area. Links to the courses are also included. Leave your own rating after you've played your favorite.

Contact Us
Submit A Rating

Computel 250

CHAPTER 7

Creating Hyperlinks

You can connect related information on different Web pages by creating hyperlinks. This chapter shows you how to turn both text and images into hyperlinks.

Submit a Rating

en't the only ones who know their golf courses;
ayers as well as the weekend golfers have their
s, too. To rate a golf course, fill in the informati

Phone   **E-mail**

Location

nts

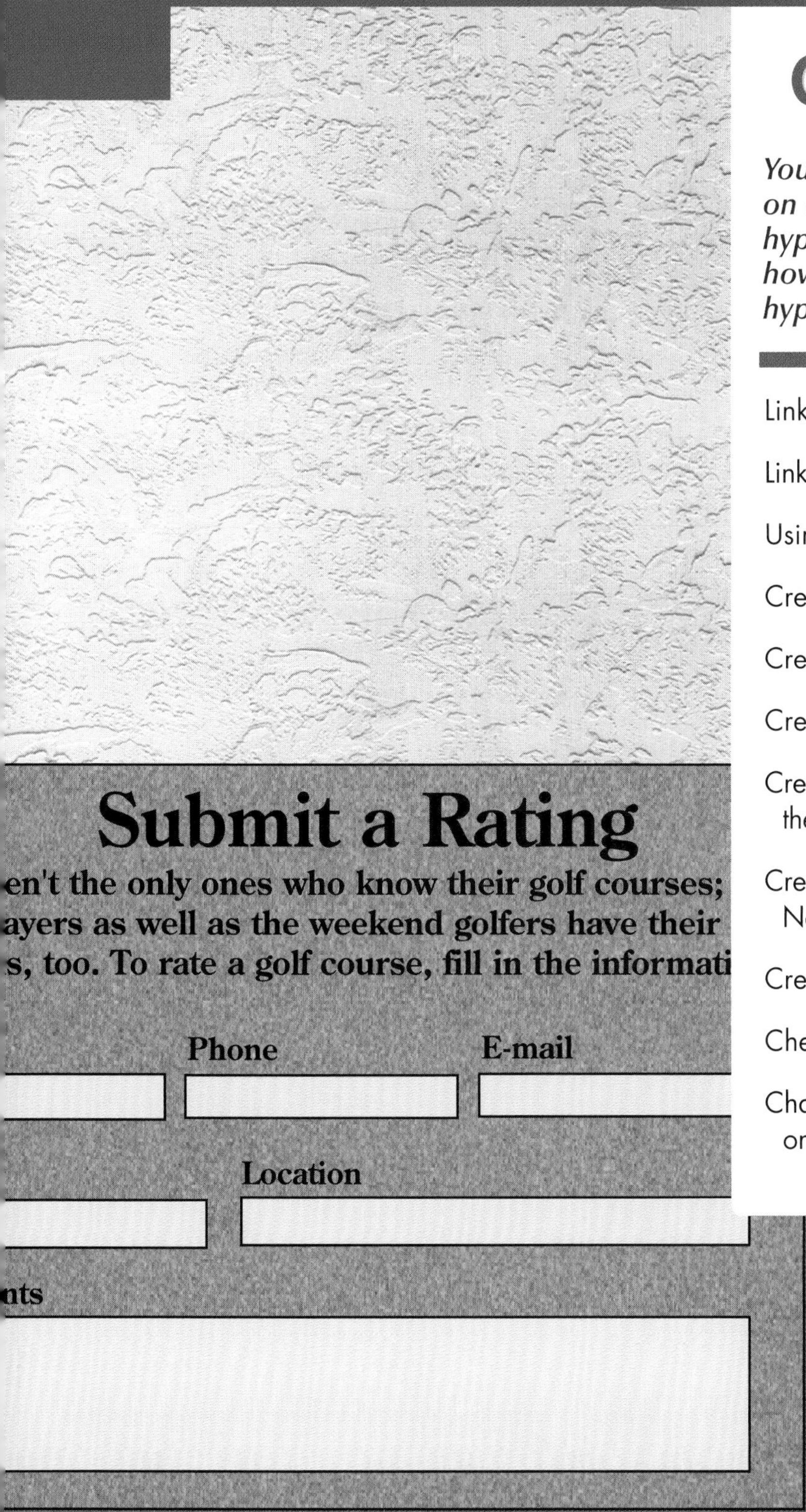

LINK TO OTHER PAGES IN YOUR SITE

You can create a link that allows readers to move from one page of your Web site to another.

LINK TO OTHER PAGES IN YOUR SITE

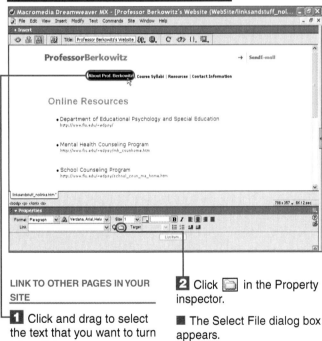

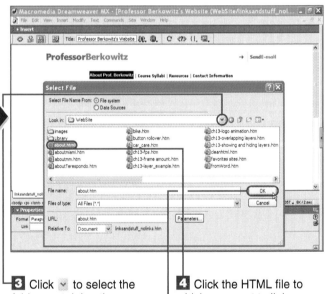

LINK TO OTHER PAGES IN YOUR SITE

1 Click and drag to select the text that you want to turn into a link.

Note: See "Using an Image as a Link" for more information on linking an image.

2 Click 📁 in the Property inspector.

■ The Select File dialog box appears.

3 Click ⬇ to select the folder containing the destination page.

4 Click the HTML file to which you want to link.

5 Click **OK**.

How should I organize the files that make up my Web site?

You should keep the files that make up your Web site in the folder that you define as your local site folder. This makes finding pages and images and creating links between your pages easier. It also ensures that all the links work correctly when you transfer the files to a live Web server. Additionally, you should store all your images in a folder called Images. If you have a lot of pages under one section, you should further divide the file structure to include subfolders for the pages in each section of the site. See Chapter 2 to set up your Web site, and Chapter 14 to transfer files to a Web server.

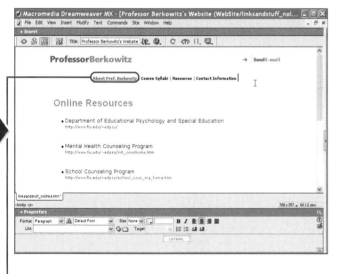

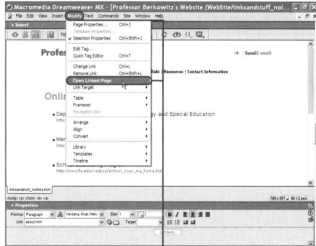

■ The new link appears in color and underlined.

■ Links are not clickable in the Document window.

■ You can test the link by previewing the file in a Web browser.

Note: See Chapter 2 to preview Web pages in a browser.

OPEN AND EDIT A LINKED PAGE

1 Click anywhere on the text of the link whose destination you want to open.

2 Click **Modify**.

3 Click **Open Linked Page**.

■ The link destination opens in a Document window. You can edit it as you would any other file.

LINK TO ANOTHER WEB SITE

You can give viewers access to additional information about topics by linking to pages in other Web sites.

LINK TO ANOTHER WEB SITE

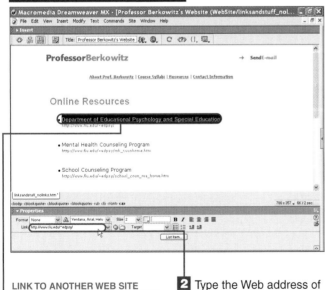

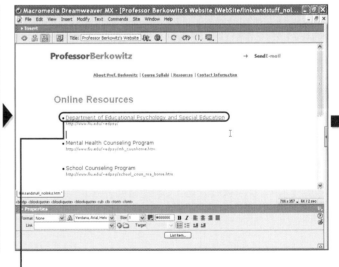

LINK TO ANOTHER WEB SITE

1 Click and drag to select the text that you want to turn into a link.

2 Type the Web address of the destination page, including the `http://`, in the Link field on the Property inspector.

■ The new link appears colored and underlined.

■ Links are not clickable in the Document window.

■ You can test the link by previewing the file in a Web browser.

Note: See Chapter 2 to preview Web pages in a browser.

How do I make sure my links to other Web sites always work?

You usually have no control over the Web pages on other sites to which you have linked. If you have linked to a Web page whose file is later renamed or taken offline, your viewers will receive an error message when they click the link. Maintain your site by periodically checking your links. You can also use software or Web site tune-up services to perform this checking for you. Neither one can bring back a page that no longer exists, but both can tell you what links you need to remove or update.

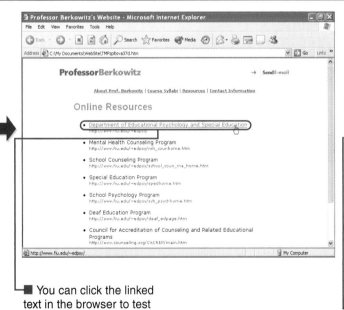

■ You can click the linked text in the browser to test the link.

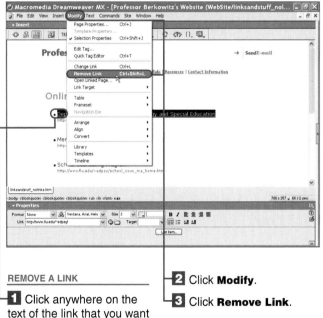

REMOVE A LINK

1 Click anywhere on the text of the link that you want to remove.

2 Click **Modify**.

3 Click **Remove Link**.

■ The link is removed, and the text no longer appears colored and underlined.

USING AN IMAGE AS A LINK

An image link allows users to click an image to go to another Web page. It is very common to build a Web site's navigation using images as links.

USING AN IMAGE AS A LINK

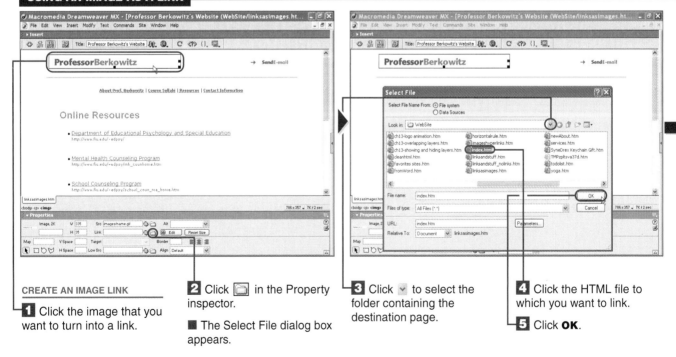

CREATE AN IMAGE LINK

1 Click the image that you want to turn into a link.

2 Click 📁 in the Property inspector.

■ The Select File dialog box appears.

3 Click ∨ to select the folder containing the destination page.

4 Click the HTML file to which you want to link.

5 Click **OK**.

How do I create a navigation bar for my Web page?

Many Web sites include sets of images that act as link buttons on the top, side, or bottom of each page. These button images let viewers navigate through the pages of the Web site. You can create these button images using an image-editing program such as Adobe Photoshop or Macromedia Fireworks.

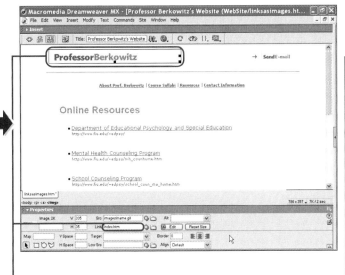

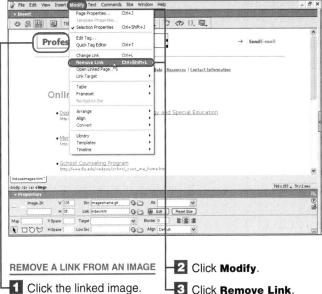

■ Your image is now a link.

■ Links are not clickable in the Document window, but you can test the link by previewing the file in a Web browser.

Note: See Chapter 2 to preview Web pages in a browser.

REMOVE A LINK FROM AN IMAGE

-1 Click the linked image.

-2 Click **Modify**.

-3 Click **Remove Link**.

■ The link is removed.

CREATE A JUMP LINK WITHIN A PAGE

You can create a link to other content on the same page. Same-page links are useful when a page is very long. A common use for this type of link is often seen on a Web site's Frequently Asked Questions (FAQ) page.

CREATE A JUMP LINK WITHIN A PAGE

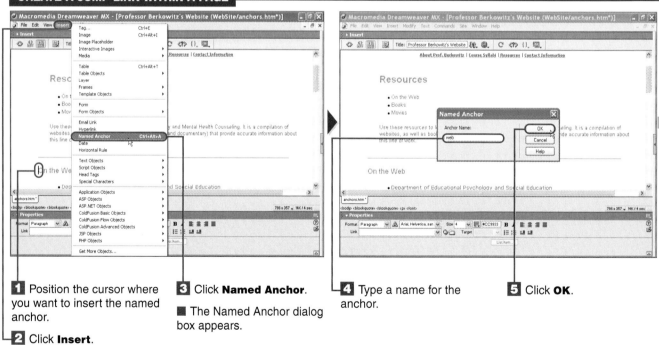

1 Position the cursor where you want to insert the named anchor.

2 Click **Insert**.

3 Click **Named Anchor**.

■ The Named Anchor dialog box appears.

4 Type a name for the anchor.

5 Click **OK**.

What is an example of a useful same-page hyperlink?

Web designers often employ same-page hyperlinks. For example, you frequently see them at the bottom of a page. The "Back to Top" link brings you to the beginning of the page when you click it. If you have a Web page that is a glossary, same-page links let you link to different parts of the glossary from a link menu at the top of the page. A Frequently Asked Questions (FAQ) page is also a common example of when to use same-page links. You can list all your questions at the top of the page, and link each one to a detailed answer further down on the page.

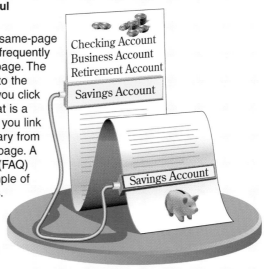

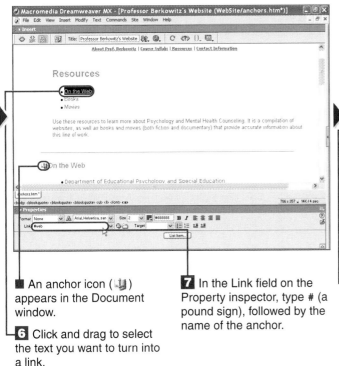

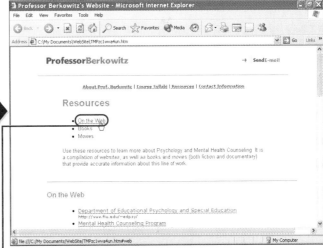

■ An anchor icon () appears in the Document window.

6 Click and drag to select the text you want to turn into a link.

7 In the Link field on the Property inspector, type # (a pound sign), followed by the name of the anchor.

■ The selected text is now linked to the named anchor.

■ The new hyperlink is not clickable in the Document window.

■ You can test the link by previewing the file in a Web browser.

Note: See Chapter 2 to preview Web pages in a browser.

CREATE A LINK TO ANOTHER FILE TYPE

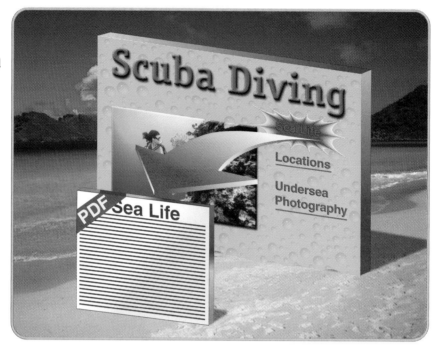

Links do not have to lead just to other Web pages. You can link to other file types, such as image files, word processing documents, PDF files or multimedia files.

CREATE A LINK TO ANOTHER FILE TYPE

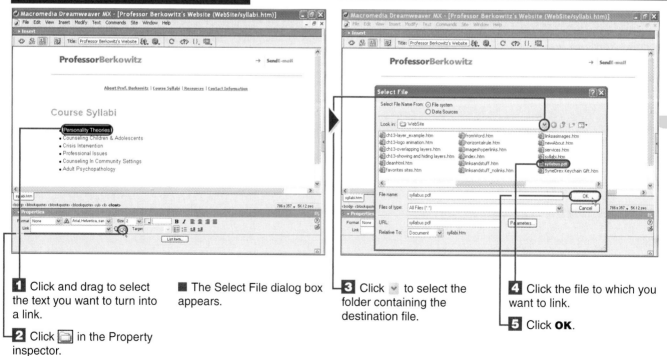

1 Click and drag to select the text you want to turn into a link.

2 Click 🖹 in the Property inspector.

■ The Select File dialog box appears.

3 Click ⌄ to select the folder containing the destination file.

4 Click the file to which you want to link.

5 Click **OK**.

How do users see files that are not HTML documents?

What users see when they click links to other types of files depends on how their Web browser is configured and what applications they have installed on their computer. For instance, if you link to a QuickTime movie (`.mov`), users need to have QuickTime software installed on their computer to see the movie. If a user does not have the software installed, the browser typically asks if the user wants to download the file and save it so they can view it later — after they have installed the correct software.

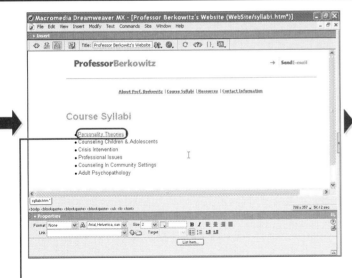

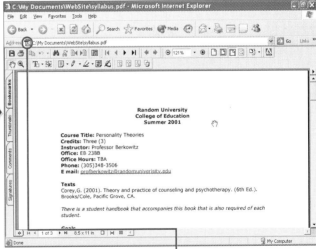

■ The new link appears in color and underlined.

■ Links are not clickable in the Document window.

■ You can test the link by previewing the file in a Web browser.

Note: See Chapter 2 to preview Web pages in a browser.

■ When you click the link in the browser, the linked file opens.

■ In this example, the linked PDF appears in the browser window when the link is clicked.

CREATE AN IMAGE MAP

To make an image serve several purposes, you can assign different links, also called hotspots, to different parts of a single image using Dreamweaver's image-mapping tools.

CREATE AN IMAGE MAP

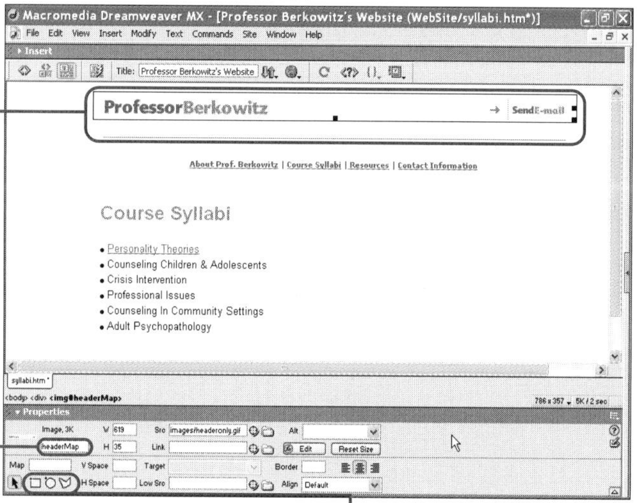

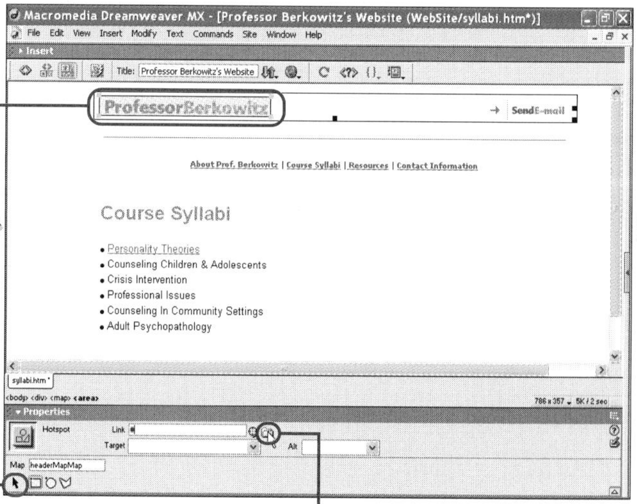

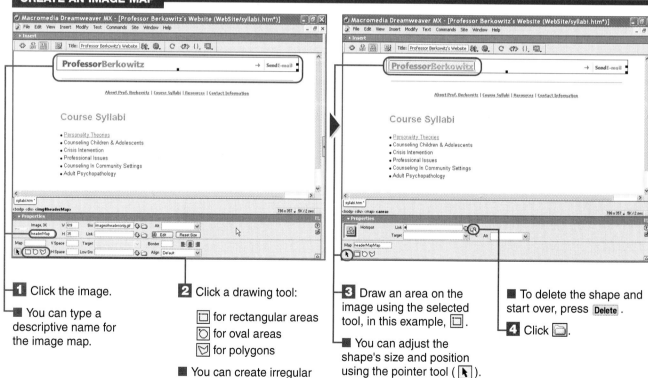

1 Click the image.

■ You can type a descriptive name for the image map.

2 Click a drawing tool:

- for rectangular areas
- for oval areas
- for polygons

■ You can create irregular shape areas with the polygon tool.

3 Draw an area on the image using the selected tool, in this example, the rectangle tool.

■ You can adjust the shape's size and position using the pointer tool.

■ To delete the shape and start over, press **Delete**.

4 Click the folder icon.

How can I create an interactive map of the United States with each state having a different link?

An interactive map is a common place to see hotspots in action. You can create one by adding a map of the U.S. to your Web page and defining a hotspot over each state. Use the polygon tool ([☑]) to draw around the states. Finally, assign a different link to each state.

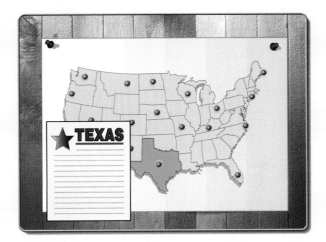

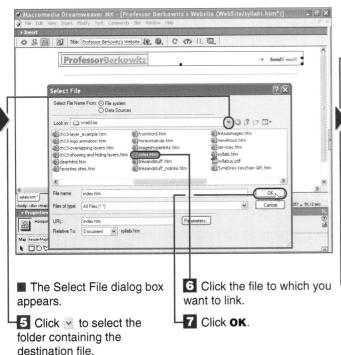

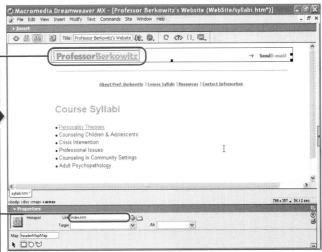

■ The Select File dialog box appears.

5 Click ☑ to select the folder containing the destination file.

6 Click the file to which you want to link.

7 Click **OK**.

■ The area defined by the shape becomes a link to the selected file. Here, the Professor Berkowitz image links to the index.htm file.

■ Repeat steps **2** to **7** to add other linked areas to your image.

■ The image-map shapes will not appear when you open the page in a Web browser.

Note: You should avoid overlapping hot spots. The results are unpredictable across browsers.

111

CREATE A LINK USING THE SITE PANEL

You can create links on your page quickly and easily by clicking and dragging to the Site panel.

CREATE A LINK USING THE SITE PANEL

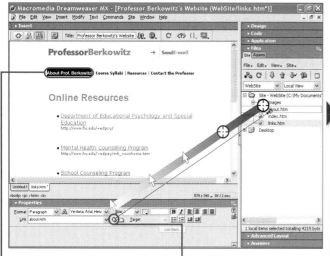

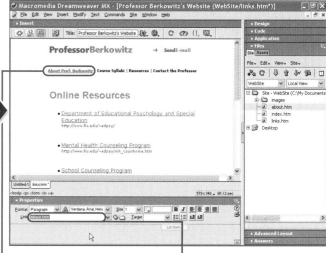

1 Arrange your workspace with both the Document window and Site panel visible.

2 Click and drag to select the text that you want to turn into a link.

3 Click and drag the Point to File icon (⊕) to the destination file in the Site panel (🖑 changes to ⊕).

■ The new link appears in color and underlined.

■ The destination file displays in the Link field in the Property inspector.

Note: You can also select an image to create an image link. See the section "Using an Image as a Link" for more information.

CREATE A LINK TO OPEN A NEW BROWSER WINDOW

You can create a link that opens a new browser window when clicked. The destination page opens in the new window.

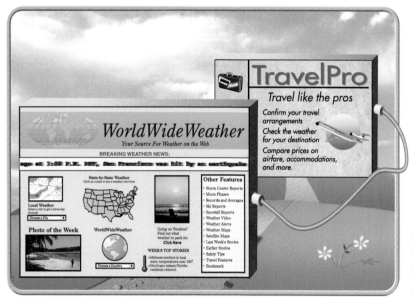

Opening a new window lets you keep a previous Web page open on a viewer's computer.

CREATE A LINK TO OPEN A NEW BROWSER WINDOW

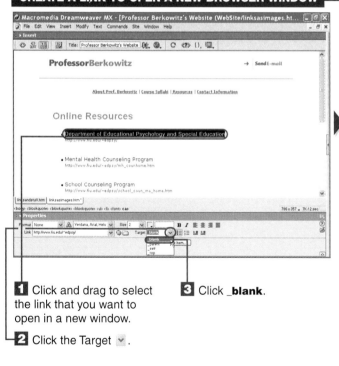

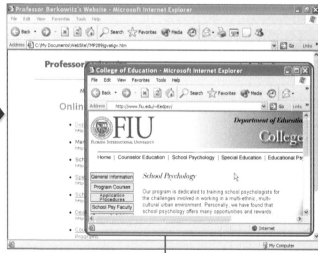

1 Click and drag to select the link that you want to open in a new window.

2 Click the Target ⌄.

3 Click **_blank**.

4 Preview the page in a Web browser and click the link.

Note: See Chapter 2 to preview Web pages in a browser.

■ The link destination appears in a new window.

CREATE AN E-MAIL LINK

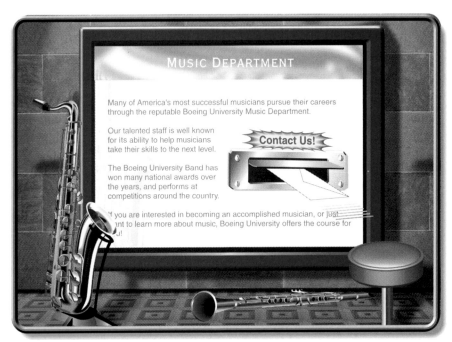

You can create a link that launches an e-mail composition window.

CREATE AN E-MAIL LINK

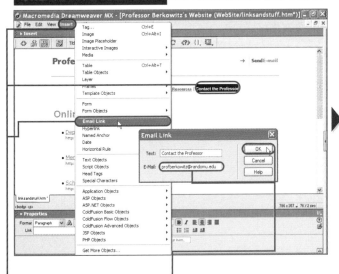

1 Click to select the text or image that you want to turn into an e-mail link.

2 Click **Insert**.

3 Click **Email Link**.

■ The selected text appears in the Text field of the Email Link dialog box.

4 Type the e-mail address to which you want to link.

5 Click **OK**.

■ You can also add an e-mail link by typing **mailto:** and the e-mail address in the Link field in the Property Inspector. Example: mailto: john@home.com.

6 To test the link, preview the page in a browser.

■ In the Web browser, you can click the link to launch your e-mail program. The e-mail address you specified in step **4** appears in the To: field.

■ If the browser does not have e-mail capability set up, clicking the link has no effect.

CHECK LINKS

You can automatically verify a Web page's links and get a report that lists any that are broken.

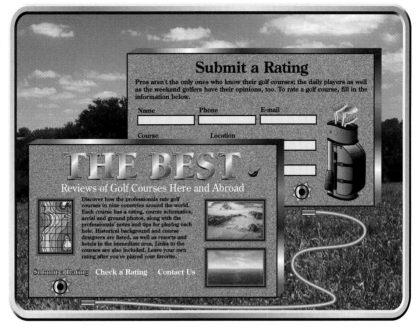

Deleting or renaming a link breaks the connection of the Web page files.

CHECK LINKS

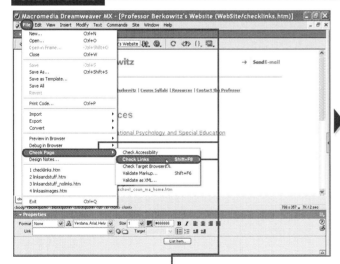

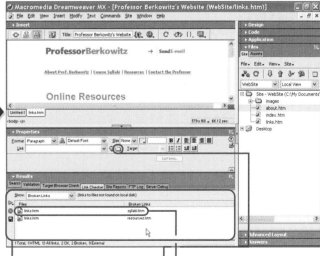

1 Open the Web page you want to check.

Note: See Chapter 2 to preview Web pages in a browser.

2 Click **File**.

3 Click **Check Page**.

4 Click **Check Links**.

■ Dreamweaver checks the local links and lists any broken links it finds.

Note: Dreamweaver is unable to verify links to Web pages on external sites.

■ You can edit a broken destination file by selecting it and editing the Broken Links field.

■ You can also click 🗀 to select a new destination for the link.

CHANGE THE COLOR OF LINKS ON A PAGE

You can change the color of the links on your Web page to make them match the visual style of the text and images on your page.

CHANGE THE COLOR OF LINKS ON A PAGE

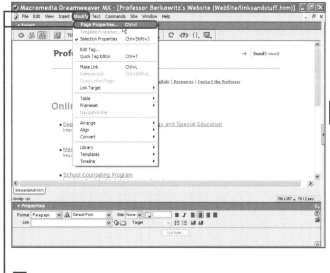

-1 Click **Modify**.

-2 Click **Page Properties**.

■ The Page Properties dialog box appears.

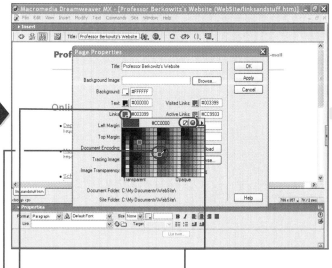

3 Click the Links ☐ to access a menu from which you can select a color for unvisited links (⬚ changes to ✎).

4 Click a color from the menu using the eyedropper tool (✎).

■ You can click the System Color Picker button (◉) to select a custom color, or the Default Color button (☑) to specify no color.

■ The color menu closes.

What color will my links appear if I do not specifically define them?

Blue is the default link color in the Dreamweaver Document window. What viewers see when the page opens in a browser depends on the browser settings. By default, most browsers display unvisited links as blue, visited links as purple, and active links as red.

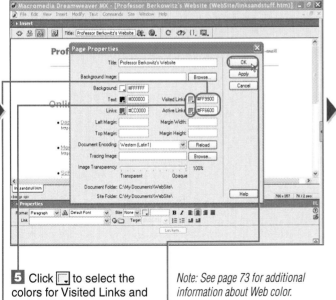

5 Click 🔲 to select the colors for Visited Links and Active Links.

■ You can also specify common colors by typing, for example, **red** or **blue** in the text field.

Note: See page 73 for additional information about Web color.

6 Click **OK**.

7 Preview the page in a Web browser.

Note: See Chapter 2 to preview Web pages in a browser.

■ The links display in the specified colors.

DESSERTS

	Chocolate chip cookies, made fresh daily in our kitchen. Served warm alone or with ice cream.	3 for $2.00 A dozen for $6.00
	Chocolate mousse in three varieties – dark chocolate, cafe au lait, and creamy chocolate.	$3.65
	Homemade ice cream in French Vanilla, Fresh Strawberry, Dark Chocolate, and Chocolate Chip.	$2.25
	Fruit pies made in our kitchen. Peach, Apple, Strawberry, Raspberry, and Three Berry.	$2.75
	Whole pies are available for takeout. Order in advance for warm pies made to order.	$15.00

CHAPTER 8

Using Tables to Design a Web Page

Tables enable you to arrange text, images, and other elements on your pages and create complex designs, even within the constraints of HTML. This chapter shows you how to create and format tables.

INSERT A TABLE INTO A WEB PAGE

You can organize content into columns and rows by inserting tables into your Web page.

Softball Standings

Team	Games	Wins	Losses	Ties	Points
The Chargers	10	9	1	0	18
Sluggers	10	8	1	1	17
The Champs	10	7	2	1	15
The Eagles	10	5	5	0	10
Barry's Battalion	10	3	7	0	6
The Professionals	10	2	8	0	4
Baseball Bombers	10	1	9	0	2

INSERT A TABLE INTO A WEB PAGE

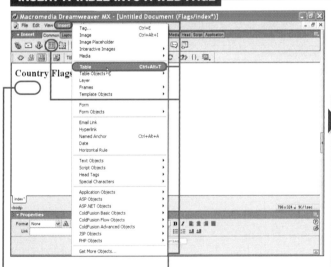

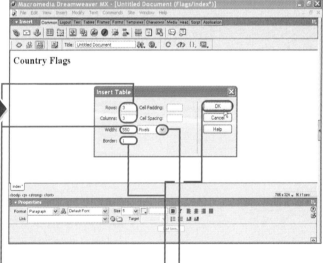

1 Position the cursor where you want to insert the table.

Note: The cursor will snap to the left margin by default, but you can insert tables between existing elements on a page, such as between two images or after a block of text.

2 Click **Insert**.

3 Click **Table**.

■ You can also insert a table by clicking the Insert Table button (⊞) in the Common Insert panel.

■ The Insert Table dialog box appears.

4 Type the number of rows and columns in your table.

5 Type the width of your table.

■ You can set the width in pixels or as a percentage of the page by clicking ⌄ and selecting your choice of measurements.

6 Type a border size in pixels.

7 Click **OK**.

120

How do I change the appearance of the content inside my table?

You can specify the size, style, and color of text inside a table the same way you format text anywhere else in a Web page. Likewise, you control the appearance of an image inside a table the same way you control it outside a table. See Chapter 5 to format text, and Chapter 6 for more about images.

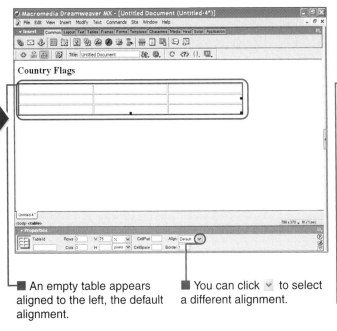

■ An empty table appears aligned to the left, the default alignment.

■ You can click ⌄ to select a different alignment.

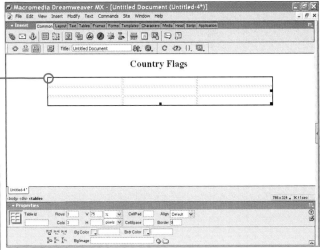

TURN OFF TABLE BORDERS

1 Click anywhere on the table border to select the entire border.

2 Type **0** in the Border field.

3 Press **Enter** (**Return**).

■ When you view the page in a Web browser, the dashed table border disappears.

INSERT CONTENT INTO A TABLE

You can fill the cells of your table with text, images, multimedia files, form elements, and other tables.

INSERT CONTENT INTO A TABLE

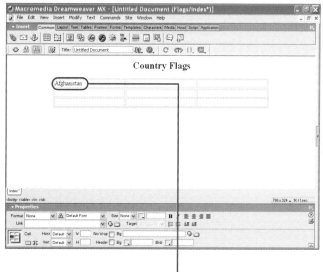

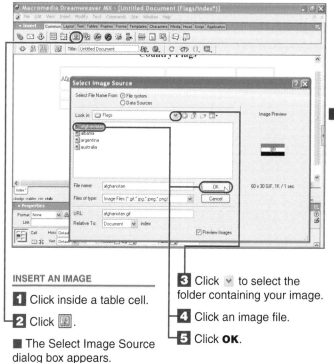

INSERT TEXT

1 Click inside a table cell.

2 Type your text in the cell.

Note: See Chapter 5 for more about formatting your text.

INSERT AN IMAGE

1 Click inside a table cell.

2 Click [icon].

■ The Select Image Source dialog box appears.

3 Click [icon] to select the folder containing your image.

4 Click an image file.

5 Click **OK**.

How can I add captions to images on my Web page?

The best way to add a caption to the top, bottom, or side of an image is by creating a two-celled table. Place the image in one cell and the caption in the other. You can then adjust the table's size and alignment to position the captioned image with the rest of your page's content.

This really is me!

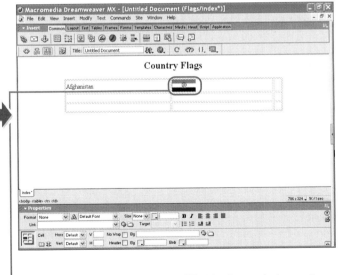

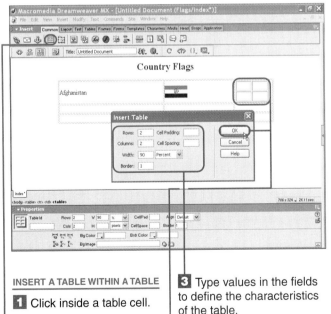

■ The image appears in the table cell.

■ If the image is larger than the cell, the cell expands to accommodate the image.

INSERT A TABLE WITHIN A TABLE

1 Click inside a table cell.

2 Click 📋 .

■ The Insert Table dialog box appears.

3 Type values in the fields to define the characteristics of the table.

4 Click **OK**.

■ The new table appears within the table cell.

CHANGE THE BACKGROUND OF A TABLE

You can change the background of a table to complement the style of your Web page. Just like a Web page's background, you can change a table's background color or fill the table's background with an image. See Chapter 6 for more about Web page backgrounds.

CHANGE THE BACKGROUND OF A TABLE

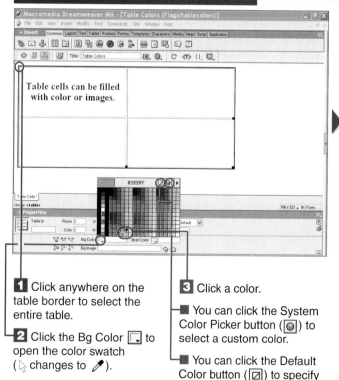

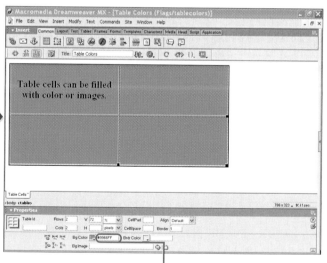

1 Click anywhere on the table border to select the entire table.

2 Click the Bg Color ☐ to open the color swatch (↳ changes to ✐).

3 Click a color.

■ You can click the System Color Picker button (◉) to select a custom color.

■ You can click the Default Color button (▱) to specify no color.

■ The color fills the background of the table.

■ You can also type a color name or a color code directly.

Note: See page 73 for additional information about Web color.

■ When both a table and a cell have a BG Color value, the background color of a cell supersedes the background color of a table.

How can I change the background of a table cell?

Click inside a cell and then specify the background color using the Bg Color ⬛ or a background image by clicking ⬛. Each cell can have a different background, or all cells can be formatted to create an appearance of a solid area with elements floating over them in the cells.

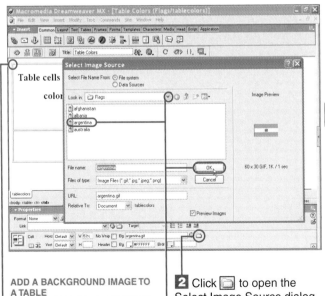

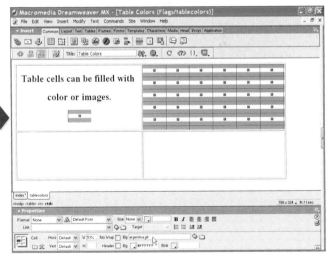

ADD A BACKGROUND IMAGE TO A TABLE

1 Click inside a table cell.

■ You can also click anywhere on the table border to select the entire table.

2 Click ⬛ to open the Select Image Source dialog box.

3 Click ⬇ to select the folder containing your image.

4 Click an image file.

5 Click **OK**.

■ The table background fills with the image.

■ If space in the cell allows, the image tiles to fill the available area.

125

CHANGE THE CELL PADDING IN A TABLE

You can change the cell padding to add space between a table's content and its borders.

CHANGE THE CELL PADDING IN A TABLE

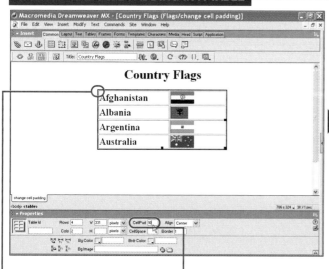

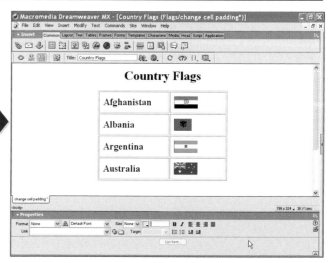

1 Click anywhere on the table border to select the entire table.

2 Type the amount of padding, in pixels, in the CellPad field.

3 Press **Enter** (**Return**).

■ The space between the table content and the table borders adjusts.

Note: Adjusting the cell padding affects all the cells in a table. You cannot adjust the padding of individual cells by using the CellPad field.

You can change the cell spacing to adjust the width of your table borders.

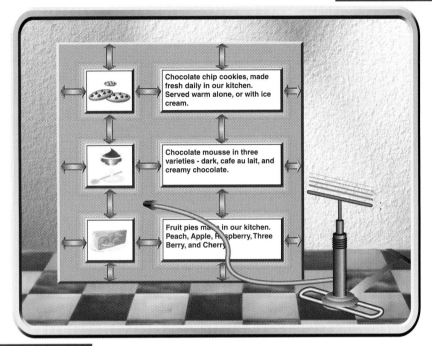

CHANGE THE CELL SPACING IN A TABLE

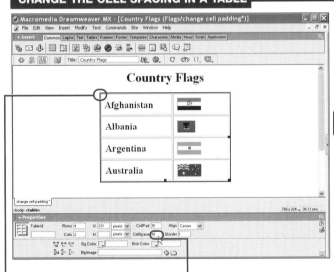

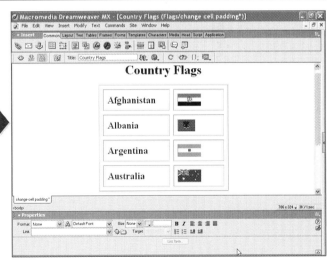

1 Click anywhere on the table border to select the entire table.

2 Type the amount of spacing, in pixels, in the CellSpace field.

■ The width of the table's cell borders adjusts.

Note: Adjusting the cell spacing affects all the cell borders in the table. You cannot adjust the spacing of individual cell borders by using the CellSpace field.

CHANGE THE ALIGNMENT OF A TABLE

You can change the alignment of a table and wrap text and other content around it.

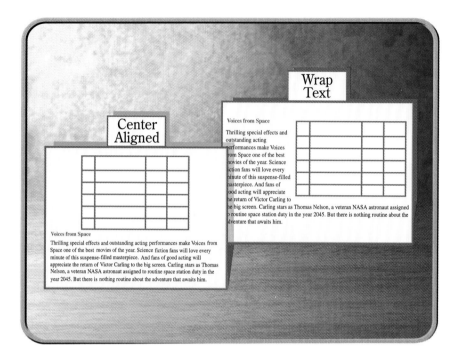

CHANGE THE ALIGNMENT OF A TABLE

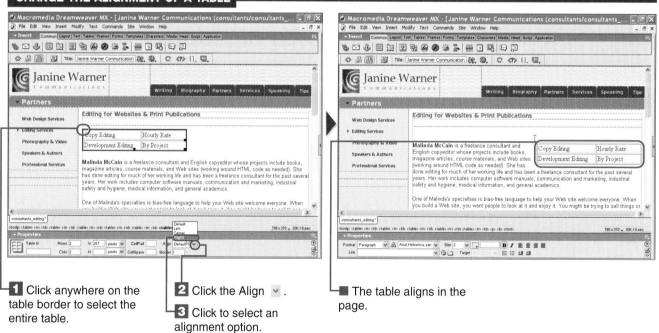

1 Click anywhere on the table border to select the entire table.

2 Click the Align ⬇.

3 Click to select an alignment option.

■ The table aligns in the page.

You can align the
content in your table
cells horizontally and
vertically.

CHANGE THE ALIGNMENT OF CELL CONTENT

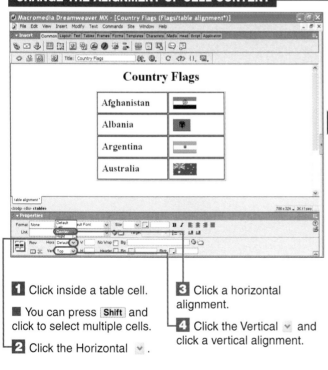

1 Click inside a table cell.

■ You can press **Shift** and
click to select multiple cells.

2 Click the Horizontal ⌄.

3 Click a horizontal
alignment.

4 Click the Vertical ⌄ and
click a vertical alignment.

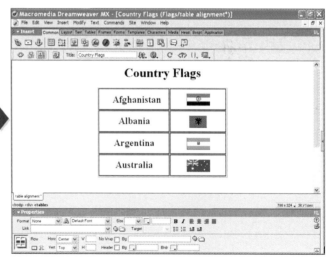

■ The content aligns.

*Note: In this example, eight cells
have been aligned as center
horizontal and top vertical.*

INSERT OR DELETE A ROW OR COLUMN

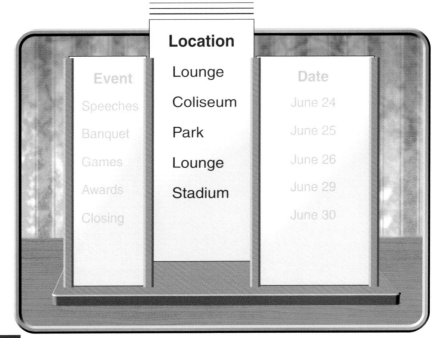

You can insert cells into your table to add content or create space between elements, and delete rows or columns to remove them.

INSERT A ROW OR COLUMN

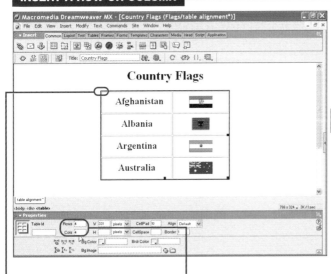

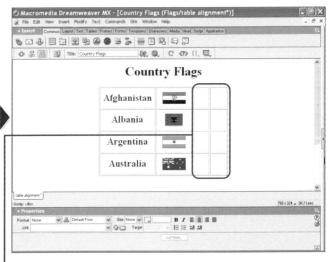

1 Click anywhere on the table border to select the entire table.

2 Type the number of rows and columns you want in the Property inspector.

3 Press Enter (Return).

■ Empty rows or columns appear in the table.

■ To add a row or column in front of an existing cell, right-click inside the cell and choose **Insert Row or Column** from the menu that appears. You can also click **Modify**, **Table**, and then **Insert Row or Column**.

**What happens to the content
of a deleted cell?**

It is deleted as well.
Dreamweaver does not warn
you if the cells you are deleting
in a table contain content. If you
accidentally remove content
when deleting rows or columns,
you can click **Edit**, and then
Undo to undo the last
command.

DELETE A ROW OR COLUMN

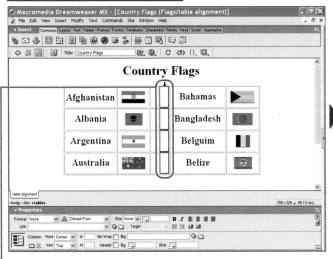

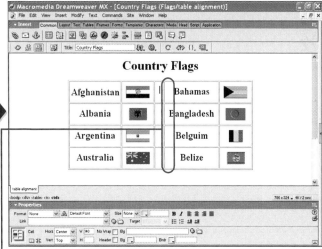

1 Press Shift and click to
select the cells that you want
to delete.

2 Click Delete.

■ The deleted row or
column disappears.

■ A cell's content is
removed from the page
when a cell is deleted.

■ You can also delete cells
by right-clicking inside the
cell, and then choosing
Delete Row or **Delete
Column** from the menu that
appears. You can also click
Modify, **Table**, and then
Delete Row or **Delete
Column**.

SPLIT OR MERGE TABLE CELLS

You can create a more elaborate arrangement of cells in a table by splitting or merging its cells.

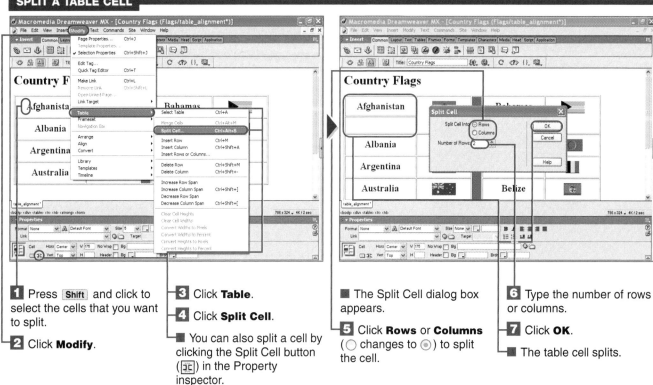

1 Press **Shift** and click to select the cells that you want to split.

2 Click **Modify**.

3 Click **Table**.

4 Click **Split Cell**.

■ You can also split a cell by clicking the Split Cell button (⬚⊏) in the Property inspector.

■ The Split Cell dialog box appears.

5 Click **Rows** or **Columns** (○ changes to ◉) to split the cell.

6 Type the number of rows or columns.

7 Click **OK**.

■ The table cell splits.

Can I merge any combination of table cells?

No. The cells must have a rectangular arrangement. For example, you can merge all the cells in a two-row-by-two-column table. But you cannot select three cells that form an "L" shape and merge them into one.

MERGE TABLE CELLS

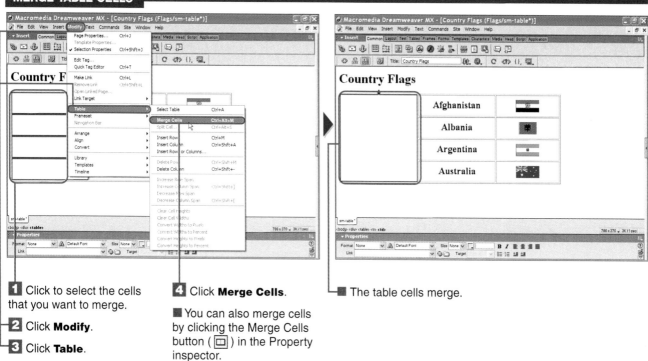

1 Click to select the cells that you want to merge.

2 Click **Modify**.

3 Click **Table**.

4 Click **Merge Cells**.

■ You can also merge cells by clicking the Merge Cells button (□) in the Property inspector.

■ The table cells merge.

CHANGE THE DIMENSIONS OF A TABLE

You can change the dimensions of your table to fit into your Web page.

CHANGE THE DIMENSIONS OF A TABLE

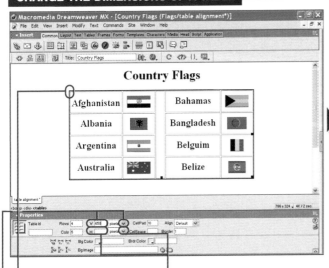

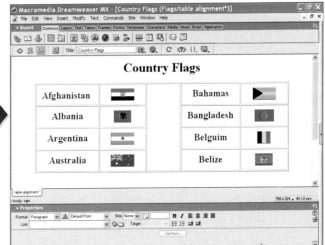

1 Click anywhere on the table border to select the entire table.

2 Type a width.

3 Click 🔽 to select the width setting in pixels or a percentage of the screen.

4 Type a height.

5 Click 🔽 and select the height setting in pixels or a percentage of the screen.

6 Press **Enter** (**Return**).

■ The table readjusts to its new dimensions.

Note: Table dimensions may be constrained by content. Dreamweaver cannot shrink a table smaller than the size of the content it contains.

Note: If no height or width is specified, the table automatically adjusts to fit the space available on the user's screen.

CHANGE THE DIMENSIONS OF A CELL

You can change the dimensions of individual table cells to organize the content in your table.

CHANGE THE DIMENSIONS OF A CELL

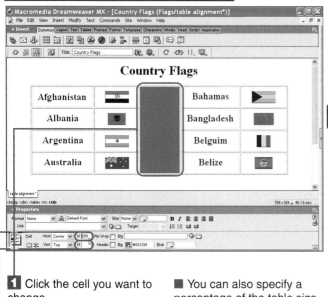

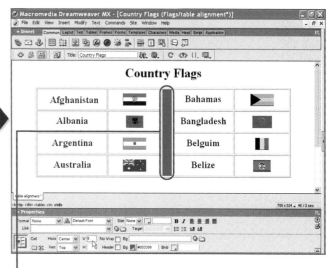

1 Click the cell you want to change.

2 Type the new width in pixels.

3 Type the new height in pixels.

■ You can also specify a percentage of the table size instead of specifying pixels. For example, type **40%** in the width or height box.

4 Press Enter (Return).

■ The cell readjusts to its new dimensions as well as to the cells next to the selection.

Note: Cell dimensions may be constrained by content. Dreamweaver cannot shrink a cell smaller than the size of the content it contains.

CREATE A LAYOUT TABLE

You can create tables to better control the layout of a Web page. Tables used for layout are typically designed to fill the entire display area, and the borders are turned off so that the table itself is not visible.

Because you cannot control the size of all of the monitors that will view your Web page, it is best to set a fixed width that will fit on a monitor with 800 by 600 resolution, the most common on the Web today. The ideal table size for 800 by 600 resolution is actually 760 pixels wide by 420 pixels high to leave room for the toolbars and borders of the user's browser.

CREATE A LAYOUT TABLE

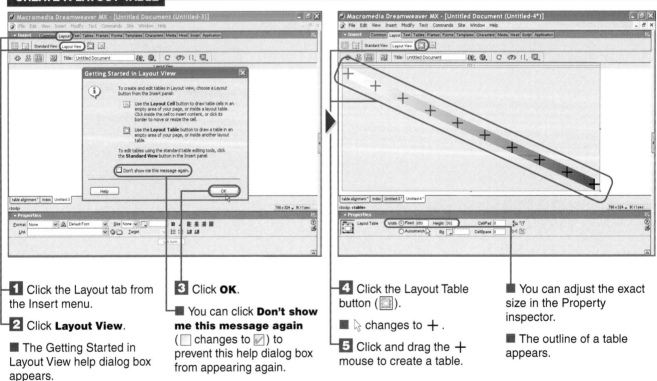

1 Click the Layout tab from the Insert menu.

2 Click **Layout View**.

■ The Getting Started in Layout View help dialog box appears.

3 Click **OK**.

■ You can click **Don't show me this message again** (☐ changes to ☑) to prevent this help dialog box from appearing again.

4 Click the Layout Table button (☐).

■ ⬚ changes to ✛.

5 Click and drag the ✛ mouse to create a table.

■ You can adjust the exact size in the Property inspector.

■ The outline of a table appears.

What can I do to help me draw my layout table cells precisely?

Click the **Layout** tab from the Insert menu, then **Layout View**. In Layout View, you can draw table cells anywhere on the page by clicking and dragging. Dreamweaver creates a complex table in the background with spacers to control the exact positioning of elements in your page design.

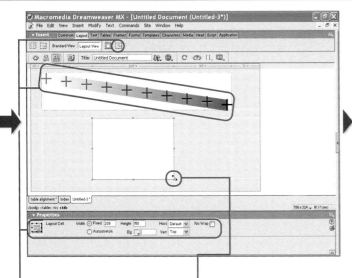

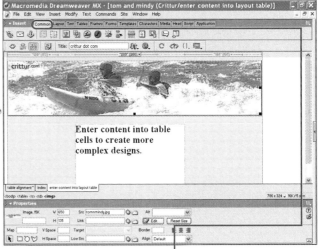

6 Click the Layout Cell button (▦).

■ ⤢ changes to +.

7 Click and drag inside the table to create a Layout Cell.

■ The attributes of the cell appear in the Property inspector.

■ You can adjust the size and position of a cell by clicking and dragging its edge or by clicking the center of the border where the dots appear.

■ You can click ▦ again to draw more cells.

8 Click to put your cursor in the cell where you want to add content.

Note: See "Insert Content into a Table," earlier in this chapter, for more information.

■ You can click the **Common** tab in the Insert menu to access the Insert Image (▦) and other buttons.

Note: You can insert content in Layout View the same way you do in Standard View, but it is easier to tab around a table in Standard View. See "Insert Content into a Table."

REARRANGE A LAYOUT TABLE

You can easily change the size and arrangement of a table's cells in Layout View.

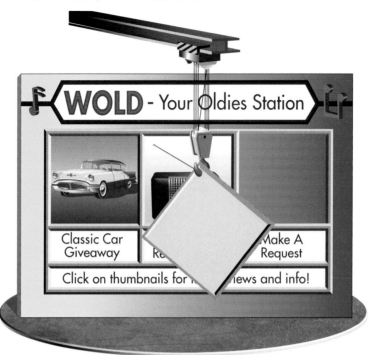

REARRANGE A LAYOUT TABLE

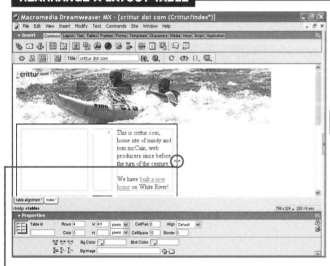

CHANGE THE SIZE OF A TABLE OR A CELL

1 Click the edge of the table or an individual cell (▷ changes to ↔).

2 Click and drag a side or corner handle to the desired size.

■ The table or cell resizes.

■ You cannot overlap other cells in a table.

How do I delete a table or cell in Layout View?

Click the edge of the cell, and then press Delete. Dreamweaver will replace the space with gray, non-editable cells. Similarly, you can delete a layout table by clicking the table's top tab and pressing Delete.

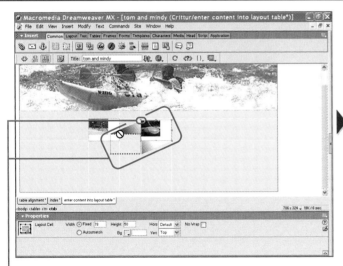

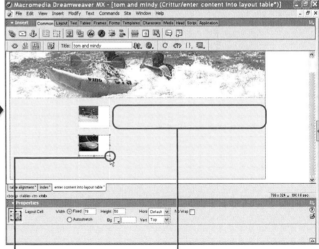

MOVE A CELL

1 Click the edge of a layout cell.

2 Click and drag the edge of the cell.

Note: Do not click and drag a handle.

■ ↳ changes to ⊘ when you drag over other layout cells, because cells cannot overlap.

3 Move the layout cell in its new position.

■ Undefined cells in the table adjust their sizes to make room for the cell's new position.

ADJUST THE WIDTH OF A LAYOUT TABLE

By using a combination of fixed and default settings to adjust table and cell dimensions, you can create a table that automatically adjusts to fit a viewer's browser size.

‹100 pixels› ‹Autostretch›

You can define the table columns as fixed-width or as autostretch, which fills the remaining space available.

ADJUST THE WIDTH OF A LAYOUT TABLE

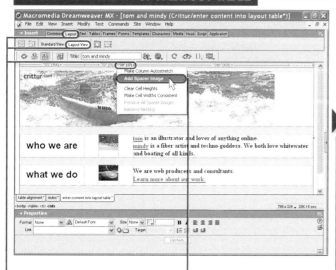

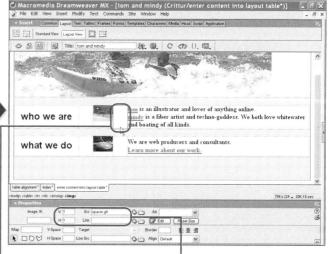

CREATE A FIXED-WIDTH COLUMN

1 Click the **Layout** tab.

2 Click **Layout View**.

3 Click a column heading.

4 Click **Add Spacer Image** from the menu that appears.

■ If your site lacks a spacer image file that it can reference, a dialog box will appear asking if you want to create one. Click **OK**.

■ The spacer image has been added to hold a fixed space in the table cell.

■ The filename of the spacer image displays in the Property inspector. The height and width of the spacer image can be altered to adjust spacing.

What is a spacer image?

A *spacer image* is a transparent GIF image file that is used as a "filler" to invisibly control spacing on a Web page. Dreamweaver inserts a spacer image into tables automatically in Layout View, and then uses the height and width attributes of the invisible image to secure table cells at specified sizes. You can also use this trick manually to control spacing wherever you want to make sure that an element stays put on your page — browsers can move things around on a Web page if you use blank spaces. A spacer image can be as small as 1x1 pixels, but 10x10 pixels is the ideal size. A spacer image of only 1x1 pixels is hard to keep track of when you insert it on a page. It is invisible, and tiny, and thus almost impossible to select when you want to move it around or adjust its size.

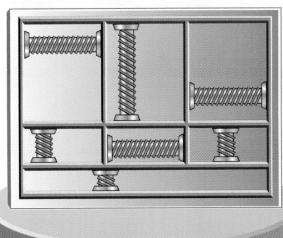

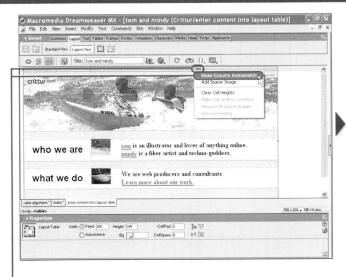

CREATE AN AUTOSTRETCH COLUMN

1 Click a column heading.

2 Click **Make Column Autostretch** from the menu that appears.

■ Dreamweaver automatically specifies a size that takes up any available space in the cell.

3 Preview the page in a Web browser.

Note: See Chapter 2 to preview Web pages in a browser.

■ To see the autostretch effects, resize the browser window.

■ You can also resize a browser by clicking and dragging a corner of the window.

Calligraphica

FRAME 2

FRAME 1

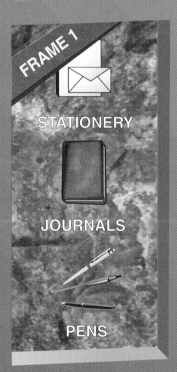

STATIONERY

JOURNALS

PENS

FRAME 3

Italian Leather-Bound Journals

Shagreen Explorer's Journal

Maybe you'll use it to record that once-in-a-lifetime adventure . . . a honeymoon cruise . . . an anniversary trip to exotic places.

Whatever you decide to place within its rich, green covers, this journal will preserve your memories for generations to come. What adventures will *you* leave them?

Handcrafted journal of shagreen, filled with 180 pages of cream, 60 lb. cotton paper. Marbled end papers.
PRICE $129.00

Qty	Gift Wrap	Personalization

Add to Shopping Cart

CHAPTER 9

Creating Pages with Frames

You can divide the site window into multiple panes by creating frames. This chapter shows you how to organize information on your pages and create links to frames.

INTRODUCTION TO FRAMES

Frames enable you to divide your Web page into multiple windows and display different content in each frame.

You can put a list of navigation links in one frame of your site, and have the links open their destination pages in a larger content frame.

Setting Up Frames

You can create a framed Web site in Dreamweaver by dividing the Document window horizontally or vertically one or more times. Each window is composed of an independent Web page and can be linked independently. All pages in a frameset are described in a *frameset page* and must be saved separately.

How Frames Work

Frames on a page operate independently of one another. As you scroll through the content of one frame, the content of the other frames remains fixed. You can create links in one frame that open in another frame.

**You can easily create
popular frame styles
using the predefined
framesets located in
the Frames tab in
the Insert panel.**

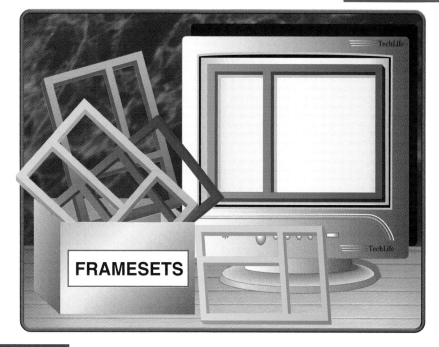

If you do not want to use
one of Dreamweaver's
framesets, you can divide
the window manually. See
the section "Divide a
Page into Frames."

INSERT A PREDEFINED FRAMESET

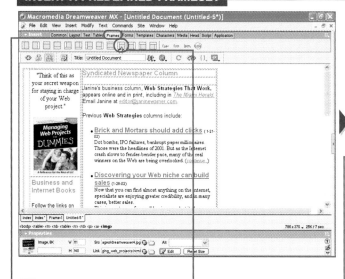

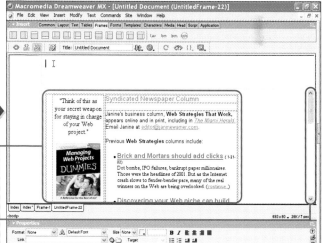

1 Click the **Frames** tab on
the Insert panel.

■ The Frames panel
appears.

2 Click a frame design
button.

■ Dreamweaver applies the
frames to your page.

*Note: See "Add Content to a Frame"
to add text, images, or other
elements to a new frame.*

■ If content existed in the
original page, it shifts to one
of the new frames.

■ Scroll bars appear if the
content extends outside the
frame borders.

■ You can also create a
frameset by clicking **File**
and then **New**. In the New
Document dialog box, click
the category **Frameset**,
click a predefined frameset,
and then click **Create**.

SAVE A FRAMED SITE

Saving your frameset requires you to save the individual pages that appear in the frames as well as the frameset that defines how each frame is displayed.

You need to save all the individual documents before you can preview your work in a browser or upload your site.

SAVE A FRAMED SITE

SAVE YOUR FRAMED PAGES

1 Click inside the frame you want to save.

2 Click **File**.

3 Click **Save Frame**.

Note: Save Frame appears gray if the current frame is already saved.

■ The Save As dialog box appears.

4 Click ⌄ to select the folder where you want to save the framed page.

5 Type a name for the page.

6 Click **Save**.

■ Dreamweaver saves the page.

■ Repeat steps **1** to **6** to save other framed pages.

■ Save each page with a different filename.

**Is there a shortcut for saving all
the pages of my framed site?**

Yes. You can click **File** and
then **Save Frameset**. This
will save all the framed
pages and framesets that
make up your site. This
is definitely a timesaver!

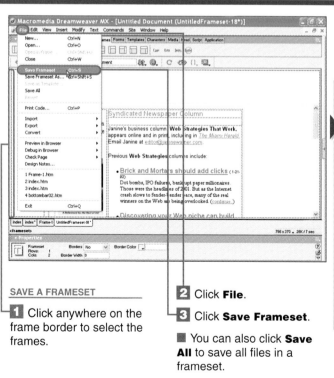

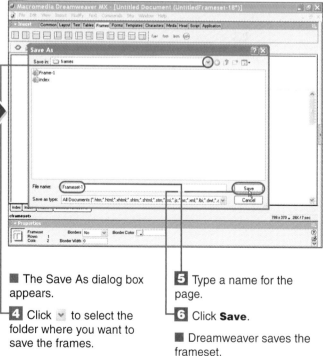

SAVE A FRAMESET

1 Click anywhere on the
frame border to select the
frames.

2 Click **File**.

3 Click **Save Frameset**.

■ You can also click **Save
All** to save all files in a
frameset.

■ The Save As dialog box
appears.

4 Click ∨ to select the
folder where you want to
save the frames.

5 Type a name for the
page.

6 Click **Save**.

■ Dreamweaver saves the
frameset.

147

DIVIDE A PAGE INTO FRAMES

You can split a Document window vertically to create a frameset with left and right frames, or split it horizontally to create a frameset with top and bottom frames.

You can also choose a predefined frameset for your site. See the section "Insert a Predefined Frameset," earlier in this chapter.

DIVIDE A PAGE INTO FRAMES

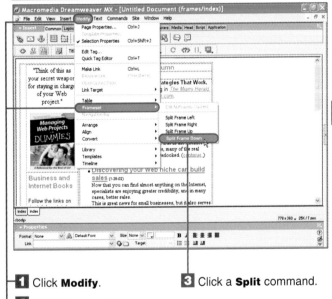

1 Click **Modify**.

2 Click **Frameset**.

3 Click a **Split** command.

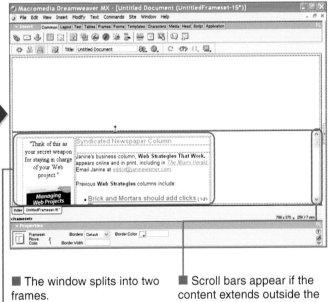

■ The window splits into two frames.

■ If content existed in the original page, it shifts to one of the new frames.

■ Scroll bars appear if the content extends outside the frame borders.

Note: See "Add Content to a Frame" to add text, images, or other elements to a new frame.

CREATE A NESTED FRAME

You can subdivide a frame of an existing frameset to create nested frames. With nested frames, you can organize the information in your site in a more complex way.

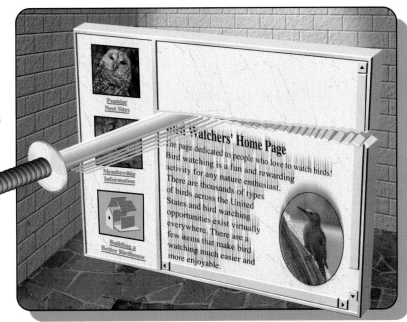

CREATE A NESTED FRAME

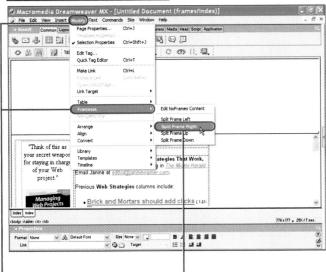

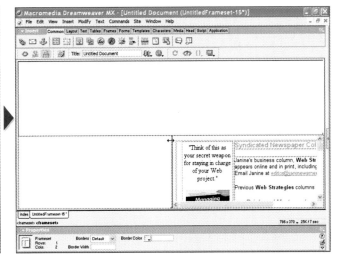

1 Click inside the frame you want to subdivide.

2 Click **Modify**.

3 Click **Frameset**.

4 Click a **Split** command.

■ You can also choose a predefined frame design. Click 🔲, for example, in the Common Insert panel.

■ Dreamweaver splits the selected frame into two frames, creating a nested frame.

■ You can continue to split your frames into more frames.

Note: See "Add Content to a Frame" to add text, images, or other elements to a new frame.

149

CHANGE THE DIMENSIONS OF A FRAME

You can change the dimensions of a frame to attractively and efficiently display the information inside it.

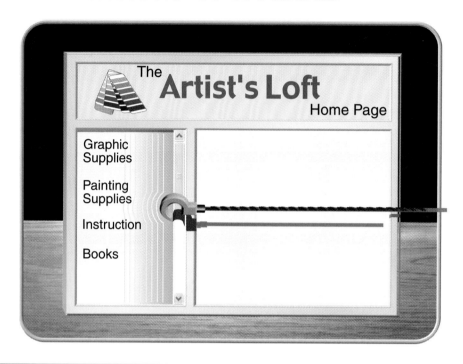

CHANGE THE DIMENSIONS OF A FRAME WITH THE PROPERTY INSPECTOR

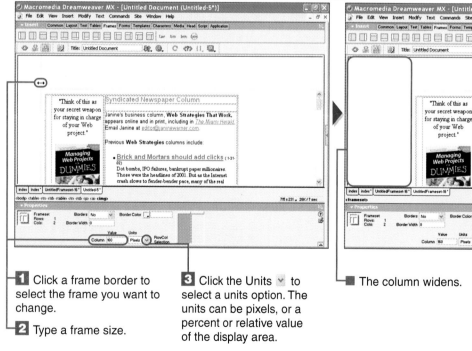

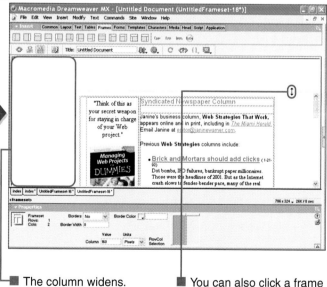

1 Click a frame border to select the frame you want to change.

2 Type a frame size.

3 Click the Units ⌄ to select a units option. The units can be pixels, or a percent or relative value of the display area.

■ In the example, a fixed width of 160 pixels is applied to the left frame.

■ The column widens.

■ You can also click a frame border and drag it to the desired size (⤡ changes to ↕).

Is there a shortcut for changing the dimensions of frames?

Yes. You can click and drag a frame border to adjust the dimensions of a frame quickly. The values in the Property inspector will change as you drag the frame border.

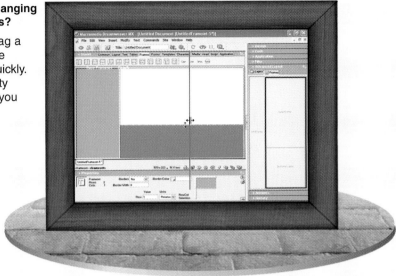

CHANGE THE DIMENSIONS OF A FRAME WITH THE FRAMES PANEL

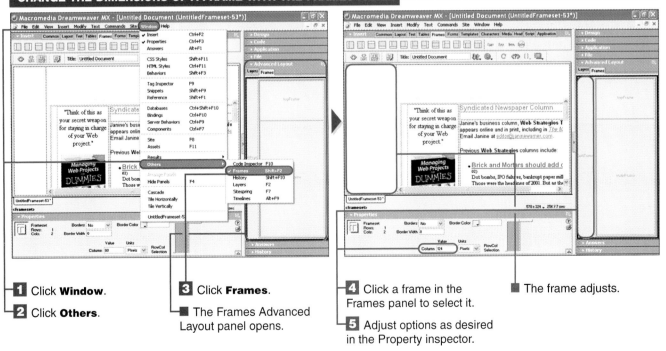

1 Click **Window**.

2 Click **Others**.

3 Click **Frames**.

■ The Frames Advanced Layout panel opens.

4 Click a frame in the Frames panel to select it.

5 Adjust options as desired in the Property inspector.

■ The frame adjusts.

ADD CONTENT TO A FRAME

You can add content to a frame by inserting an existing HTML document into the frame. You can also create a new page in a frame by typing text or inserting elements such as images and tables, just as you would in an unframed page.

ADD CONTENT TO A FRAME

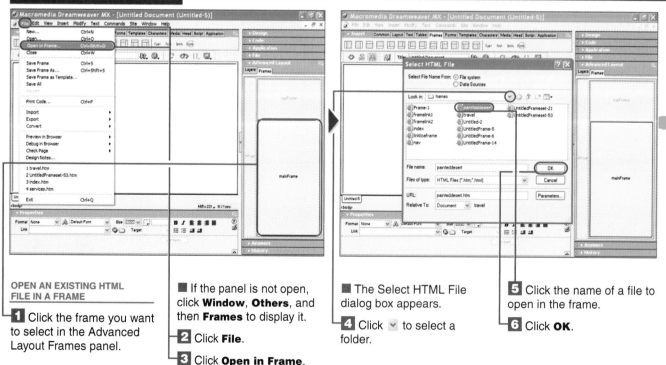

OPEN AN EXISTING HTML FILE IN A FRAME

1 Click the frame you want to select in the Advanced Layout Frames panel.

■ If the panel is not open, click **Window**, **Others**, and then **Frames** to display it.

2 Click **File**.

3 Click **Open in Frame**.

■ The Select HTML File dialog box appears.

4 Click ⌄ to select a folder.

■ 5 Click the name of a file to open in the frame.

6 Click **OK**.

Can I link a frame to a page somewhere else on the Web?

Yes. You can link to an external Web-page address in the URL field in the Property inspector, just as you would link to any other page, except you need to specify the target. See the section "Link to a Frame," later in this chapter. Because Dreamweaver cannot display external files, the Web page will not appear in the Document window. However, it will appear if you preview your site in a Web browser. See Chapter 2 to preview a Web page in your browser.

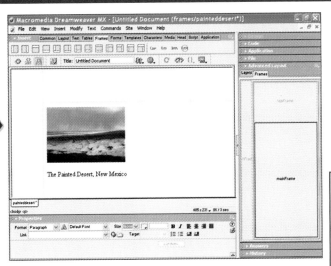

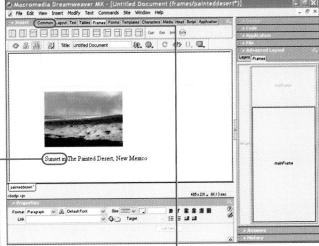

■ The selected page appears in the frame area.

■ If the content extends beyond the frame, scroll bars appear automatically. To turn off scroll bars, see "Control Scroll Bars in Frames," later in this chapter.

ADD NEW CONTENT TO A FRAME

1 Click inside the frame.

2 Type any text you want to display.

■ You can also add images, tables, or other elements as you would in any other page. Click the **Common** tab, and click ▣ or ▤, for example, in the Insert panel.

DELETE A FRAME

You can delete or create a frame in your frameset to change or expand your design.

DELETE A FRAME

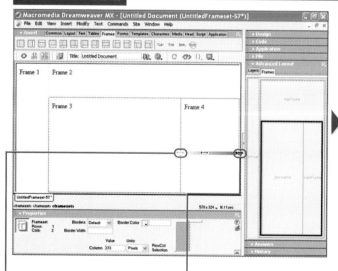

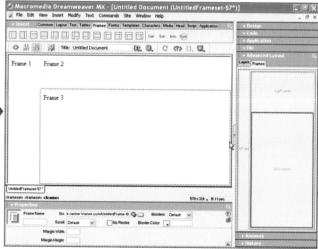

1 Position the mouse on the border of the frame you want to delete (changes to ↔).

2 Click and drag the border to the edge of the window.

■ Dreamweaver deletes the frame.

NAME A FRAME

To create links in one frame that open in another, you need to give your frames names. The name targets the link destination, indicating where the linked page should open in the frameset.

NAME A FRAME

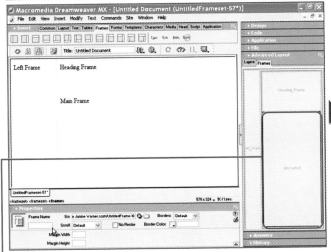

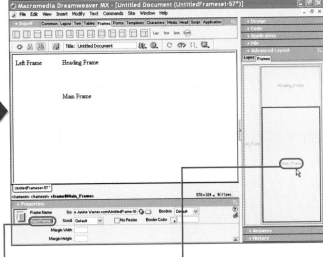

1 Click to select the frame you want to name in the Advanced Layout Frames panel.

■ If the panel is not open, click **Window**, **Others**, and then **Frames** to display it.

2 Type a name for the frame.

3 Press [Enter] ([Return]).

■ The name of the frame appears in the Frames panel.

LINK TO A FRAME

You can create a link that opens a page in a different frame. You will want to do this for frames that contain navigation hyperlinks.

For more information about links, see Chapter 7.

LINK TO A FRAME

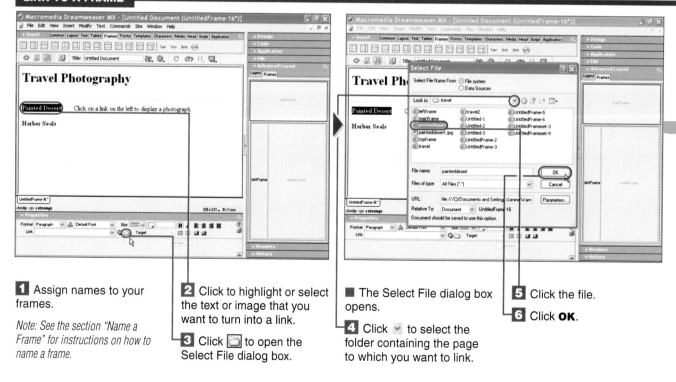

1 Assign names to your frames.

Note: See the section "Name a Frame" for instructions on how to name a frame.

2 Click to highlight or select the text or image that you want to turn into a link.

3 Click [ ] to open the Select File dialog box.

■ The Select File dialog box opens.

4 Click [ ] to select the folder containing the page to which you want to link.

5 Click the file.

6 Click **OK**.

How do I target links in my frames?

You can target a link to open in any section of the frame by selecting the name of the frame. Selecting **_top**, instead of a frame name, opens the linked page on "top" of the existing frameset. This action takes the user out of the frameset as is recommended when linking to another Web site.

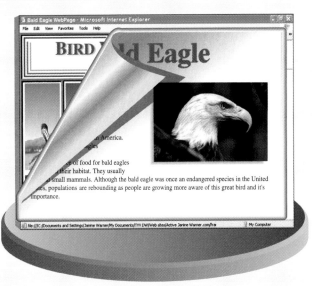

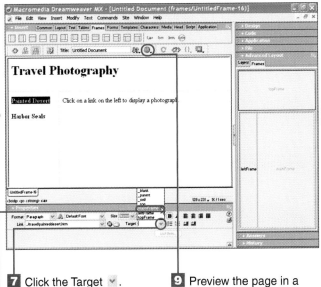

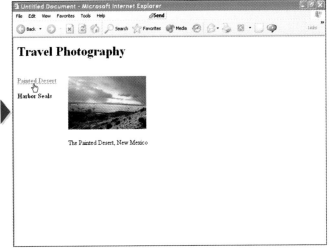

7 Click the Target ⌄.

8 Click to select a frame where the target file will open.

■ If you have named the frame, it appears in the menu.

9 Preview the page in a Web browser by clicking the Preview button (⬚).

Note: See Chapter 2 for more about previewing a Web page in your browser.

■ When you open the framed page in a Web browser and click the link, the destination page opens inside the targeted frame.

FORMAT FRAME BORDERS

You can modify the appearance of your frame borders to make them complement your design by specifying the color and width of your borders, or you can turn them off so they are not visible.

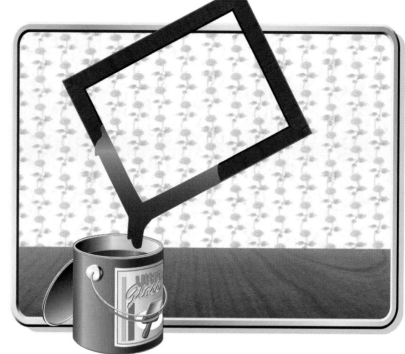

FORMAT FRAME BORDERS

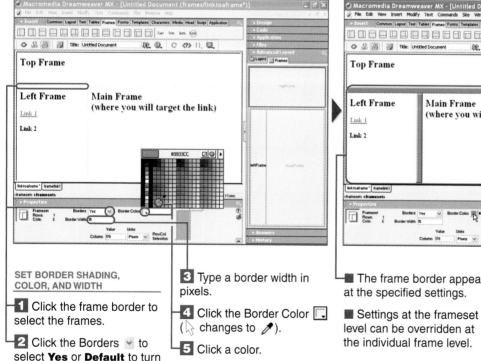

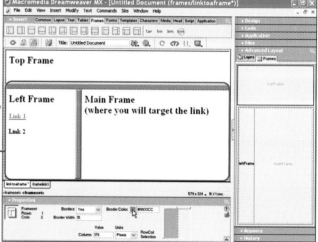

SET BORDER SHADING, COLOR, AND WIDTH

1 Click the frame border to select the frames.

2 Click the Borders ⏷ to select **Yes** or **Default** to turn on borders.

3 Type a border width in pixels.

4 Click the Border Color ▦ (⏷ changes to ✐).

5 Click a color.

■ The frame border appears at the specified settings.

■ Settings at the frameset level can be overridden at the individual frame level.

■ You can also press and hold **Alt** (**option**) and click inside a frame to select it, and then specify formatting in the Property inspector.

Why would I want to make my frame borders invisible?

Turning borders off can disguise the fact that you are using frames in the first place. If you want to further disguise your frames, you can set the pages inside your frames to the same background color. See Chapter 6 to change background colors.

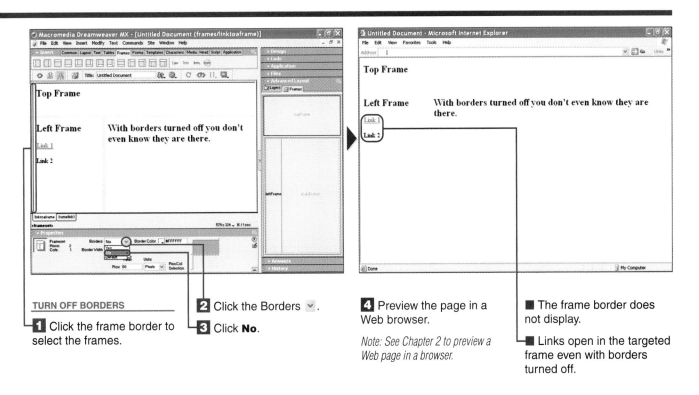

TURN OFF BORDERS

1 Click the frame border to select the frames.

2 Click the Borders ✓.

3 Click **No**.

4 Preview the page in a Web browser.

Note: See Chapter 2 to preview a Web page in a browser.

■ The frame border does not display.

■ Links open in the targeted frame even with borders turned off.

CONTROL SCROLL BARS IN FRAMES

You can control whether or not scroll bars will appear in your frames. Hiding scroll bars enables you to have more control over the presentation of your site, but may also prevent some users from seeing all your site content.

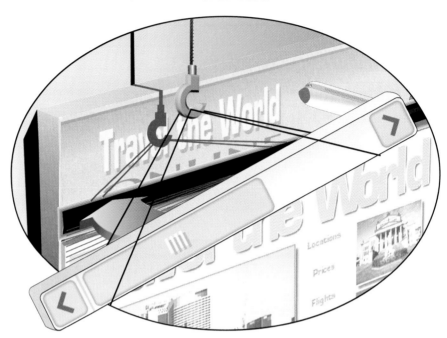

CONTROL SCROLL BARS IN FRAMES

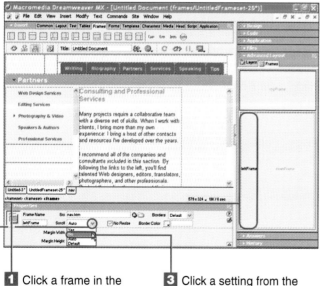

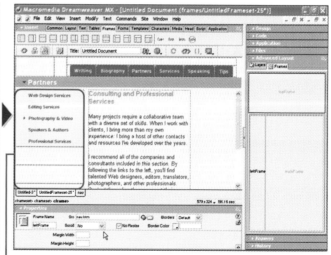

1 Click a frame in the Advanced Layout Frames panel to select it.

2 Click the Scroll ∨.

3 Click a setting from the options: **Yes**, to keep scroll bars on; **No**, to turn scroll bars off; or **Auto**, recommended, because it keeps scroll bars on if necessary. In most browsers, Default and Auto have the same result.

■ The frame appears with the new setting.

■ In this example, scroll bars are turned off in the left frame where they are not necessary. They remain on in the right frame so that the viewer can access all content in that frame.

The default behavior for most browsers allows users to resize frames by clicking and dragging frame borders.

You can prevent users from resizing the frames of a site. However, depending on the size of their monitor, you may make it impossible for them to view all your content.

CONTROL RESIZING IN FRAMES

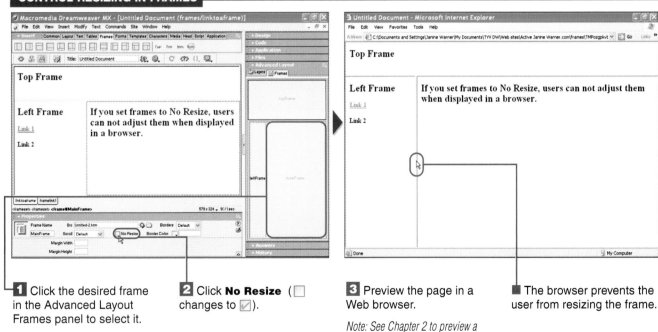

1 Click the desired frame in the Advanced Layout Frames panel to select it.

2 Click **No Resize** (☐ changes to ☑).

3 Preview the page in a Web browser.

Note: See Chapter 2 to preview a Web page in a browser.

■ The browser prevents the user from resizing the frame.

ADD NOFRAMES CONTENT

Not every browser in use on the Internet can display frames. If you want to ensure that all possible users can view something on your Web site, you can use the NoFrames option and create an alternate message for visitors with old or limited browsers.

This Web page uses frames. Your current Web browser does not display frame or frame viewing has been turned o

ADD NOFRAMES CONTENT

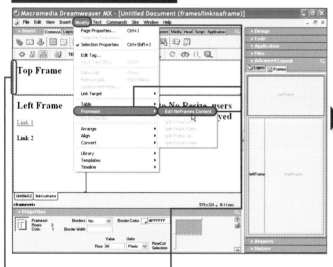

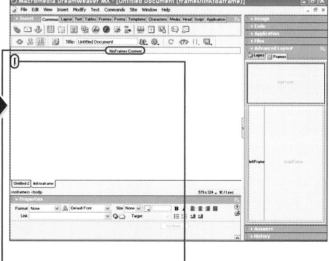

1 Click the outermost frame border to select the frameset.

Note: You must select the outermost frameset in a Document window that has nested framesets.

2 Click **Modify**.

3 Click **Frameset**.

4 Click **Edit NoFrames Content**.

■ Dreamweaver displays a blank NoFrames Content window.

5 Click inside the window to add the content you want to display.

What kinds of users are unable to view frames?

Users with text-based (nongraphical) browsers are usually unable to view frames, as are users with older versions of graphical browsers released for use before frames became popular on the Web. Special browsers for the blind and others with disabilities also have problems with frames. In general, it's best to avoid frames unless you know your audience can view them, and you have a compelling navigation challenge that only frames can solve.

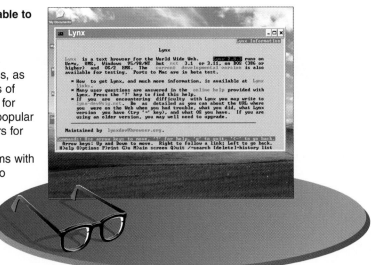

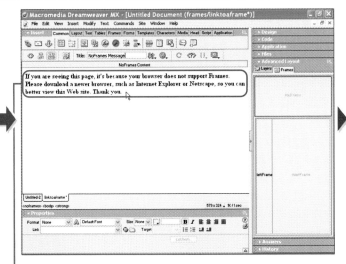

6 Enter the text and images you want to display for visitors who have limited browsers and cannot display your site in frames.

■ This message will only be displayed in limited browsers. Changes to the NoFrames content will not affect any of the other content in your site.

7 Open your page in a text-based browser, or any other browser that cannot display frames.

■ This is how it would look in a browser that does not support frames.

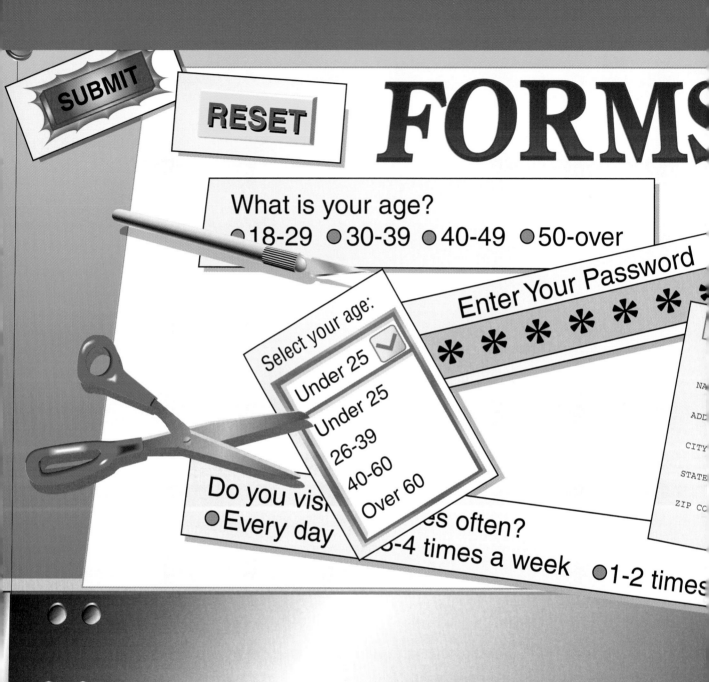

CHAPTER 10

Creating Web-Based Forms

You can enable your site visitors to send you information by creating forms on your Web pages. This chapter shows you how to create forms with different types of fields, buttons, and menus.

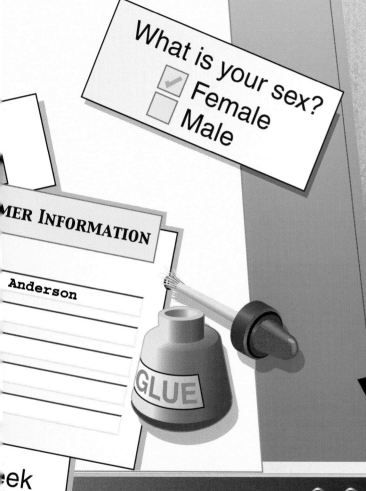

UNDERSTANDING FORMS

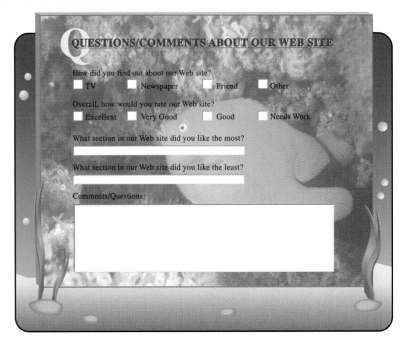

Adding forms to your Web site makes it more interactive, enabling viewers to enter and submit information to you through your Web pages.

Every form works in conjunction with a *form handler*, a type of program or script that processes the form information.

Create a Form

You can construct a form by inserting text fields, pull-down menus, check boxes, and other interactive elements into your page. You can also assign the Web address of a form handler to the form so that the information can be processed. Visitors to your Web page fill out the form and send the information to the form handler by clicking a Submit button.

Process Form Information

The *form handler* is a program or script that processes the form information and does something useful with it, such as forwarding the information to an e-mail address or entering it into a database. Many ready-made form handlers are available free on the Web in ASP, CGI, PHP, or ColdFusion. Your Web hosting company may also have forms available for you to use with your site.

You set up a form on your Web page by first creating a container that holds the text fields, menus, and other form elements. Dreamweaver assigns the Web address of the *form handler* — the program that processes the form — to this container.

DEFINE A FORM

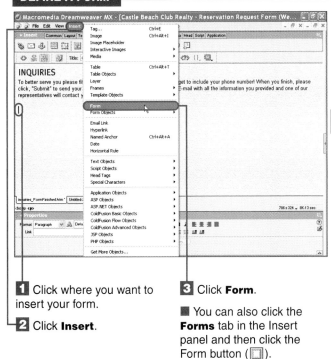

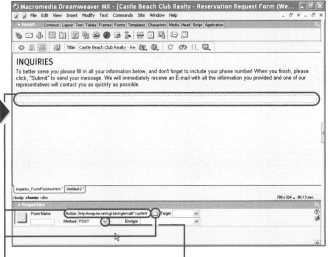

1 Click where you want to insert your form.

2 Click **Insert**.

3 Click **Form**.

■ You can also click the **Forms** tab in the Insert panel and then click the Form button (▣).

■ A red, dashed box appears on the page.

4 Type the address of the form handler file in the Action field.

■ You can also click 🗀 to select the form handler file.

5 Click ⌄ and select **POST** or **GET**.

■ GET is the default and most common method used by Webmasters.

■ The form container is set up. To build the form, add form elements inside the red box.

167

ADD A TEXT FIELD TO A FORM

You can add a text field to enable viewers to submit text through your form. Text fields are probably the most common form element, enabling users to enter names, addresses, brief answers to questions, and other short pieces of text.

ADD A TEXT FIELD TO A FORM

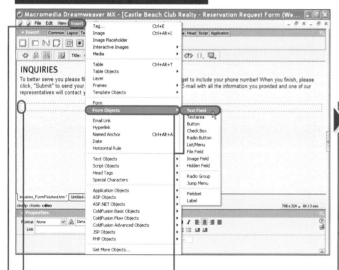

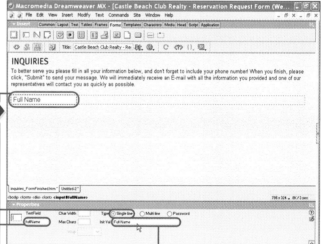

1 Click inside the form container where you want to insert the text field.

Note: See the previous section to set up a form.

2 Click **Insert**.

3 Click **Form Objects**.

4 Click **Text Field**.

■ You can also click the **Forms** tab in the Insert panel and then click the Insert Text Field button (▣).

■ A text field appears in your form.

■ The Single line radio button is selected by default (◉), but you can click **Multi line** (○ changes to ◉) if you want a text box with more than one line available for text.

5 Type a name in the text field.

■ This name lets the browser distinguish the field from other form elements and tells the form handler what to do with the information in the field.

6 Type an optional initial value for the text field.

■ This value appears in the form when the Web page is viewed in a browser.

Can I define the style of text that appears in the text field?

The browser determines what style of text appears in the form fields by default. It is not possible to format this type of text with plain HTML. Using style sheets, you can manipulate the way the text in the form fields looks. However, be aware that only the newer browsers support this feature.

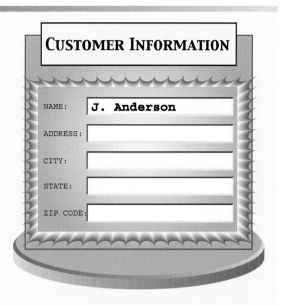

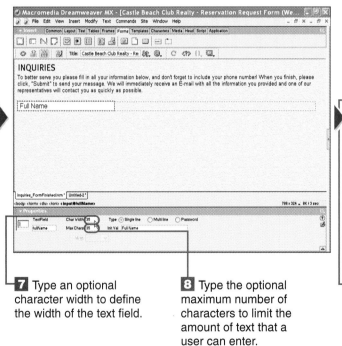

7 Type an optional character width to define the width of the text field.

8 Type the optional maximum number of characters to limit the amount of text that a user can enter.

9 Type a label for the text field so that users know what to enter.

■ Dreamweaver applies your specifications to the text field.

ADD A CHECK BOX TO A FORM

Check boxes enable you to present multiple options in a form and allow the user to select one, several, or none of the options.

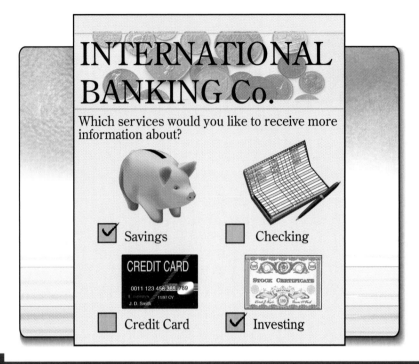

INTERNATIONAL BANKING Co.

Which services would you like to receive more information about?

☑ Savings   ☐ Checking

☐ Credit Card   ☑ Investing

ADD A CHECK BOX TO A FORM

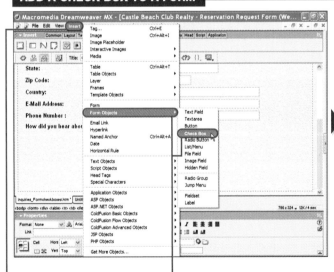

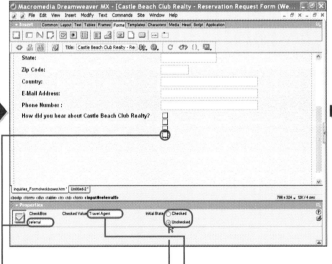

1 Click inside the form container where you want to insert your check boxes.

Note: See "Define a Form," earlier in this chapter, to set up a form.

2 Click **Insert**.

3 Click **Form Objects**.

4 Click **Check Box**.

■ You can also click the **Forms** tab in the Insert panel and then click the Insert Check Box button (☑).

5 Repeat steps **2** to **4** until you have the desired number of check boxes in your Web page.

6 Click a check box.

7 Type a name for the check box.

8 Type a checked value for the check box.

■ This value is assigned to the box when the user checks it.

9 Click **Checked** or **Unchecked** (○ changes to ◉) to select the check box's initial status.

Can I have several different groups of check boxes in the same form?

Yes. How you organize the check boxes in a form — in one group, several groups, or each check box by itself — is up to you. If you want to provide various choices in one group, you can assign the same name to all the check boxes in that group and give each one a different Checked Value. The form handler treats those check boxes as a group.

Favorite Food:
☐ **Lasagna**
☐ **Steak**
☐ **Spaghetti**
☐ **Hamburgers**

Favorite Drink:
☐ **Fruit Juice**
☐ **Soft Drinks**
☐ **Lemonade**
☐ **Iced T**

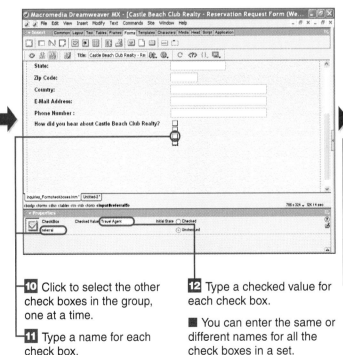

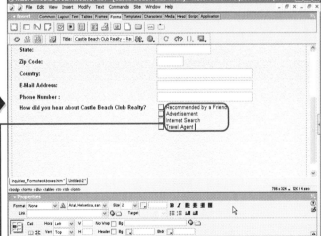

10 Click to select the other check boxes in the group, one at a time.

11 Type a name for each check box.

12 Type a checked value for each check box.

■ You can enter the same or different names for all the check boxes in a set.

13 Type labels for the check boxes so that users know what to check.

■ Dreamweaver applies your specifications to the check boxes.

ADD A RADIO BUTTON TO A FORM

You can let users select one option from a set of several options by adding a set of radio buttons to your form. With radio buttons, a user cannot select more than one option from a set.

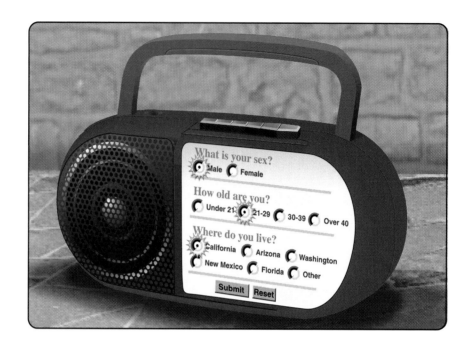

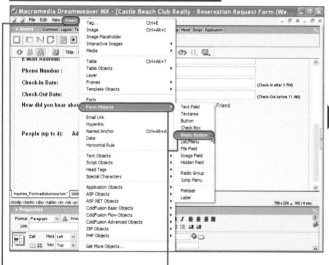

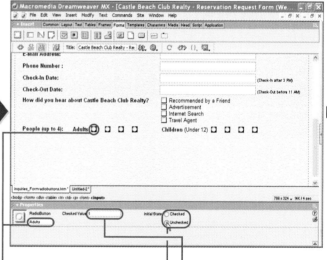

1 Click inside the form container where you want to insert your radio buttons.

Note: See "Define a Form," earlier in this chapter, to set up a form.

2 Click **Insert**.

3 Click **Form Objects**.

4 Click **Radio Button**.

■ You can also click the **Forms** tab in the Insert panel and then click the Insert Radio Button button (⬛).

5 Repeat steps **2** to **4** until you have the desired number of radio buttons in your Web page.

6 Click a radio button.

7 Type a name for the radio button.

8 Type a checked value for the radio button.

9 Click **Checked** or **Unchecked** (○ changes to ◉) to select the radio button's initial status.

What happens if I give each radio button in a set a different name?

If you do this, a user can select more than one button in the set at a time, and after a button is selected, the user cannot deselect it. This defeats the purpose of radio buttons. If you want your users to be able to select more than one choice or to deselect a choice, use check boxes instead of radio buttons.

How old are you?

Under 21

21-29

30-39

Over 40

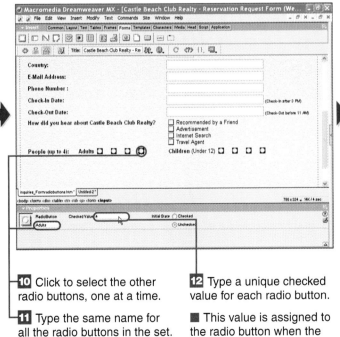

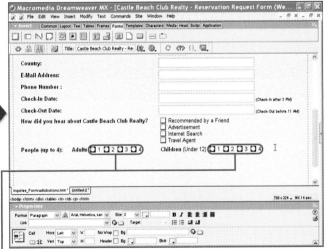

10 Click to select the other radio buttons, one at a time.

11 Type the same name for all the radio buttons in the set.

■ Assigning each button the same name ensures that only one in the set is on at a time.

12 Type a unique checked value for each radio button.

■ This value is assigned to the radio button when the user checks it.

13 Type labels for the radio buttons so that users know what to select.

■ Dreamweaver applies your specifications to the radio buttons.

ADD A MENU OR LIST TO A FORM

A menu allows users to choose one option from a list of options. It works in much the same way as a set of radio buttons. A list allows users to choose one or more options from a list of options, similar to a set of check boxes.

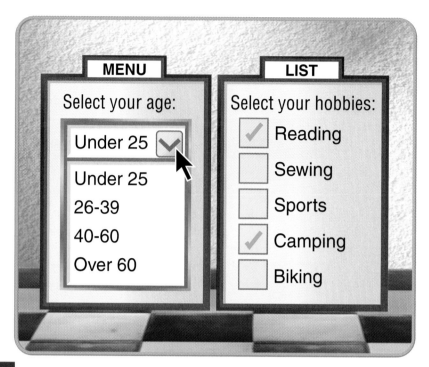

MENU	LIST
Select your age:	Select your hobbies:
Under 25	✓ Reading
Under 25	Sewing
26-39	Sports
40-60	✓ Camping
Over 60	Biking

ADD A MENU OR LIST TO A FORM

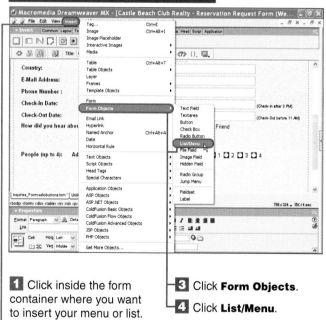

1 Click inside the form container where you want to insert your menu or list.

Note: See "Define a Form," earlier in this chapter, to set up a form.

2 Click **Insert**.

3 Click **Form Objects**.

4 Click **List/Menu**.

■ You can also click the **Forms** tab in the Insert panel and then click the Insert List/Menu button (📋).

5 Click the menu that appears to select it.

■ To display a list instead of a menu, you can click **List** (○ changes to ◉).

6 Type a name for the menu.

7 Click **List Values**.

■ The List Values dialog box appears.

What determines the width of a menu or list?

The widest item determines the width of your menu or list. To change the width, you can change the width of your item descriptions.

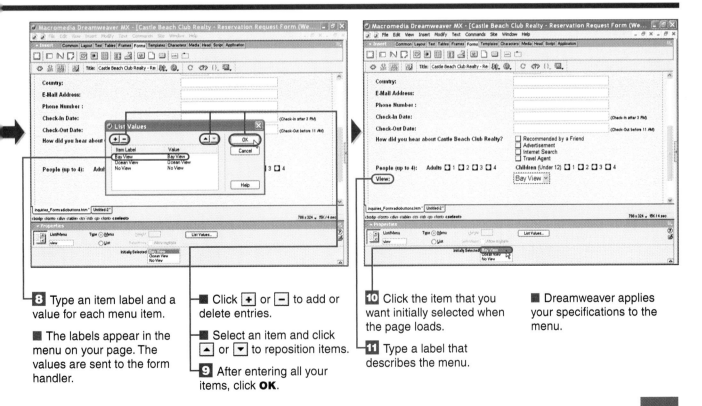

8 Type an item label and a value for each menu item.

■ The labels appear in the menu on your page. The values are sent to the form handler.

■ Click ➕ or ➖ to add or delete entries.

■ Select an item and click ▲ or ▼ to reposition items.

9 After entering all your items, click **OK**.

10 Click the item that you want initially selected when the page loads.

11 Type a label that describes the menu.

■ Dreamweaver applies your specifications to the menu.

ADD A PASSWORD FIELD TO A FORM

A password field is similar to a text field, except the text in the field is hidden as the user enters it. The characters display as asterisks or bullets, depending on the type of operating system used to view the page.

The password field alone *does not* prevent someone from intercepting your information as it travels between a user's computer and the form handler.

ADD A PASSWORD FIELD TO A FORM

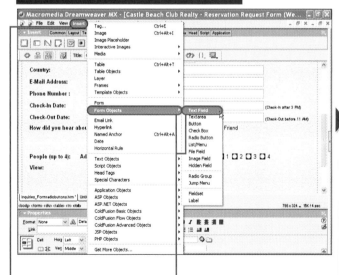

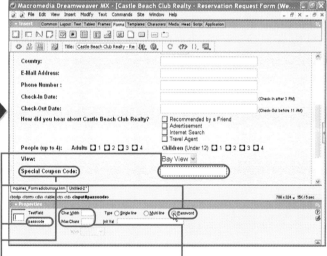

1 Click inside the form container where you want to insert the password field.

Note: See "Define a Form," earlier in this chapter, to set up a form.

2 Click **Insert**.

3 Click **Form Objects**.

4 Click **Text Field**.

■ You can also click the **Forms** tab in the Insert panel and then click the Insert Text Field button (□).

■ A single-line text field appears in your form.

5 Click **Password** (○ changes to ◉).

6 Type a name for the password field.

7 Type a label for the field so that users know what to enter.

■ You can also type in an optional width and maximum number of characters for the password field.

■ When you preview the page in a browser and type into the password field, asterisks or bullets appear in place of letters and numbers.

You can add a button
that enables users to
submit information in a
form, sending it to the
specified form handler.
Adding a Reset button
allows users to erase
their form entries so
they can start over.

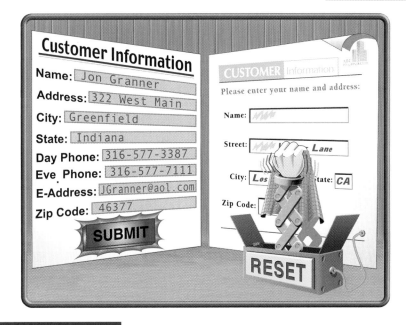

ADD A SUBMIT OR RESET BUTTON TO A FORM

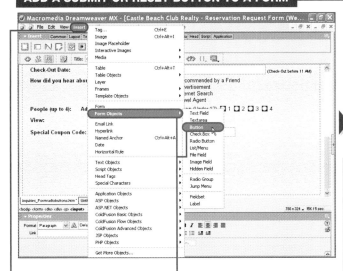

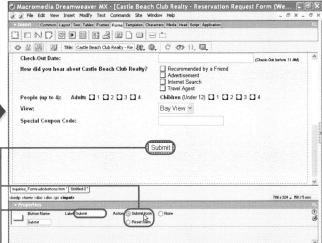

1 Click inside the form
container where you want to
insert the button.

*Note: See "Define a Form," earlier in
this chapter, to set up a form.*

2 Click **Insert**.

3 Click **Form Objects**.

4 Click **Button**.

■ You can also click the
Forms tab in the Insert panel
and then click the Insert
Button button (▭).

■ A button appears in your
Web page.

5 Click the **Submit Form**
or the **Reset Form** radio
button (○ changes to ◉).

6 Type a label for the
button.

■ The label appears on the
button.

■ When a user clicks the
Submit button, the browser
sends the form information
to the form handler.

■ When a user clicks the
Reset button, the browser
resets the form to its initial
values.

CREATE A JUMP MENU

A *jump menu* lets users easily navigate to other Web pages using the menu form object. Dreamweaver uses JavaScript in the form handler to make the jump menu work.

Breaking News

Interesting Discussions

Low-Priced Books

CREATE A JUMP MENU

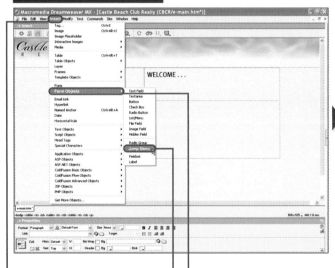

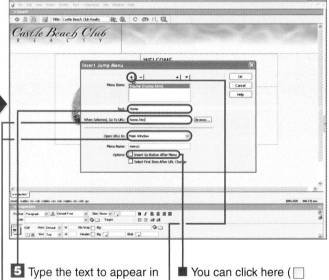

1 Click inside the Document window where you want to insert the jump menu.

Note: See "Define a Form," earlier in this chapter, to set up a form.

2 Click **Insert**.

3 Click **Form Objects**.

4 Click **Jump Menu**.

■ You can also click the **Forms** tab in the Insert panel and then click the Insert Jump Menu button (📄).

■ The Insert Jump Menu dialog box appears.

5 Type the text to appear in the menu for an item.

6 Type the corresponding Web address for the item.

■ If your site has frames, you can specify that the URL opens in a particular frame.

■ You can click here (□ changes to ✓) if you want to insert a Go button after the menu.

7 Click ➕ to specify another item.

178

Does a jump menu require a form handler?

No. For a jump menu, JavaScript code processes the menu information instead of a form handler. If you view the code used to display a jump menu, you may notice that the `<form>` tag is missing the action attribute that usually specifies the form handler.

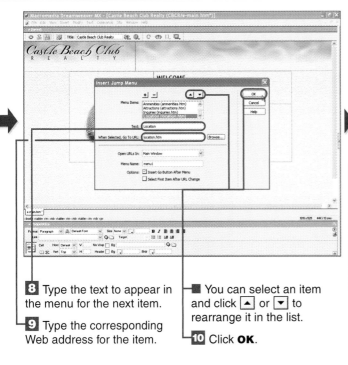

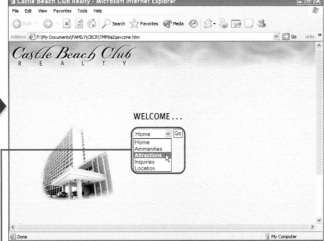

8 Type the text to appear in the menu for the next item.

9 Type the corresponding Web address for the item.

■ You can select an item and click ▲ or ▼ to rearrange it in the list.

10 Click **OK**.

■ The jump menu appears on the page.

■ To test the menu, preview the page in a Web browser.

Note: See Chapter 2 for details on previewing Web pages in a browser.

CHAPTER 11

Using Library Items and Templates

You can save time by storing frequently used Web page elements and layouts as library items and templates. This chapter shows you how to use these features to your advantage.

INTRODUCTION TO LIBRARY ITEMS AND TEMPLATES

With library items and templates, you can avoid repetitive work by storing copies of page elements and layouts that you frequently use. You can access the library items and templates that you create for your site by accessing the Assets panel.

Library Items

You can define parts of your Web pages that are repeated in your site as library items, so you do not have to create them from scratch repeatedly. Each time you need a library item, you can just insert it from your library. If you ever make changes to a library item, Dreamweaver automatically updates all instances of the item across your Web site. Good candidates for library items include advertising banners, company slogans, and any other feature that appears many times across a site.

Templates

You can define commonly used Web page layouts as templates to save you time as you build your pages. Templates can also help you maintain a consistent page design throughout a site. After you make changes to a template, Dreamweaver automatically updates all the pages of your site that are based on that template. If you use just a few page layouts across all the pages in your site, consider defining those layouts as templates.

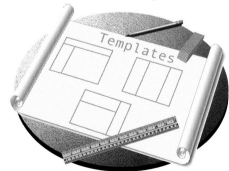

You can access the library and templates of a site by using commands in the Window menu. You can also access them via the Assets panel.

VIEW LIBRARY ITEMS AND TEMPLATES

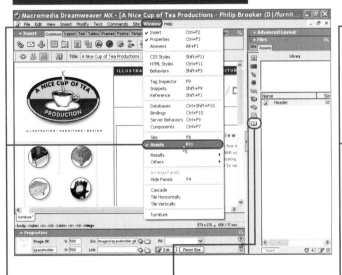

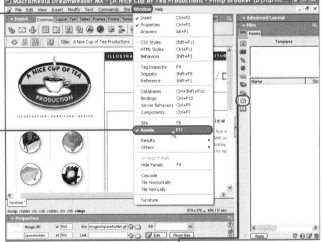

VIEW THE LIBRARY

1 Click **Window**.

2 Click **Assets**.

■ The Assets panel opens, displaying the library for the site.

■ If you already have the Assets panel open, you can click 🔲 to view the library.

VIEW TEMPLATES

1 Click **Window**.

2 Click **Assets**.

3 Click 🔲 to view the templates.

■ The Templates window opens in the Assets panel.

CREATE A LIBRARY ITEM

You can define text, images, and other Dreamweaver objects that you want to appear frequently in your Web site as library items. Library items enable you to quickly insert such page elements without having to re-create them from scratch every time.

If you edit a library item, Dreamweaver automatically updates each instance of the item throughout your site.

CREATE A LIBRARY ITEM

1 Click and drag to select an element or section of your page that you want to define as a library item.

Note: Before you can use the library item feature in Dreamweaver, you must first set up and define your local site. See Chapter 2 to set up a local site.

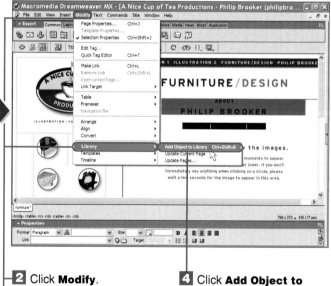

2 Click **Modify**.

3 Click **Library**.

4 Click **Add Object to Library**.

■ A new untitled library item appears in the Library window.

What page elements should I consider defining as library items?

Anything that appears multiple times in a Web site is a good candidate to become a library item. These elements include headers, footers, navigational menus, contact information, and disclaimers. Any element that appears in the body of an HTML document, such as text, images, tables, forms, layers, and multimedia, may be defined as a library item.

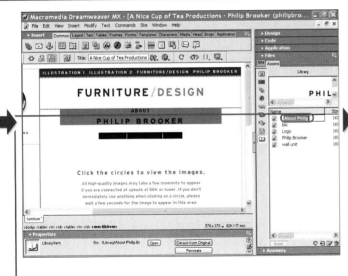

5 Type a name for the library item.

6 Press **Enter** (**Return**).

■ The new library item appears in the yellow highlighting.

Note: See Chapter 3 to change the highlighting color for library items in Preferences.

■ Defining an element as a library item prevents you from editing it in the Document window.

Note: See "Detach Library Content for Editing" to edit library items.

INSERT A LIBRARY ITEM

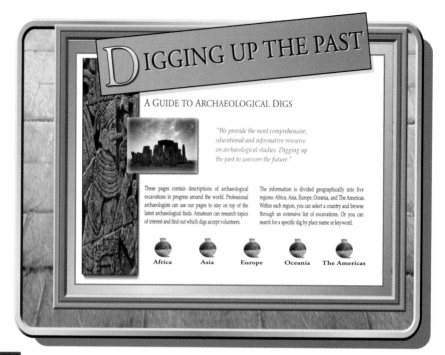

Inserting an element onto your page from the library saves you from having to create it from scratch. It also ensures that the element is identical to other instances of that library item in your site.

INSERT A LIBRARY ITEM

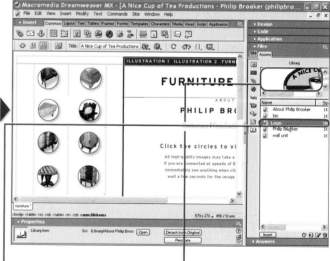

1 Position your cursor where you want to insert the library item.

2 Click **Window**.

3 Click **Assets**.

■ If you already have the Assets panel open, you can click ▥ to open the Library window.

4 Click a library item.

■ The library item appears in the top of the Library window.

186

How do I edit a library item that has been inserted into a page?

Instances of library items in your pages are locked and cannot be edited. To edit a library item, you need to edit the original version of that item from the library. You can also detach an instance of a library item from the library for editing, but then the instance is no longer a part of the library. See the sections "Update Your Web Site with the Library" and "Detach Library Content for Editing" later in this chapter.

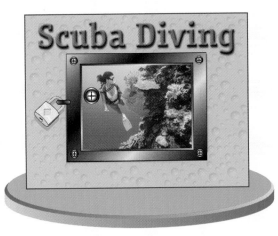

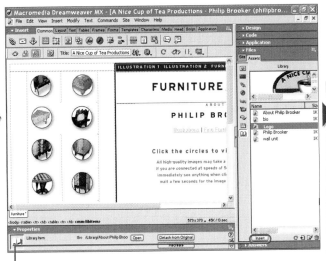

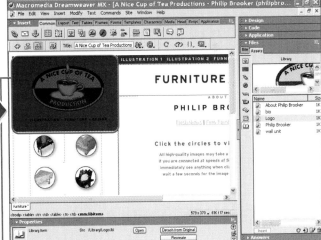

5 Click **Insert**.

■ You can also click and drag library items from the Library panel to the page to insert them.

■ Dreamweaver inserts the highlighted library item into the Document window.

UPDATE YOUR WEB SITE WITH THE LIBRARY

You can edit a library item to automatically update all the pages in your site that feature that item. This feature can save you time when maintaining a Web site.

You can also edit a specific instance of a library item on a page. See "Detach Library Content for Editing."

UPDATE YOUR WEB SITE WITH THE LIBRARY

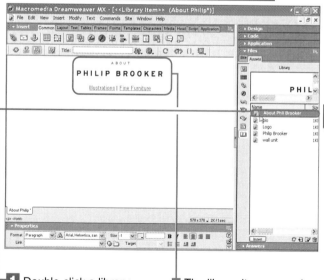

1 Double-click a library item to open it.

■ The library item opens in a new window.

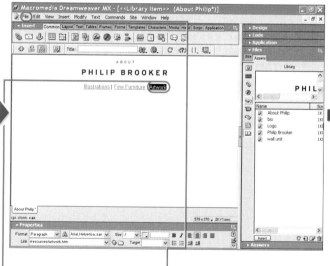

2 Edit the library item as you would edit any similar element in Dreamweaver, using the Property inspector and other features.

■ In this example, a link is added to the new Artwork section.

Note: See Chapter 7 for more about links.

3 Click **File**.

4 Click **Save**.

What will my pages look like after I have edited a library item and updated my site?

All the pages in your site that contain an instance of the library item will have those instances replaced with the edited version. By using the library feature, you can make a change to a single library item and have hundreds of Web pages updated automatically.

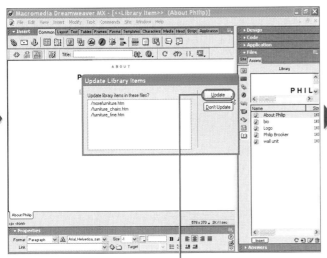

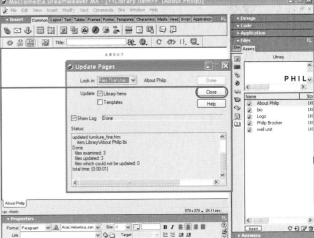

■ The Update Library Items dialog box appears, and Dreamweaver asks if you want to update all instances of the library item in the site.

5 Click **Update**.

■ The Update Pages dialog box shows the progress of the updates.

6 After Dreamweaver updates the site, click **Close**.

■ All instances of the library item are updated.

DETACH LIBRARY CONTENT FOR EDITING

You can detach an instance of a library item from the library and then edit it just like regular content.

DETACH LIBRARY CONTENT FOR EDITING

1 Open a document that contains a library item you want to edit independently.

2 Click the library item to select it.

3 Click **Detach from Original**.

■ The element is no longer a library item and no longer has the distinctive highlighting.

Why might I use the Detach from Original command on a regular basis?

You can use it if you are using library items as templates for specific design elements on your pages. For instance, if you need numerous captioned images in your Web site, you can create a library item that has a two-cell table with a generic image and caption. To place an image and caption, you insert the library item and then detach the item from the library to make it editable. You can then replace the generic image and caption with appropriate content. See Chapter 8 for more about tables.

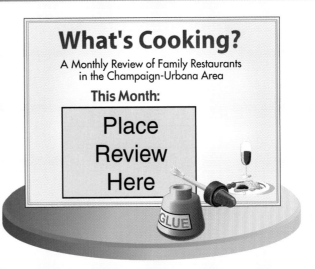

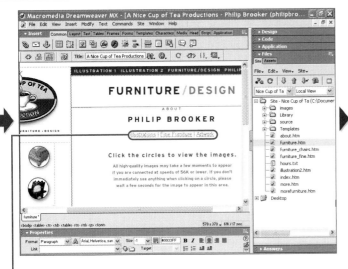

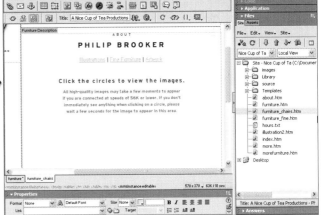

4 Edit the content.

■ In this example, the link color is changed.

5 Open another page that uses the same library item.

■ Editing a detached library item has no effect on the library items that are used on other pages.

CREATE A TEMPLATE

To help you save time, you can create generic template pages to use as starting points for new pages.

CREATE A TEMPLATE

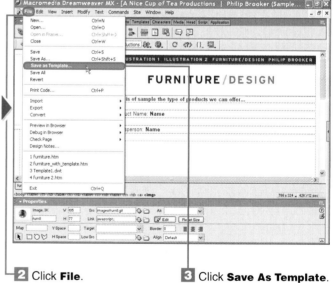

1 Create the page that will serve as a template.

■ You can add placeholders where information will change from page to page.

Note: To create templates for your Web pages, you must already have defined a local site. See Chapter 2 to set up a local site.

2 Click **File**.

3 Click **Save As Template**.

What are the different types of content in a template?

A template contains two types of content: editable and locked. After you create a new Web page based on a template, you can only change the parts of the new page that are defined as editable. To change locked content, you must edit the original template. See the section "Set a Template's Editable Regions" for more information.

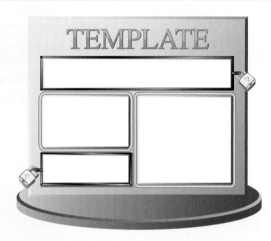

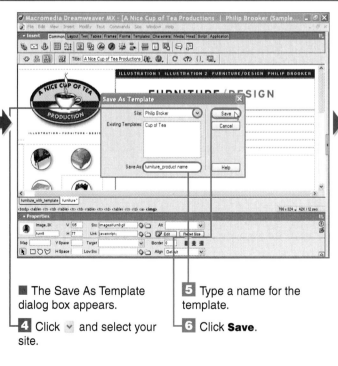

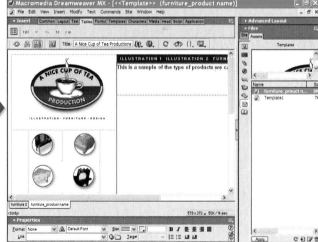

■ The Save As Template dialog box appears.

4 Click ⌄ and select your site.

5 Type a name for the template.

6 Click **Save**.

■ If a template folder does not already exist, Dreamweaver automatically creates one when it saves the new template.

Note: To make the template functional, you must define the editable regions where you want to be able to modify content. See the section "Set a Template's Editable Regions," later in this chapter, for more information.

SET A TEMPLATE'S EDITABLE REGIONS

After you create a Web page template, you must define which regions of the template are editable. These regions are changeable in a page according to its template design.

SET A TEMPLATE'S EDITABLE REGIONS

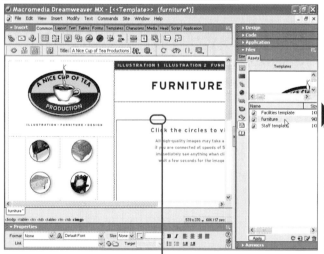

1 Open a template.

■ You can open templates from the Assets panel by clicking **Window**, **Assets**, 📄, and then double-clicking the template file to open it.

■ You can also click **File**, **Open**, and then open the template from inside the Templates folder.

2 Click to select the image or text area that you want to define as editable.

3 Click **Insert**.

4 Click **Template Objects**.

5 Click **Editable Region**.

What parts of a template should be defined as editable?

You should define any part that needs to be changed from page to page as editable. Generally, variable areas in the page body are defined as editable while site navigation, disclaimers, and copyright information are kept locked.

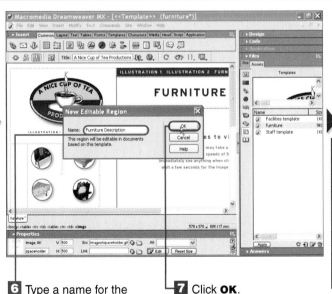

6 Type a name for the editable region that distinguishes it from other editable regions on the page.

Note: You cannot use the characters &, ", ', <, or > in the name.

7 Click **OK**.

■ The editable region is indicated by light blue highlighting and a box with the region name as you have defined it.

Note: See Chapter 3 to change the highlighting color for editable text in Preferences.

8 Repeat steps **1** to **7** for other regions on the page to be editable in the template.

9 Click **File**, and then **Save**.

■ Editable regions in the template are defined.

CREATE A PAGE BY USING A TEMPLATE

You can create a new Web page based on a template that you have already defined. This step saves you from having to build all the generic elements that appear on many of your pages from scratch.

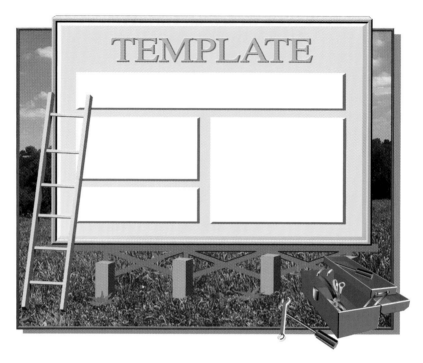

CREATE A PAGE BY USING A TEMPLATE

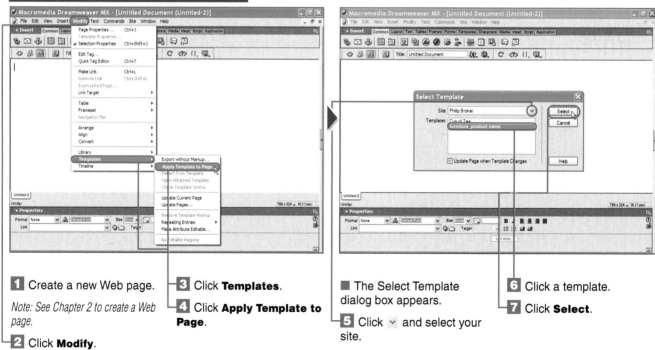

1 Create a new Web page.

Note: See Chapter 2 to create a Web page.

2 Click **Modify**.

3 Click **Templates**.

4 Click **Apply Template to Page**.

■ The Select Template dialog box appears.

5 Click ⌄ and select your site.

6 Click a template.

7 Click **Select**.

How do I detach a page from a template?

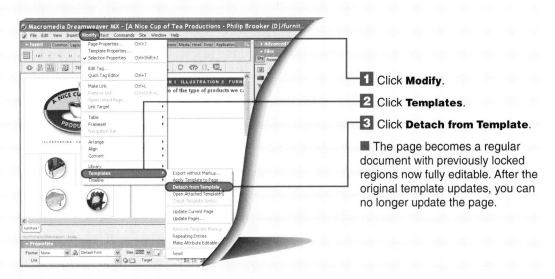

1 Click **Modify**.

2 Click **Templates**.

3 Click **Detach from Template**.

■ The page becomes a regular document with previously locked regions now fully editable. After the original template updates, you can no longer update the page.

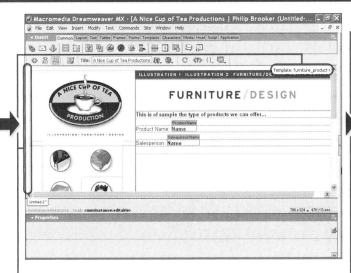

■ The template is denoted with a yellow border and a tab with the template name.

■ You can find the editable regions in the blue highlighting.

■ You can select a specific editable region by clicking **Modify**, **Templates**, and then a region name from the bottom of the menu that appears.

8 Type content in the editable regions.

9 Click **File**.

10 Click **Save**.

■ The new page, based on the template, is saved.

EDIT A TEMPLATE AND UPDATE YOUR WEB SITE

As you make updates to an original template file, Dreamweaver transmits those updates to the pages that are supported by the template. This enables you to make wholesale changes to the page design of your site in seconds.

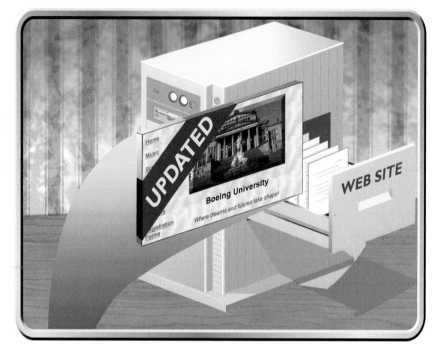

EDIT A TEMPLATE AND UPDATE YOUR WEB SITE

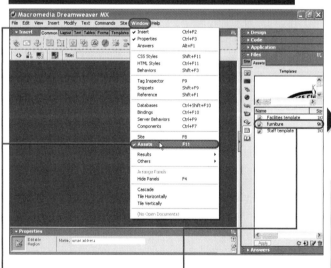

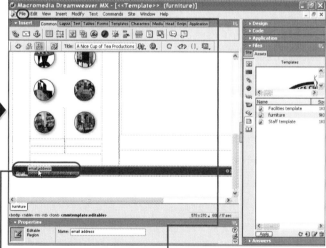

1 Click **Window**.

2 Click **Assets**.

3 Double-click the template to open it.

4 Edit the template.

■ Editing a template includes adding, modifying, or deleting editable or locked content in the page.

Note: See "Set a Template's Editable Regions," earlier in this chapter, for more information.

■ In this example, an e-mail entry has been added to a template. The Email: label is noneditable; the e-mail address, tabbed and highlighted in blue, is editable.

5 Click **File**, and then **Save**.

How does Dreamweaver store page templates?

Dreamweaver stores page templates in a folder called Templates inside the local site folder. You can open templates by clicking **File**, **Open**, and then ⌄ to select the Template folder. You can click a template file to select it. You can also open templates from inside the Assets panel.

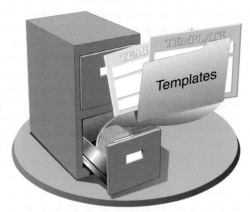

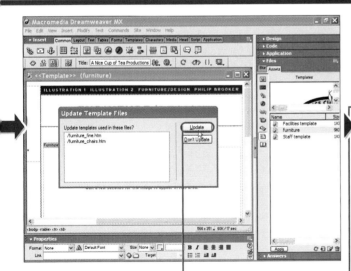

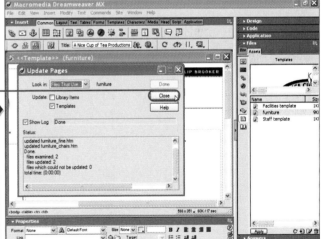

■ Dreamweaver asks if you want to update all documents in the local site that use the template.

6 Click **Update**.

■ The Update Pages dialog box shows the update progress.

7 After Dreamweaver updates the site, click **Close**.

■ All pages that use the template are updated to reflect the changes.

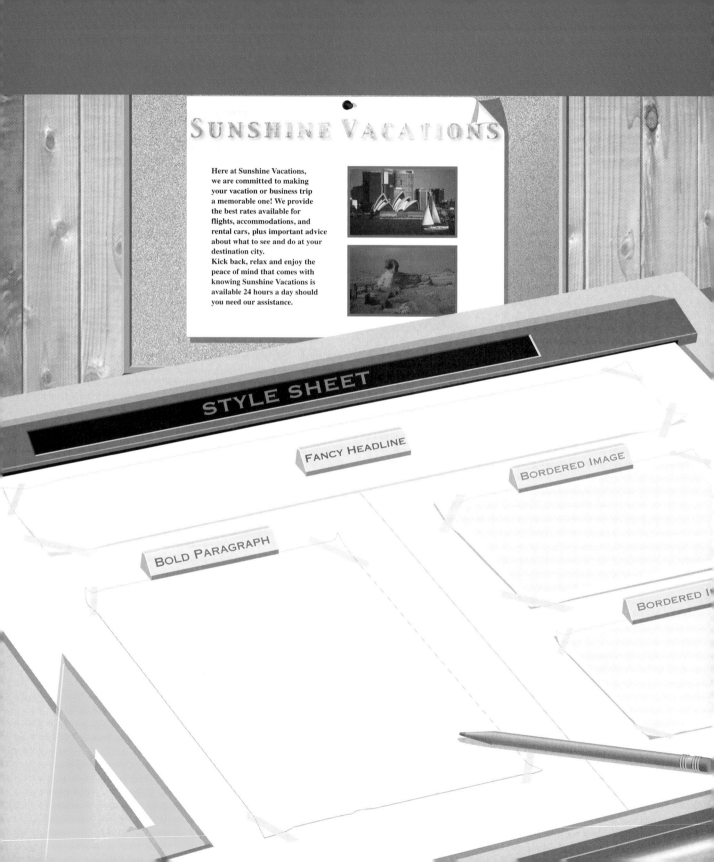

SUNSHINE VACATIONS

Here at Sunshine Vacations, we are committed to making your vacation or business trip a memorable one! We provide the best rates available for flights, accommodations, and rental cars, plus important advice about what to see and do at your destination city.

Kick back, relax and enjoy the peace of mind that comes with knowing Sunshine Vacations is available 24 hours a day should you need our assistance.

STYLE SHEET

FANCY HEADLINE

BORDERED IMAGE

BOLD PARAGRAPH

BORDERED I

CHAPTER 12

Creating and Applying Style Sheets

This chapter shows you how to apply complex formatting to your pages using cascading style sheets and HTML styles. These features will save you lots of time, especially on big Web sites.

INTRODUCTION TO STYLE SHEETS

You can apply many different types of formatting to your Web pages with style sheets, also known as *cascading style sheets,* or *CSS.*

Format Text

A separate standard from HTML, style sheets enable you to format fonts; adjust character, paragraph, and margin spacing; customize the look of hyperlinks; tailor the colors on your page; and more.

Create Global Web Page Styles

You can use style sheets to globally change the attributes of images, text, and other elements to create consistent formatting styles across your Web page, more efficiently than you can with HTML.

HTML and CSS Style Sheets

You can create new custom cascading style sheets, or you can redefine existing HTML tags to create HTML styles. You can use HTML styles to apply more than one formatting option at a time. You can use CSS style sheets to apply styles across a single page, or across an entire Web site.

Embedded Style Sheets

A style sheet saved inside a particular Web page is an *embedded* style sheet. Embedded style sheet rules apply only to the page in which they are embedded.

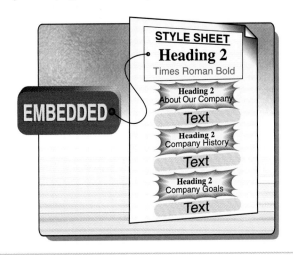

External Style Sheets

You can save style sheets as separate files; these *external* style sheets exist independently of your HTML pages. You can use external style sheets to control formatting across multiple pages and even an entire site. You can also make global changes to formatted elements when you edit style sheet definitions.

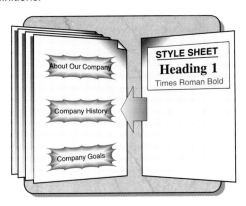

Style Sheets and Browsers

Some older browsers do not support style sheet standards, and browsers display style sheets differently. Always test pages that use style sheets on different browsers to ensure that content displays as you expect it.

Netscape Communicator

Microsoft Internet Explorer

REDEFINE AN HTML STYLE

You can use style sheets to customize the style that an HTML tag applies to text or other elements. Doing this enables you to apply multiple style options with one HTML tag.

REDEFINE AN HTML STYLE

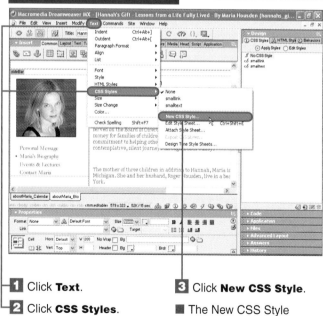

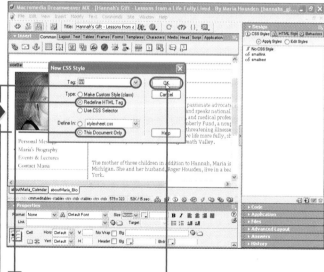

1 Click **Text**.

2 Click **CSS Styles**.

3 Click **New CSS Style**.

■ The New CSS Style dialog box appears.

4 Click **Redefine HTML Tag** (○ changes to ⊙).

5 Click ⌄ and select a tag.

6 Click **This Document Only** to create an embedded style sheet for the file on which you are working (○ changes to ⊙).

Note: See "Create an External Style Sheet" to create style sheets for more than one document.

7 Click **OK**.

How do I edit the style that I have applied to a tag?

6 In the left pane of the CSS Style definition dialog box, click a style. Specify the style settings in the right pane, and then click **OK**.

7 Click **Done**.

■ Dreamweaver saves the edits to the style.

4 Click a tag.

5 Click **Edit**.

1 Click **Text**.

2 Click **CSS Styles**.

3 Click **Edit Style Sheet**.

■ A dialog box displays the current customized tags and style sheet classes.

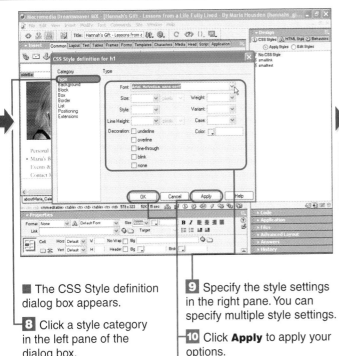

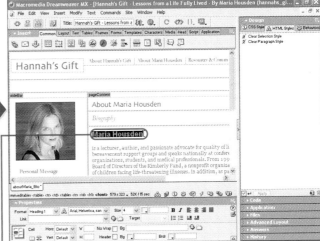

■ The CSS Style definition dialog box appears.

8 Click a style category in the left pane of the dialog box.

9 Specify the style settings in the right pane. You can specify multiple style settings.

10 Click **Apply** to apply your options.

11 Click **OK** to accept your options.

■ Dreamweaver adds the new style to any content formatted with the redefined tag.

■ In this example, the <H1> was redefined to use a different font face and size.

■ You can also apply the style by formatting new content with the redefined tag.

CREATE A CUSTOM STYLE

You can define specific style attributes as a custom style sheet. You can then apply that style to text or other elements on your Web page.

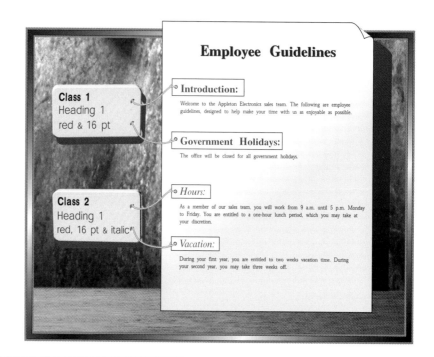

CREATE A CUSTOM STYLE

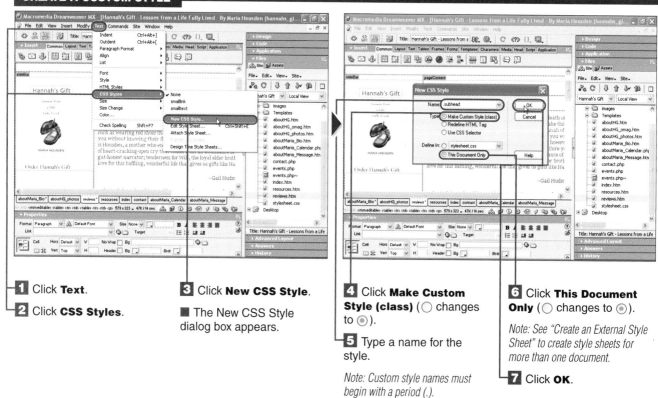

1 Click **Text**.

2 Click **CSS Styles**.

3 Click **New CSS Style**.

■ The New CSS Style dialog box appears.

4 Click **Make Custom Style (class)** (○ changes to ◉).

5 Type a name for the style.

Note: Custom style names must begin with a period (.).

6 Click **This Document Only** (○ changes to ◉).

Note: See "Create an External Style Sheet" to create style sheets for more than one document.

7 Click **OK**.

How does customizing an HTML tag differ from creating a custom style?

Customizing an HTML tag links a style rule to an existing HTML tag. The new style affects every instance of that tag on your Web page. For example, if you customize your paragraph tags as green using style sheets, every paragraph in your page will be green. With custom styles, you can define style sheets that are independent of HTML tags. You can apply new styles without affecting existing HTML tags.

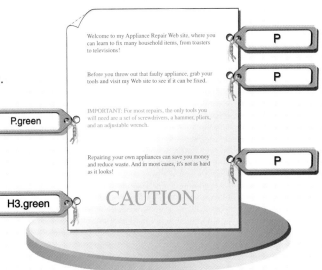

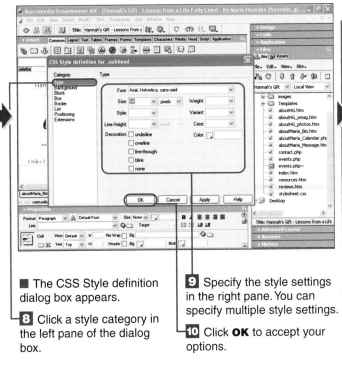

■ The CSS Style definition dialog box appears.

8 Click a style category in the left pane of the dialog box.

9 Specify the style settings in the right pane. You can specify multiple style settings.

10 Click **OK** to accept your options.

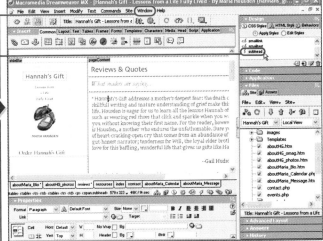

11 Click **Window**.

12 Click **CSS Styles** to open the CSS Styles panel.

■ The new style appears in the CSS Styles panel.

■ In this example, the font settings are changed.

■ The new style can be applied to new or existing content.

Note: See the section "Apply a Style" for more about applying a style.

APPLY A STYLE

Applying a style sheet to elements on your Web page enables you to make global changes to the color, font, size, background, and other characteristics of content on your page.

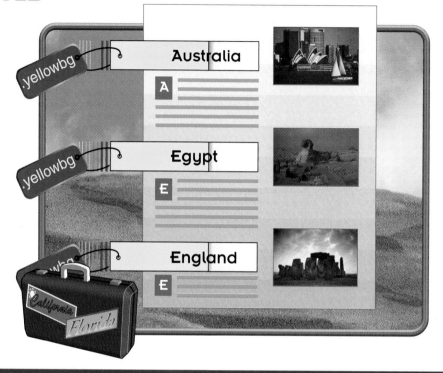

APPLY A STYLE

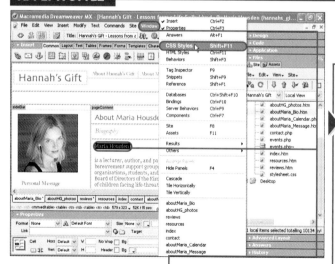

Note: This section uses custom styles. See the section "Create a Custom Style" to create a new custom style.

APPLY A STYLE TO AN OBJECT

-1 Click and drag to select the text or other element to which you want to apply the style.

-2 Click **Window**.

-3 Click **CSS Styles**.

■ The CSS Styles panel opens in the Design panel.

-4 Click the name of a style.

■ Dreamweaver applies the style sheet definition to the selected content in the Document window.

■ In this example, the font changes to reflect the selected style.

CSS Styles vs. HTML Styles

CSS styles are part of the official HTML specification, but HTML styles, which are a special feature of Dreamweaver, provide a variation Macromedia offers as an alternative because HTML styles are currently supported by more browsers. As a result, you can create HTML styles and have the benefits of the acceptability of HTML with the power of style sheets. See "Create an HTML Style," later in this chapter, to create an HTML style.

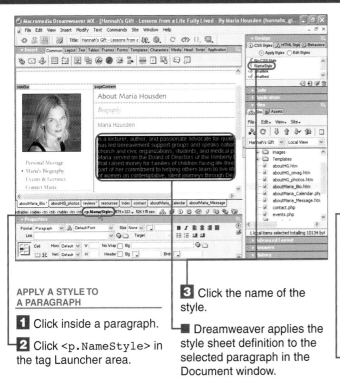

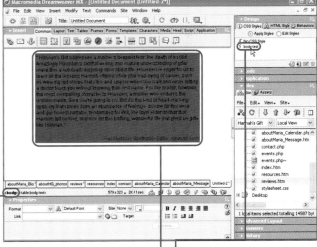

**APPLY A STYLE TO
A PARAGRAPH**

1 Click inside a paragraph.

2 Click <p.NameStyle> in the tag Launcher area.

3 Click the name of the style.

■ Dreamweaver applies the style sheet definition to the selected paragraph in the Document window.

**APPLY A STYLE TO THE
ENTIRE BODY OF A PAGE**

1 Click inside the Document window.

2 Click <body> in the tag Launcher area.

3 Click the name of the style in the CSS Styles panel.

■ Dreamweaver applies the style sheet class to the entire body of the page in the Document window.

EDIT A STYLE SHEET

You can edit style sheet definitions and automatically apply the changes across all of the text or other elements to which you have applied the style on your site.

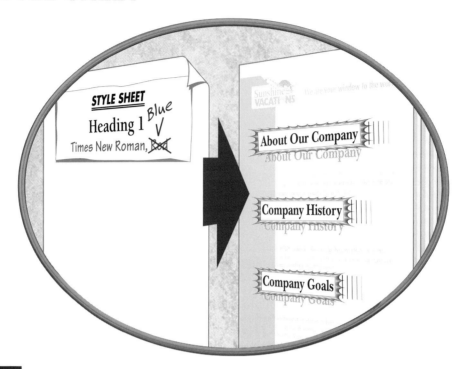

EDIT A STYLE SHEET

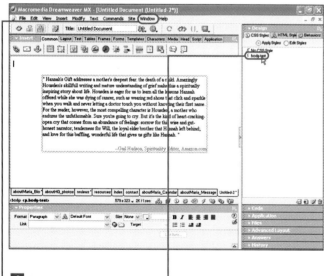

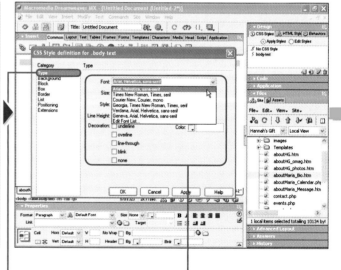

1 Click **Window**.

2 Click **CSS Styles**.

■ The CSS Styles panel opens and displays the styles available to that page.

3 Double-click the style you want to edit.

■ The CSS Style definition dialog box opens.

4 Click a style category in the left pane of the dialog box.

5 Specify the style settings in the right pane. You can specify multiple style settings.

■ In this example, the font settings are changed.

What are some type-based features that I can apply with style sheets that I cannot with HTML?

With style sheets, you can specify a numeric value for font weight, enabling you to apply varying degrees of boldness, instead of just a single boldness setting as with HTML. You can also define type size in absolute units — pixels, points, picas, in, cm, or mm — or relative units — ems, exs, or percentage. Keep in mind that these features work only with certain fonts and will not display in all browsers.

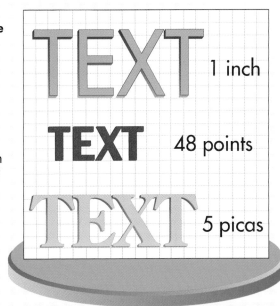

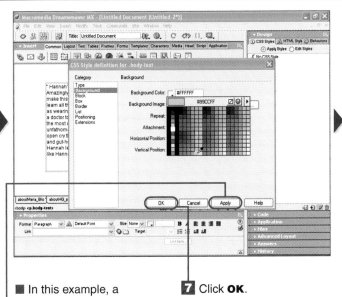

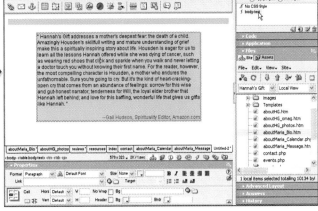

■ In this example, a background color is specified.

6 Click **Apply** to accept the changes.

7 Click **OK**.

■ Dreamweaver saves the style sheet changes.

■ In this example, the background color and font are changed when the new style definition is applied.

USING CSS SELECTORS TO MODIFY LINKS

You can use style sheet *selectors* to customize the links on your page. Selectors enable you to customize your links in ways that you cannot with HTML, such as removing the underline from linked text.

USING CSS SELECTORS TO MODIFY LINKS

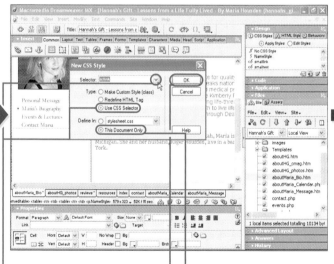

1 Click **Text**.

2 Click **CSS Styles**.

3 Click **New CSS Style**.

■ The New CSS Style dialog box appears.

4 Click **Use CSS Selector** (○ changes to ◉).

5 Click ⌄ and choose a selector.

6 Click **This Document Only** to create an embedded style sheet (○ changes to ◉).

Note: See "Create an External Style Sheet" to create style sheets for more than one document.

7 Click **OK**.

How do I attach a style sheet to an existing document or entire site?

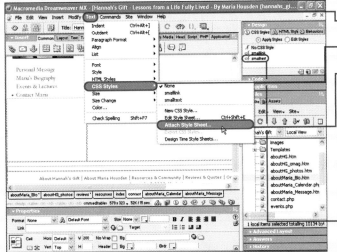

1 Open the page to which you want to attach the style sheet.

2 Click **Text**.

3 Click **CSS Styles**.

4 Click **Attach Style Sheet** to open the Link External Style Sheet dialog box.

5 Click **Browse** to open the Select Style Sheet File dialog box. Click the file, and then click **OK**.

6 Click **OK** in the Link External Style Sheet dialog box.

■ The style from the style sheet appears in the CSS Styles panel and can be attached to the page.

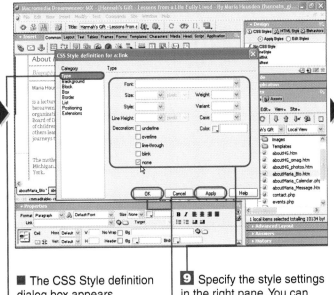

■ The CSS Style definition dialog box appears.

8 Click a style category in the left pane of the dialog box.

9 Specify the style settings in the right pane. You can specify multiple style settings.

10 Click **Apply** to apply your options.

11 Click **OK** to accept your options.

12 Preview the page in a Web browser

Note: See Chapter 2 to preview a page in Web browsers.

■ Dreamweaver applies the style changes to the link.

■ In this example, the name at the beginning of the paragraph in the text is not underlined, even though it is a link.

CREATE AN EXTERNAL STYLE SHEET

External style sheets enable you to define a set of style sheet rules and apply them to many different pages — even pages on different Web sites. With this capability, you can keep a consistent look and feel across many pages and streamline style updates.

CREATE AN EXTERNAL STYLE SHEET

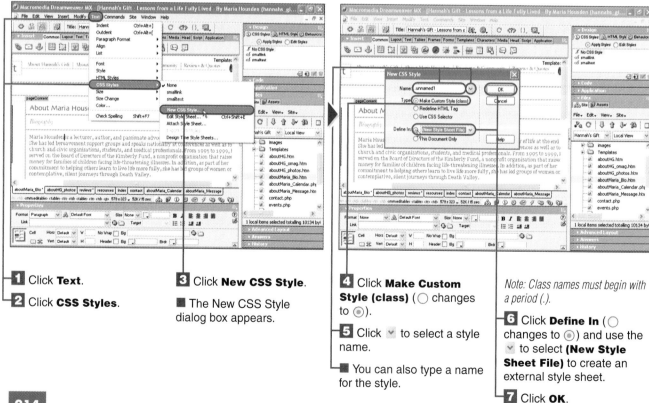

1 Click **Text**.

2 Click **CSS Styles**.

3 Click **New CSS Style**.

■ The New CSS Style dialog box appears.

4 Click **Make Custom Style (class)** (○ changes to ⊙).

5 Click ⌄ to select a style name.

■ You can also type a name for the style.

Note: Class names must begin with a period (.).

6 Click **Define In** (○ changes to ⊙) and use the ⌄ to select **(New Style Sheet File)** to create an external style sheet.

7 Click **OK**.

**How do I export a set of embedded
styles to create an external style sheet?**

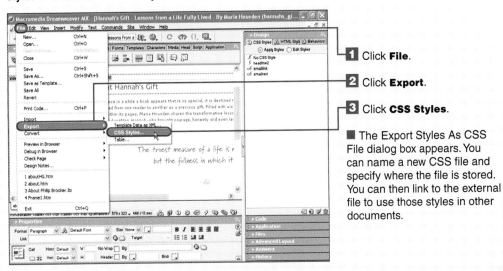

1 Click **File**.

2 Click **Export**.

3 Click **CSS Styles**.

■ The Export Styles As CSS
File dialog box appears. You
can name a new CSS file and
specify where the file is stored.
You can then link to the external
file to use those styles in other
documents.

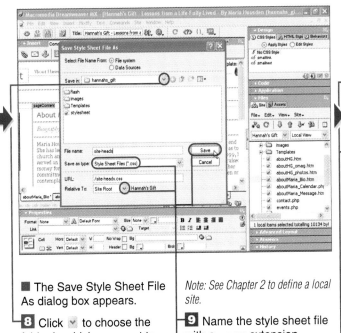

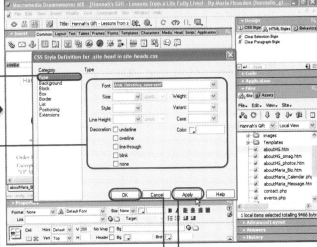

■ The Save Style Sheet File
As dialog box appears.

*Note: See Chapter 2 to define a local
site.*

8 Click ⬇ to choose the
folder in which you want to
store the external style sheet.

■ You should store the
external style sheet
somewhere inside your
local site folder.

9 Name the style sheet file
with a `.css` extension.

10 Click the Relative To ⬇
and select **Site Root**.

11 Click **Save**.

■ The CSS Style Definition
dialog box appears.

12 Click a style category
in the left panel of the
dialog box.

13 Specify the style settings
in the right pane. You can
specify multiple style
settings.

14 Click **Apply** to apply your
options.

15 Click **OK** to accept your
options.

■ Dreamweaver applies
changes to the style sheet
definition.

215

CREATE AN HTML STYLE

HTML styles were created by Macromedia to provide an alternative to custom style sheets (CSS). HTML styles provide most of the benefits of CSS, but they display better in a wider range of browsers. HTML styles do not have all the power of CSS styles, but they offer many of the timesaving benefits, especially if you want to make global formatting changes to content. See "Create a Custom Style," earlier in this chapter, to create a CSS style.

CREATE AN HTML STYLE

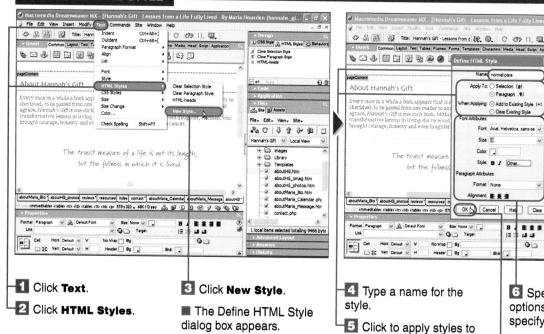

1 Click **Text**.

2 Click **HTML Styles**.

3 Click **New Style**.

■ The Define HTML Style dialog box appears.

4 Type a name for the style.

5 Click to apply styles to a selection or a paragraph. Click to add new styles to existing styles or clear existing styles first (○ changes to ◉).

6 Specify the formatting options for the style. You can specify multiple options.

7 Click **OK**.

■ The new style appears in the HTML Styles panel.

APPLY AN HTML STYLE

You can format text using the HTML Styles panel, which allows you to apply a complicated style with a single click.

APPLY AN HTML STYLE

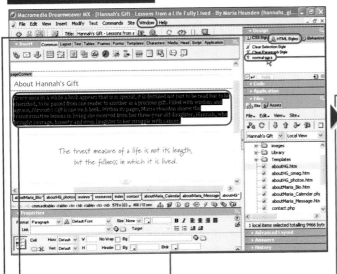

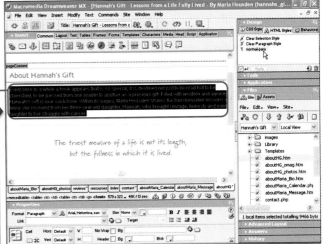

1 Click and drag to select the text you want to format in the Document window.

2 Click the **HTML Styles** tab in the Design panel.

■ You can also click **Window** and then **HTML Styles**.

■ The HTML Styles panel appears.

3 Select a style from the list.

■ The text appears formatted according to the style. In this example, the font changes.

■ Dreamweaver comes with several HTML styles predefined. To add custom styles to the HTML Styles panel, see the section "Create an HTML Style."

Ancient Treasure

See the most rece
discoveries in the
world of archaeo

CUSTOMER INFORMATION

NAME: J. Anderso

ADDRESS: 322 W

CITY:

STAT

VALIDATED

ZIP CODE: 47777-8844

CHAPTER 13

Using Dynamic HTML

In addition to static Web pages, Dreamweaver can also create Dynamic HTML, or DHTML, to make your site come to life. This chapter shows you how to add logic and interactivity to your Web pages.

INTRODUCTION TO DHTML

DHTML is not a programming language; it is a subset of technologies that extend static HTML Web pages. DHTML enables you to create interactive elements within your pages.

Behavior Basics

Behaviors are cause-and-effect events that you can insert into your Web pages. Creative behaviors can make pictures on the page change when they are touched by the mouse or make headlines fly across the page. Logical behaviors tell people what Web browser they are using, or remind them to fill out their name in your site's questionnaire form.

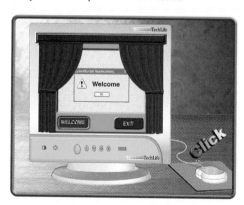

Behind the Scenes

Dreamweaver behaviors insert brief programs called "scripts" between lines of your Web pages. Dreamweaver creates these scripts in a language called *JavaScript*; however, many available behaviors rely on other technologies such as ActiveX and SSI. JavaScript is by far the most accepted and widely used client-side programming language due to wide browser acceptance and its powerful abilities.

Behaviors and Browsers

Behaviors vary in complexity and can be written in various ways to ensure compatibility with older browsers. Both Internet Explorer 4 and Netscape 4 adopted the majority of DHTML technologies after version 4. However, there is no standard adoption, so each browser's result may vary. Dreamweaver knows the limitations of each browser and lets you disable behaviors that may not work in older browsers. As of this book's publication date, the most widely used Web browser is Internet Explorer, so these exercises are tailored to it.

Creating Rollovers

A *rollover* behavior is a cursor-sensitive event commonly used to swap a picture file with another when the cursor moves across an image. Many Web designers apply the rollover image behavior to make buttons light up or appear to press down to the touch. Rollovers can be programmed in a variety of ways, such as swapping multiple images when you click a button.

Validate Forms

You can prevent users from entering erroneous information in Web page forms by using a behavior to validate form fields. The behavior can be programmed to generate an alert if a required field has not been filled out, or has been filled out improperly, prior to clicking the Submit button. This gives users the ability to correct their mistake without having to start over or reload the page.

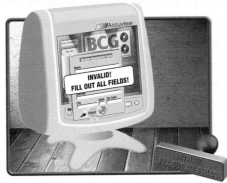

Check Browser Versions

Designing a page that works equally well in all browsers generally means that you have to refrain from using the latest Web-design technologies available. Many of the features in this chapter, such as layer animation, are not available for older browser versions. While you can create two versions of your site, one for current browsers and one for older browsers, and Dreamweaver can automatically redirect users to the page appropriate for their browser, most Webmasters do not want the added work of maintaining two versions of their sites. More commonly, you can use a behavior that lets people know they need to upgrade their browser for the best possible experience.

CREATE A LAYER AND INSERT CONTENT

Layers **are scalable rectangles inside of which you can place text and pictures, similar to tables. However, layers can float above the body of a document. You can move layers wherever you please with pixel-perfect precision. If you have worked with the layer feature of Adobe Photoshop, you will find that DHTML layers are very similar.**

Layers do not obey normal HTML flow — they can sit on top of page content and can be placed anywhere on the page. Layers can be placed to overlap other layers.

CREATE A LAYER

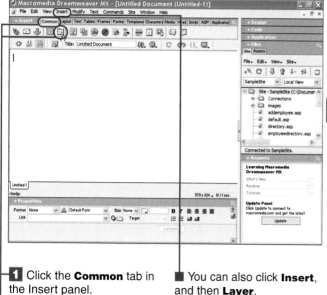

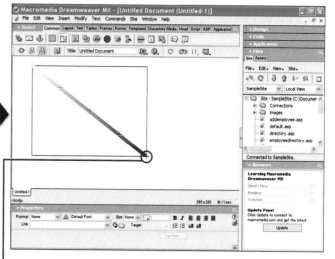

1 Click the **Common** tab in the Insert panel.

2 Click the Draw Layer button (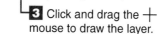).

■ You can also click **Insert**, and then **Layer**.

■ changes to +.

3 Click and drag the + mouse to draw the layer.

■ The outline of the layer appears.

How do I place one layer inside another?

This technique is called *nesting* layers, and you can toggle it on and off. To activate it, click **Edit**, and then **Preferences**. Click **Layers** from the category list, and make sure the Nesting check box is checked (☐ changes to ☑). Click the Draw Layer button (🔲) on the Insert panel. Click and drag inside an existing layer to nest a new layer inside it. When a layer is nested inside another, the layer's icon (📄) appears inside the enclosing layer.

ADD CONTENT TO A LAYER

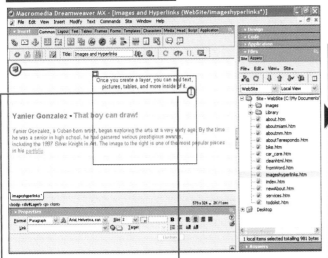

1 Click inside the layer (arrow changes to I).

■ You can now type within the layer.

■ The 📄 icon represents the inserted layer. If 📄 does not appear, click **View**, **Visual Aids**, and then **Invisible Elements**.

■ You can also add an image by clicking 🖼.

■ In this example, the text and image are inside of the layer.

■ You can do anything within a layer that you can do within the document body. You can stylize text, align it, and even insert tables. See Chapter 5 to style text, and Chapter 8 for more about tables.

RESIZE AND REPOSITION LAYERS

When you create a layer with the Draw Layer button, Dreamweaver calculates the layer's width and height, as well as its X and Y coordinates relative to the document. These four values are not set in stone after you create a layer — you can adjust the position and dimensions of a layer to make it fit attractively with the rest of the content on your page.

RESIZE A LAYER

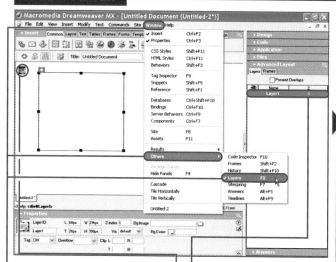

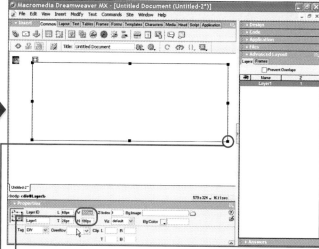

1 Click **Window**.

2 Click **Others**.

3 Click **Layers**.

■ Dreamweaver automatically names and numbers layers in the order they were created.

4 In the Layers panel, click the layer that you want to resize.

■ Layer values appear in the Property inspector.

■ You can also select a layer by clicking its icon (▣).

5 Type new width and height values.

■ You can also click and drag the layer's border handles to change its dimensions.

■ Dreamweaver applies the new dimensions to the layer.

■ In this example, Dreamweaver calculates the dimensions of the layer in pixels, indicated by typing **px** after the value. You can also type **in** for inches or **cm** for centimeters, although pixels are most practical.

How do I change a layer's visibility?

Select a layer, and then click the Vis ❏ in the Property inspector. You can make a layer visible or invisible, or have it inherit its characteristic from its *parent*, which is the enclosing layer.

There is also a visibility column available in the Layers panel within the Advanced Layout panel. Click in the column to adjust visibility. The open eye (👁) indicates the layer is visible; the closed eye (👁) indicates the layer is invisible; and no icon showing indicates default visibility, which means the layer is visible.

REPOSITION A LAYER

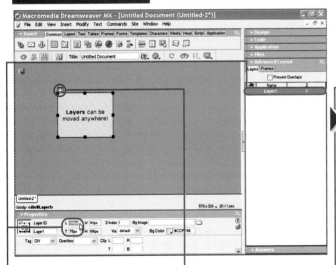

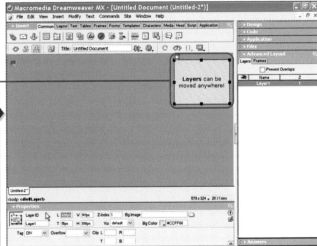

1 Click the layer you want to reposition.

2 Type the new distance from the left side of the window in the L field and from the top of the window in the T field.

■ You can also click and drag the Layer tab (▢) to change a layer's position.

■ Dreamweaver applies the new positioning to the layer.

CHANGE THE STACKING ORDER OF LAYERS

You can change the stacking order of layers on a page to change how they overlap one another. You can then hide parts of some layers under other layers.

CHANGE THE STACKING ORDER OF LAYERS

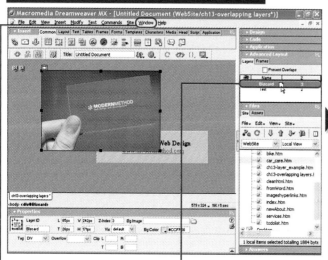

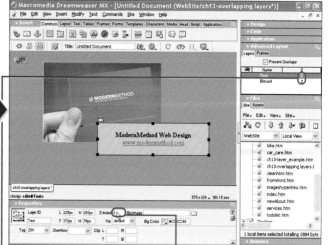

Note: A portion of the text layer is being covered by the picture layer.

1 Click **Window**, **Others**, and then **Layers**.

■ The Advanced Layout panel appears.

2 Click the layer name.

■ You can drag the name up to move a layer higher in the stack; drag it down to send it down.

■ As you drag the layer name, ↖ changes to ↘.

■ Dreamweaver changes the stacking order of the layers. Note the difference in Z-Index values in the Layers panel.

■ You can also select a layer in the document window and change its Z-Index value in the Property inspector or in the Layers panel. Layers with greater Z-Index values are placed higher in the stack.

With DHTML and layers, you can enable site visitors to pick up and move elements around your Web page.

ENABLE LAYER DRAGGING

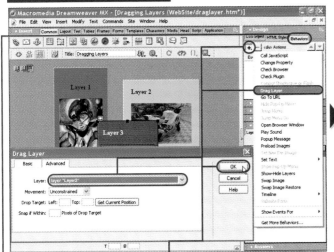

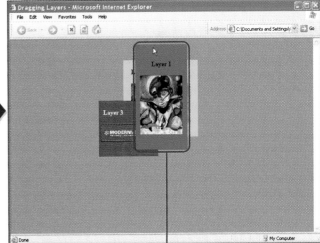

1 Create three layers.

■ You can insert images and text in layers, or click ☐ to change the color.

Note: See "Create a Layer and Insert Content" for information.

2 Click the **Behaviors** tab.

3 Click ⊞.

4 Click **Drag Layer**.

5 In the Drag Layer dialog box, click ☑, and then click a layer.

6 Click **OK**.

7 Repeat steps **2** to **6** to make each layer draggable.

8 Preview the file in a Web browser.

Note: See Chapter 2 to preview Web pages in a browser.

■ Each layer can be moved around the Web page by clicking and dragging it.

APPLY THE SHOW-HIDE LAYERS BEHAVIOR

Behaviors can be used to show, hide, and animate layers. You can add interactivity to your pages by creating *buttons* that interact with the visible or hidden layers.

HIDE A VISIBLE LAYER

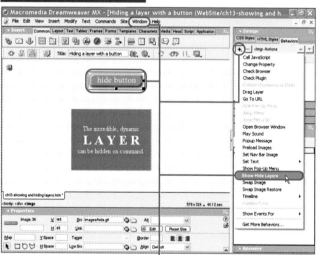

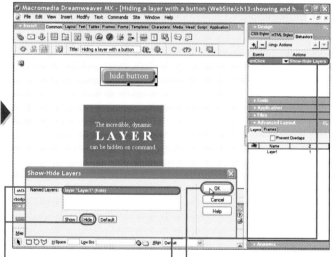

1 Create a layer containing images or text.

Note: See "Create a Layer and Insert Content" for information.

2 In the Document window, insert a graphic.

■ In this example, use the graphic as a button to hide your layer.

3 Click **Window**, and then **Behaviors** to open the Behaviors panel.

4 Click the graphic.

5 Click ➕.

6 Click **Show-Hide Layers**.

Note: Dreamweaver prevents you from choosing behaviors that your browser does not support. Netscape supports layers but is not fully compatible with this Show-Hide Layer behavior.

7 In the Show-Hide Layers dialog box, click the layer.

8 Click **Hide**.

9 Click **OK**.

■ The behavior is now associated with the action. In this example, clicking the graphic hides the layer.

Note: The layer remains hidden after the behavior executes until you create another behavior that makes it visible again or until you reload the page.

What are some practical uses for showing and hiding layers?

Many sites use these types of behaviors to create Windows-style navigational menus that expand in a tree-like structure over content. You can also use this technique to display a large amount of content on one page, simply by showing one layer while simultaneously hiding other layers. This is similar to showing and hiding index cards. Because the person never has to leave the page, you can literally create a small Web site on one page!

SHOW A HIDDEN LAYER

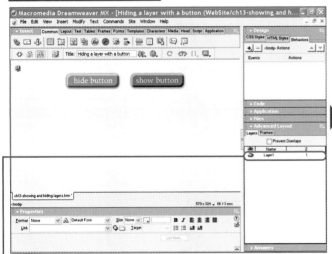

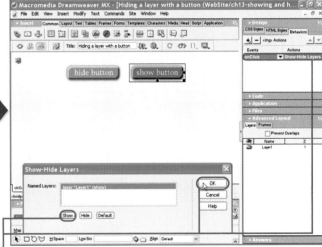

■ A closed eye icon (👁) in the visibility column of the Layers panel indicates a layer is hidden. You can also set the visibility of layers by clicking this icon.

1 Insert a graphic.

Note: See Chapter 6 to insert an image.

■ In this example, use the graphic as a button to show the layer.

2 Repeat steps **3** to **7** from the previous page.

3 Click **Show**.

4 Click **OK**.

■ The behavior is now associated with the action. In this example, clicking the graphic shows the layer.

5 Preview the file in a Web browser.

■ You can now show and hide the layer by clicking either graphic in a Web page.

■ You can apply this technique to images, buttons, and other objects to interact with layers.

CREATE A ROLLOVER IMAGE

The rollover behavior quickly swaps one image for another when the cursor touches a specified hotspot on the page. Rollover images are most commonly used on buttons to show a depressed or lit-up state when touched or clicked.

CREATE A ROLLOVER IMAGE

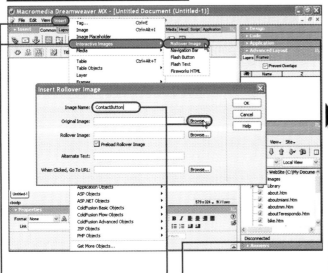

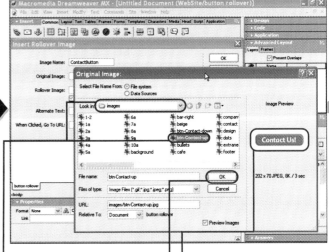

Note: The rollover image and original image should have identical dimensions for best results. They do not, however, need to have the identical file size (bytes).

1 Click **Insert**.

2 Click **Interactive Images**.

3 Click **Rollover Image**.

■ The Insert Rollover Image dialog box appears.

4 Type a name for the image.

5 Click **Browse**.

■ The Original Image dialog box appears.

6 Click ⌄ to select the folder that contains the original image.

7 Click the original image file.

■ A preview of the image appears in the right panel.

8 Click **OK**.

■ If you have not saved your document, Dreamweaver warns you that it will create a temporary path. Save your file before previewing it in the Web browser.

How do I create interesting rollover button images for my page navigation?

You can create interesting navigation buttons in an image editor such as Macromedia Fireworks, Adobe Photoshop, or Adobe ImageReady. With all three programs, you can easily create contoured, colored shapes with text inside for interesting graphical buttons. After creating an original button, you can save an alternate image that has the colors inversed, the shape beveled, or the image slightly shifted so that it looks like the graphic has been pressed on a rollover.

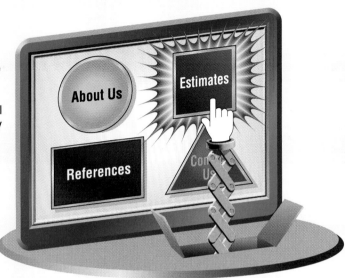

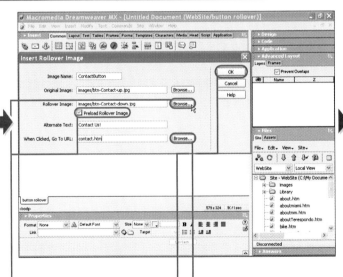

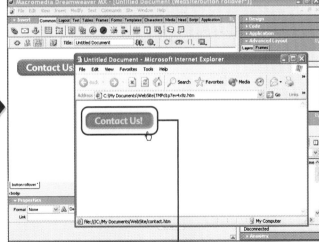

9 Click **Browse** to browse for your rollover image just as you did in the previous steps for the original image.

10 Click **Preload Rollover Image** (☐ changes to ☑).

11 Click **Browse** to select the hyperlink destination for the button.

12 Click **OK**.

13 Preview the rollover image in a Web browser.

Note: See Chapter 2 to preview Web pages in a browser.

■ The rollover image quickly swaps with your original when you pass your cursor over the image.

■ To modify this behavior, click the image and then click **Swap Image** in the Behaviors panel.

ANIMATION WITH TIMELINES

You can use a Dreamweaver timeline to visually plan a layer's movement on your Web page by plotting keyframes. Prior to timelines, Web designers had to write very complex JavaScript programs by hand to achieve this.

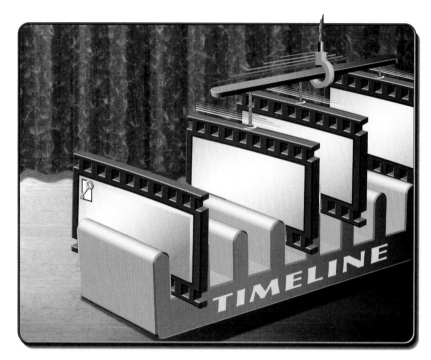

Timelines, unlike layers, are not HTML tags.

No Animation Background Necessary

With a timeline, you do not have to express each frame by hand like a hand-drawn cartoon. Instead, you can indicate the layer's position in the timeline over a period of time and then let Dreamweaver take care of the rest. These programmed layer coordinates are called *keyframes*. Each layer can operate on its own timeline, and keyframes can be chained to one another to create complex animations.

Raise the Bar on Site Interactivity

When combined with JavaScript behaviors such as drop actions and layer dragging, Timelines can really add sizzle to your Web site. Instead of just showing and hiding layers, you can program them to animate and move dynamically to buttons or timed events on your page. The possibilities are vast and Dreamweaver makes it easy.

Dreamweaver makes animating layers easy with its Timelines panel. Click Window, Others, then Timelines to open the Timelines panel. If you have ever worked with Adobe Premiere or Macromedia Flash, you will find many similar elements within this interface.

Play Button

Moves the playback head forward one frame, or plays the entire animation if you click and hold it. This is also known as the forward button.

Autoplay

Causes the animation to repeat indefinitely after it begins when checked.

Loop

Causes the animation to repeat indefinitely after it begins when checked.

Timelines Menu

Gives you access to timeline commands.

Back Button

Moves the playback head back one frame.

Rewind Button

Moves the playback head to the first frame.

Animation Path

A guideline showing how the layer travels during its animation.

Playback Head

Defines which frame is currently playing in the document window.

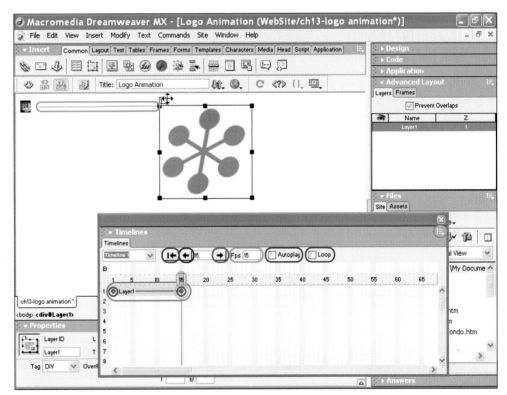

Keyframes

Contains details about a specific point of an object in an animated layer.

Current Frame

Shows the current position of the playback head.

Playback Rate

Defines how many frames of the animation play each second.

Animation Row

Defines the frames on an animation for a layer on your page.

CREATE A SIMPLE ANIMATION WITH THE TIMELINE

You can create a timeline animation that moves a layer around on your Web page. This task shows you how to create a straight-line animation to a layer that causes text and images to fly across your Web page.

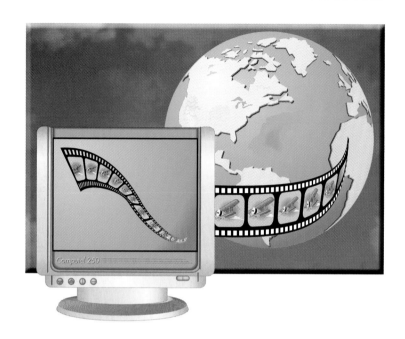

Timelines rely on heavy DHTML support from browsers, meaning this feature is only supported by 4.0 and later browsers. See "Introduction to DHTML" for more information.

CREATE A SIMPLE ANIMATION WITH THE TIMELINE

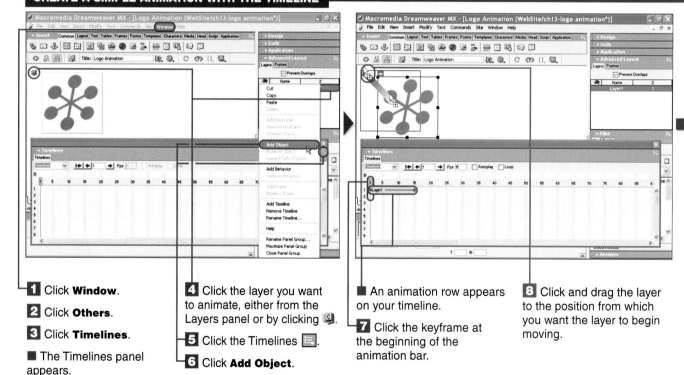

1 Click **Window**.

2 Click **Others**.

3 Click **Timelines**.

■ The Timelines panel appears.

4 Click the layer you want to animate, either from the Layers panel or by clicking 🖳.

5 Click the Timelines 🖳.

6 Click **Add Object**.

■ Dreamweaver may inform you of Web browser limitations or layer properties. Click **OK**.

■ An animation row appears on your timeline.

7 Click the keyframe at the beginning of the animation bar.

8 Click and drag the layer to the position from which you want the layer to begin moving.

Can I create several straight-line animations on a single Web page?

Yes. Put each piece of content that you want to animate in its own layer, and then define an animation bar in the Timelines panel for each layer. To add each additional animation bar to the Timelines panel, click a layer, click the Timelines ▦, and then click **Add Object**.

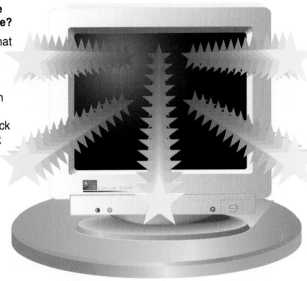

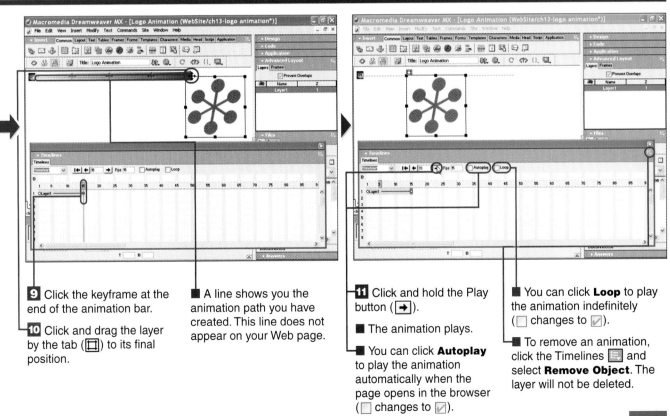

■9 Click the keyframe at the end of the animation bar.

■10 Click and drag the layer by the tab (▦) to its final position.

■ A line shows you the animation path you have created. This line does not appear on your Web page.

■11 Click and hold the Play button (➡).

■ The animation plays.

■ You can click **Autoplay** to play the animation automatically when the page opens in the browser (☐ changes to ☑).

■ You can click **Loop** to play the animation indefinitely (☐ changes to ☑).

■ To remove an animation, click the Timelines ▦ and select **Remove Object**. The layer will not be deleted.

DRAG A PATH TO CREATE AN ANIMATION

You can save time by recording a path instead of describing animation with many keyframes. To create animations that loop and curve, you can drag a layer along the intended path and have Dreamweaver record the keyframes as you go. This feature takes the work out of describing keyframes and tweens by hand.

DRAG A PATH TO CREATE AN ANIMATION

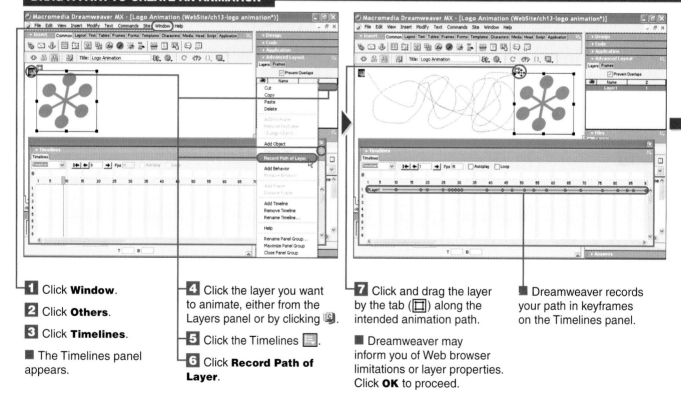

■1 Click **Window**.

■2 Click **Others**.

■3 Click **Timelines**.

■ The Timelines panel appears.

■4 Click the layer you want to animate, either from the Layers panel or by clicking ▣.

■5 Click the Timelines ▦.

■6 Click **Record Path of Layer**.

■7 Click and drag the layer by the tab (▦) along the intended animation path.

■ Dreamweaver may inform you of Web browser limitations or layer properties. Click **OK** to proceed.

■ Dreamweaver records your path in keyframes on the Timelines panel.

236

Can I rotate a layer using the Timelines panel?

Rotation is one of the limitations of animated layers. Layers remain perpendicular as they move across the screen. However, there are workarounds. You can create animated content and place it inside a moving layer. You can animate a rotation within an Animated GIF using Macromedia Fireworks, or create an animated shockwave file with Macromedia Flash or Director. The image animation within the moving layer creates the illusion that the layer is rotating.

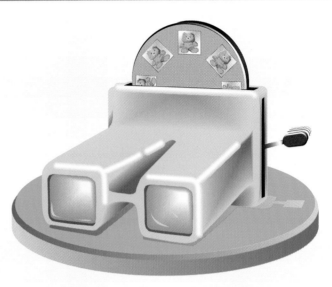

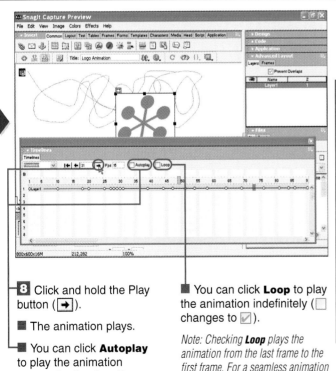

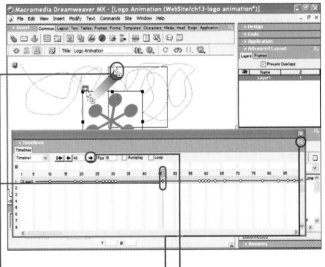

8 Click and hold the Play button (▶).

■ The animation plays.

■ You can click **Autoplay** to play the animation automatically when the page opens in the browser (☐ changes to ☑).

■ You can click **Loop** to play the animation indefinitely (☐ changes to ☑).

*Note: Checking **Loop** plays the animation from the last frame to the first frame. For a seamless animation loop, your last keyframe should end very close to where your first one begins.*

EDIT AN ANIMATION

1 Click the keyframe that you want to change.

2 Click and drag the layer by the tab (▦) to the new desired location.

3 Click and hold the Play button (▶).

■ The animation plays with your changes.

■ To remove an animation, click the Timelines ▦ and click **Remove Object**. The layer will not be deleted.

You can speed up or slow down a timeline animation by changing its frame rate or by adjusting the number of frames between the keyframes that make up the animation.

CHANGE ANIMATION SPEED AND REPETITION

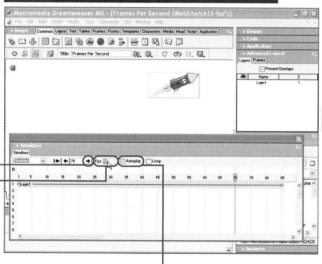

CHANGE THE FRAME RATE

1 Click and hold the Play button (▶) to preview the timeline animations on your page.

2 Type a new fps (frames per second) value for the animations.

■ A higher value increases the animation speed; a lower value decreases it. The default fps is 15. Changing the fps value affects all the animations on the timeline equally.

3 Click **Autoplay** (☐ changes to ☑).

4 Preview your changes in a Web browser.

Note: See Chapter 2 to preview Web pages in a browser.

5 In Dreamweaver, click and hold the Play button (▶).

■ The animation plays in the Web browser.

■ Your web browser plays the animation in the actual frame rate. The Dreamweaver Play button does NOT obey the frame rate.

■ You can click **Loop** to play the animation indefinitely (☐ changes to ☑).

How high should I set my frame rate for animations?

For smoother animations, increase the fps value and increase the total amount of frames in between keyframes. However, the end result on the user's screen varies based on computing power. For most computers, 15 is a safe number, while 60 may play smoothly only on high performance computers. To offer smooth animations without alienating everyone, many Webmasters choose 30 fps as a ceiling rate.

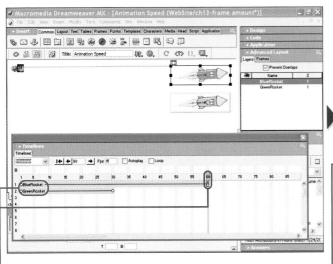

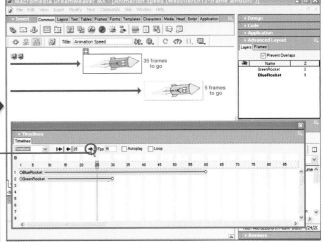

CHANGE THE FRAME AMOUNT

1 Create two layer animations that begin and end at the same points.

Note: See "Create a Simple Animation with the Timeline."

2 Click and drag the last frame of one animation outward.

■ This increases the number of frames between the start and endpoints.

■ Keyframes further apart mean more "tweened" frames and a slower animation. Keyframes closer together mean fewer "tweened" frames and a faster animation.

3 Click and hold the Play button (→) to preview your changes.

■ The animation plays.

■ The layer that has more frames in its animation plays more slowly.

■ The end speed of both animations is also affected by the fps. To view the actual speed, you must preview the animation in a Web browser.

TRIGGER AN ANIMATION WITH A BEHAVIOR

You can combine Dreamweaver behaviors and timelines so that clicking an image or hyperlink in your page plays a layer animation. This is an alternative to selecting the Autoplay feature of the Timelines panel that starts the animation when the page loads.

TRIGGER AN ANIMATION WITH A BEHAVIOR

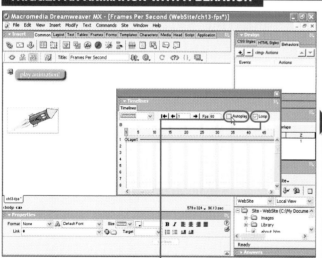

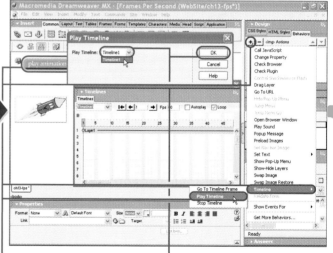

ASSIGN THE PLAY BEHAVIOR TO A BUTTON

1 Insert a graphical button.

Note: See Chapter 6 to insert an image.

2 Create a layer animation.

Note: See "Create a Simple Animation with the Timeline."

3 Uncheck **Autoplay** (☑ changes to ☐) from the Timelines panel.

■ You can click **Loop** to play the animation indefinitely (☐ changes to ☑).

4 Click the button.

5 Click ➕ in the Behaviors panel.

6 Click **Timeline**.

7 Click **Play Timeline**.

■ The Play Timeline dialog box appears.

8 Click ˅ to select the timeline that you want to animate.

9 Click **OK**.

How do I stop my animated layer animations with behaviors?

Stopping a timeline with a button behavior is very similar to the process of creating an animation. Simply follow the steps in the task below. Instead of clicking **Play Timeline** in step **7**, click **Stop Timeline**. Then, continue with steps **8** to **11**. The behavior works with both Autoplay animations and triggered animations like the one in this task.

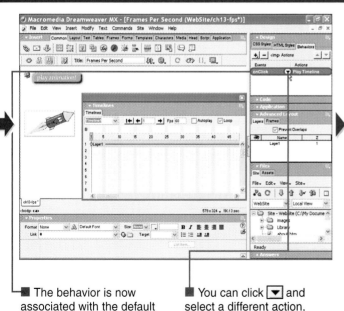

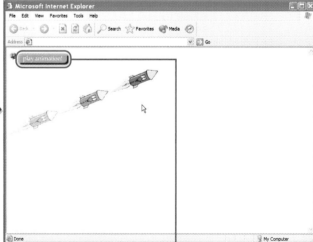

■ The behavior is now associated with the default action, onClick. In this example, clicking the graphic plays the Timeline animation.

■ You can click ▼ and select a different action, such as onMouseOver.

10 Preview the page in a Web browser.

Note: See Chapter 2 to preview Web pages in a browser.

11 Click the button or text link that you assigned the behavior to.

■ The animation plays.

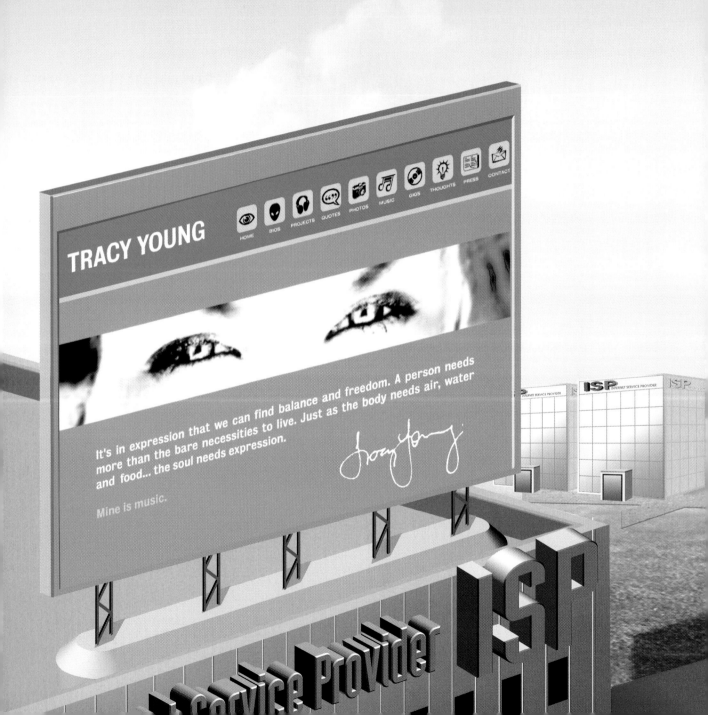

CHAPTER 14

Publishing a Web Site

You can publish your completed Web pages on a server to allow the rest of the world to view them. This chapter shows you how to use the various publishing features of Dreamweaver.

PUBLISH YOUR WEB SITE

To make the pages that you have built in Dreamweaver accessible on the Web, you must transfer them to a Web server. A *Web server*, as referred to in this chapter, is an Internet-connected computer running special software (also called a Web server) that enables the computer to serve files to Web browsers. Dreamweaver includes tools that enable you to connect and transfer pages to a Web server.

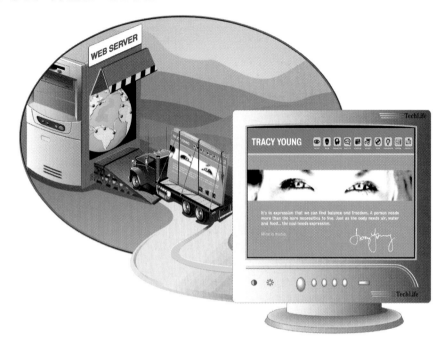

Steps for Publishing Your Web Site

Publishing your site content using Dreamweaver involves the following steps:

1 Specify where on your computer the site files are kept.

Note: This is done by defining a local site. See Chapter 2 for more information.

2 Specify the Web server to which you want to publish your files.

Note: This is done by defining a remote site. See the section "Set Up a Remote Site," later in this chapter.

Note: Most people publish their Web pages on servers maintained by their Internet service provider (ISP), a hosting company, or their company or school.

3 Connect to the Web server and transfer the files.

Note: The Site window gives you a user-friendly interface for organizing your files and transferring them to the remote site.

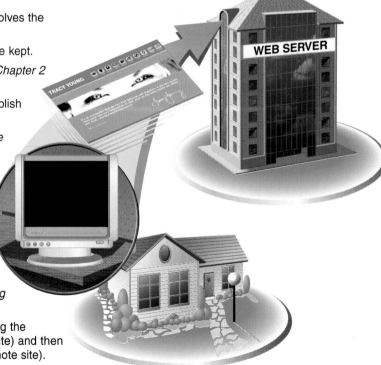

After uploading your site, you can update it by editing the copies of the site files on your computer (the local site) and then transferring those copies to the Web server (the remote site).

With the Site window, you can view the organization of all files in your site. You can also upload local files to the remote site and download remote files to the local site through the Site panel. You can access the Site window by clicking the Expand/Collapse Site Window button (▢) in the Site panel.

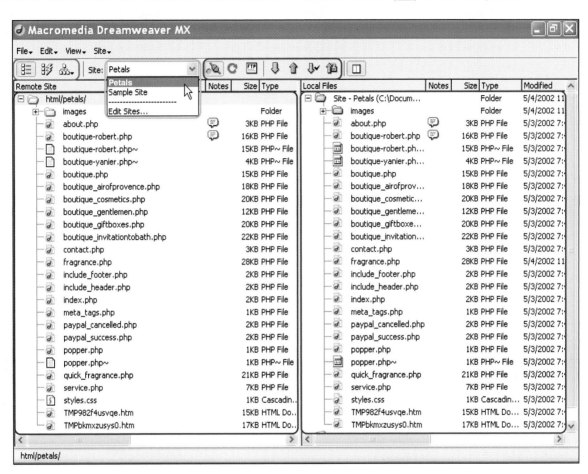

Remote Site

The left pane displays the contents of your site as it exists on the remote Web server. To define a remote site, see the section "Set Up a Remote Site."

Site Window View

You can click ▦ or ▦ to switch between viewing your site as lists of files or as a site map. See Chapter 15 for more about using the site map. You can click ▦ to access a testing server. See Chapter 16 for more about using a testing server.

Site Menu

Lets you select from the different sites you have defined in Dreamweaver.

File Transfer

Buttons enable you to connect to your remote site, refresh the file lists, upload files to the remote server, download files to the local site, and view the FTP log.

Local Site

The right pane displays the content of your site as it exists on your local computer. To define a local site, see Chapter 2.

ORGANIZE YOUR FILES AND FOLDERS

You can use the Site window to organize the elements that make up your local and remote sites. With this window, you can create and delete files and folders, as well as move files between folders.

Creating subfolders to organize files of a similar type can be useful if you have a large Web site.

ORGANIZE YOUR FILES AND FOLDERS

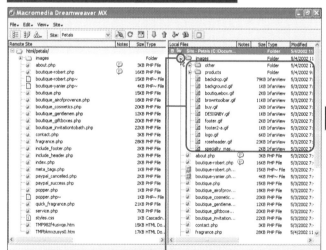

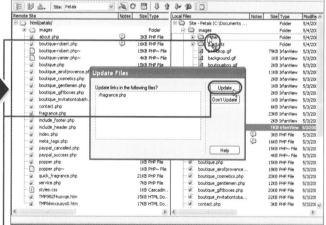

REARRANGE SITE FILES

1 Click 🔲 in the Site panel to expand the Site window.

Note: See Chapter 3 for more information about the Site panel.

2 Click ⊞ to view the files in a subfolder (⊞ changes to ⊟).

■ The folder contents display.

■ You can click ⊟ to close the subfolder.

3 Click and drag a file from the local site folder into a subfolder (⬚ changes to ⬚).

■ A prompt appears asking if you want to update your links.

4 Click **Update**. This keeps your local site links from breaking.

■ You can rearrange files the same way in the remote site pane. However, Dreamweaver cannot automatically update your links in pages on your remote site. To fix bad links on your site, you must override those pages on the remote site by uploading the pages with fixed links.

What happens to links when I move files?

When you move files into and out of folders, the hyperlinks and images referenced on those pages will most likely need to be updated, because document-relative references become invalid. Dreamweaver keeps track of any affected code when you rearrange files and can update it for you when you move a file. This capability can save you time and help keep your site links from breaking.

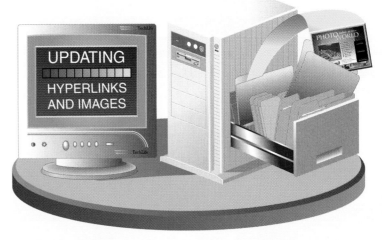

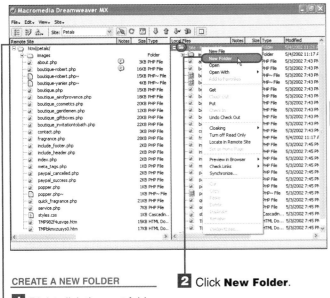

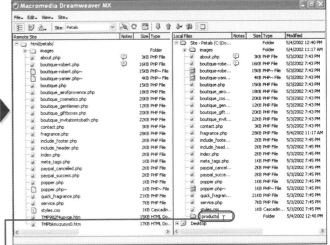

CREATE A NEW FOLDER

1 Right-click the root folder on the local site pane.

2 Click **New Folder**.

3 Type a name for the new folder.

■ To create a new folder on the remote site, right-click the root folder on the remote site pane and follow steps **2** and **3**.

SET UP A REMOTE SITE

The *remote site* is a
place where the files
of your site are made
available to the rest of
the world. You set up a
remote site by specifying
a directory on a Web
server where your site
will be hosted.

SET UP A REMOTE SITE

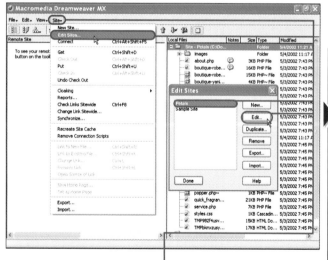

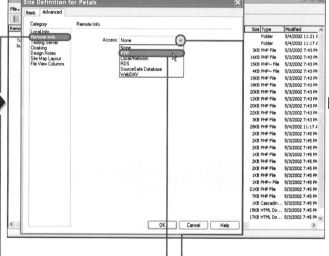

1 Set up a local site.

Note: See Chapter 2 to set up a local site.

2 Open the Site window.

Note: See the section "Using the Site Window," earlier in this chapter.

3 Click **Site**.

4 Click **Edit Sites**.

■ The Edit Sites dialog box appears.

5 Click a site name from the list.

6 Click **Edit**.

■ The Site Definition dialog box appears.

7 Click **Remote Info**.

8 Click ⌄ to select an access method.

9 Click **FTP**.

What happens if I change my Internet Service Provider (ISP) and need to move my site to a different server?

You need to change your remote site settings to enable Dreamweaver to connect to the new ISP's server. Your local site settings can stay the same.

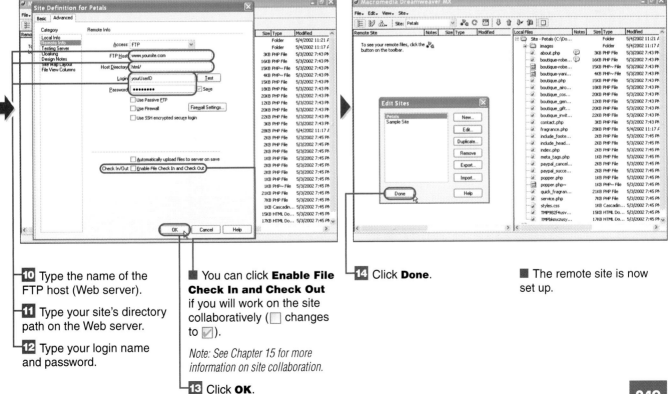

10 Type the name of the FTP host (Web server).

11 Type your site's directory path on the Web server.

12 Type your login name and password.

■ You can click **Enable File Check In and Check Out** if you will work on the site collaboratively (☐ changes to ☑).

Note: See Chapter 15 for more information on site collaboration.

13 Click **OK**.

14 Click **Done**.

■ The remote site is now set up.

CONNECT TO A REMOTE SITE

You can connect to the Web server that hosts your remote site and transfer files between it and Dreamweaver. Dreamweaver connects to the Web server by a process known as *File Transfer Protocol* or *FTP*.

CONNECT TO A REMOTE SITE

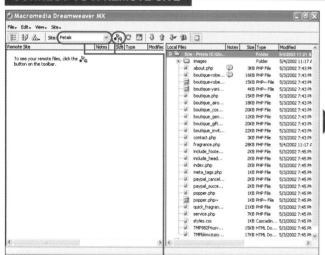

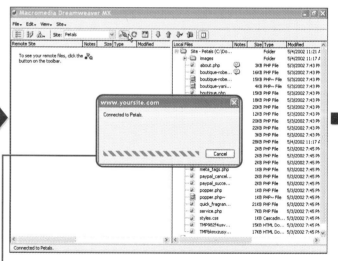

1 Set up a local site.

Note: See Chapter 2 to set up a local site.

2 Set up a remote site.

Note: See the previous section for information.

3 Open the Site window.

Note: See the section "Using the Site Window," earlier in this chapter.

4 Click ⌄ and select your Web site.

5 Click 🗽 to connect to the Web server.

■ Dreamweaver attempts to connect to the remote site.

Note: Dreamweaver displays an alert box if it cannot connect to the site. If you have trouble connecting, double-check the host information you entered for the remote site.

**How do I keep Dreamweaver
from prematurely disconnecting
from the Web server?**

You can click **Edit**, **Preferences**,
and then **Site**. You can adjust the
time that Dreamweaver lets pass
between commands before it
logs you off the server — the
default is 30 minutes. Note that
Web servers also have a similar
setting on their end. So the
server, not Dreamweaver, may
sometimes log you off.

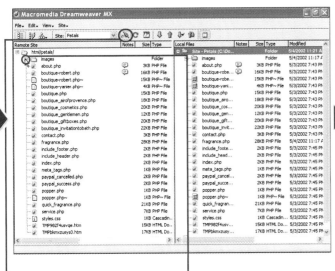

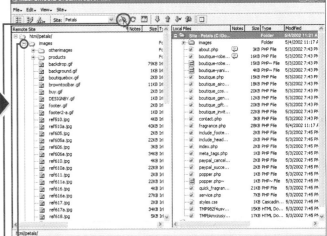

■ Dreamweaver displays
the contents of the remote
site's host directory, which
you specified when you set
up the remote site.

■ 🐾 changes to 🐾,
indicating a successful
connection.

6 Click ⊞ to open the
content of a directory on
the Web server (⊞ changes
to ⊟).

■ Dreamweaver displays
the contents of the directory.

■ You can click ⊟ to close
a directory.

7 Click 🐾 to disconnect
from the Web server.

■ Dreamweaver disconnects
from the Web server.

■ If you do not transfer
any files for 30 minutes,
Dreamweaver automatically
disconnects from a Web
server.

UPLOAD FILES TO A WEB SERVER

You can upload site files from Dreamweaver to your remote site to make the files available to others on the Web.

UPLOAD FILES TO A WEB SERVER

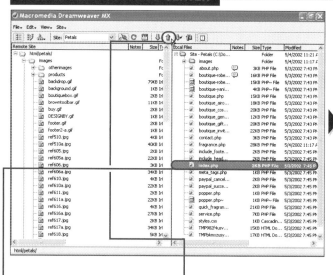

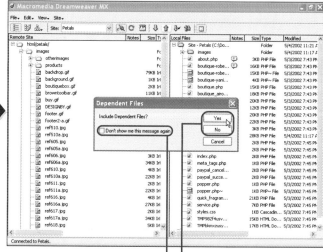

1 Connect to the Web server by using the Site window.

Note: See the previous section for information.

2 Click the file you want to upload.

3 Click the Put button (⬆).

*Note: You can also right-click the file and select **Put** from the menu that appears.*

■ An alert box appears asking if you want to include dependent files.

Note: Dependent files are images and other files associated with a particular page. If you are uploading a frameset, dependent files include the files for each frame in the frameset. See Chapter 9 for more about frames.

4 Click **Yes** or **No**.

■ You can click here to avoid the alert box in the future (☐ changes to ☑).

How do I stop a file transfer in progress?

You can click **Cancel** from the Status window that appears while a transfer is in progress. You can also press Esc .

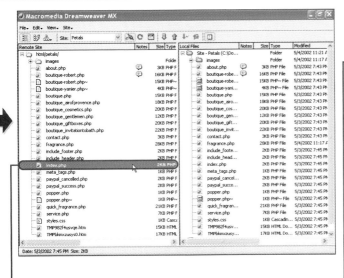

■ The files transfer from your computer to the Web server.

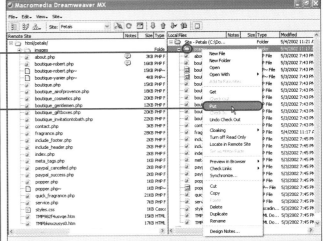

UPLOAD A FOLDER

1 In the right pane, right-click the folder you want to upload.

2 Click **Put** from the menu that appears.

■ You can also click the folder and then click 🔼.

■ Dreamweaver transfers the folder and its contents from your computer to the Web server.

DOWNLOAD FILES FROM A WEB SERVER

You can download files from your remote site to Dreamweaver if you need to retrieve copies of your pages from the Web server.

DOWNLOAD FILES FROM A WEB SERVER

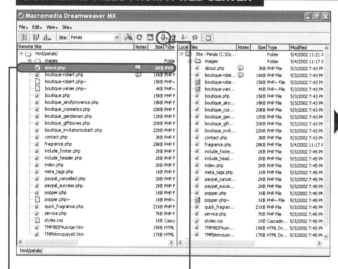

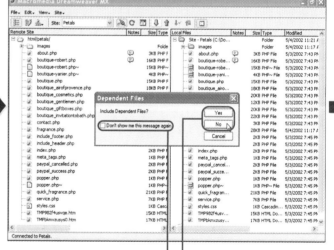

1 Connect to the Web server by using the Site window.

Note: See the section "Connect to a Remote Site," earlier in this chapter.

2 Click the file you want to download.

3 Click the Get button (⬇).

*Note: You can also right-click the file in the remote site and select **Get** from the menu that appears.*

■ An alert box appears asking if you want to include dependent files.

Note: Dependent files are images and other files associated with a particular page. If you are downloading a frameset, dependent files include the files for each frame in the frameset. See Chapter 9 for more on frames.

4 Click **Yes** or **No**.

■ You can click here to avoid the alert box in the future (☐ changes to ☑).

**Where does Dreamweaver log
errors that occur during transfer?**

Dreamweaver logs all transfer
activity, including errors, in a file-
transfer log. You can view it by
clicking **Window**, **Results**, and
then **FTP Log**. The FTP log panel
appears at the bottom of the
screen.

May 22, 2002

ERROR!

File Transfer Logs

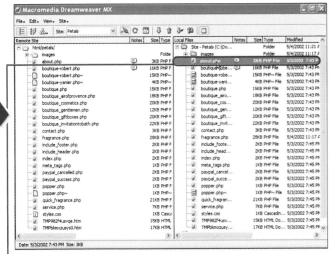

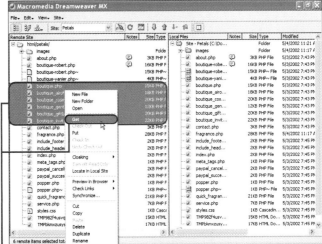

■ The files transfer from
the Web server to your
computer.

DOWNLOAD MULTIPLE FILES

1 Press and hold **Ctrl**
(**Shift**) and then click to
select the files you want to
download.

2 Right-click the selection
and click **Get** from the menu
that appears.

■ You can also click the
selection and then click 🔽.

■ The files transfer from
the Web server to your
computer.

SYNCHRONIZE YOUR LOCAL AND REMOTE SITES

Dreamweaver can transfer files between your local and remote sites so that both sites have an identical set of the most recent files. This can be useful if other people are editing the files on the remote site, and the files on your local site may not be the most recent.

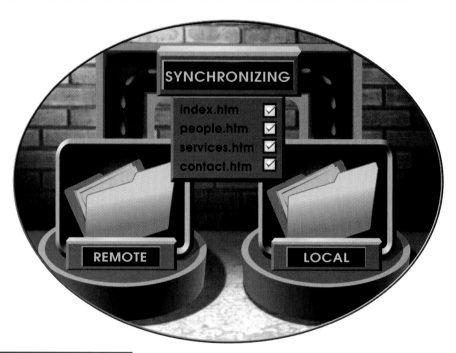

SYNCHRONIZE YOUR LOCAL AND REMOTE SITES

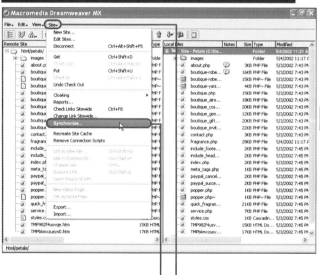

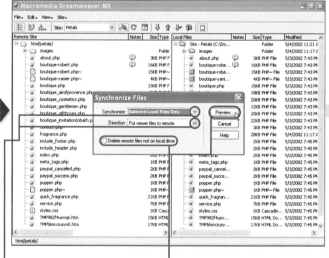

1 Open the Site window.

Note: See the section "Using the Site Window," earlier in this chapter.

2 Click **Site**.

3 Click **Synchronize**.

■ The Synchronize Files dialog box appears.

4 Click ⌄ to select the files you want to synchronize.

5 Click ⌄ to select a direction in which you want to copy the files.

■ Transferring files in both uploading and downloading directions places the newest copies on both sites.

■ You can click here (☐ changes to ☑) to delete files on the remote site that have no counterpart on the local site.

6 Click **Preview**.

TEACH YOURSELF
TY

Are there other FTP tools out there besides Dreamweaver's?

Dreamweaver offers the convenience of transferring files without having to open other programs. However, it uses a lot of system resources and can slow down some machines significantly. There are various popular — and usually free — alternatives for transferring files via FTP, including CuteFTP, LeechFTP, WS_FTP, and CoffeeCup Direct FTP.

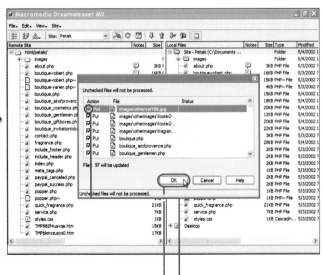

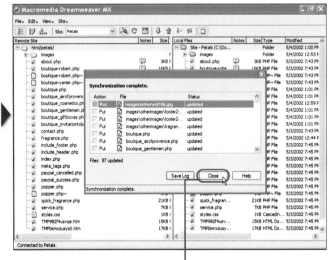

■ Dreamweaver compares the sites, and a list of files that should be transferred appears.

7 Uncheck any files that you do not want transferred (☑ changes to ☐).

8 Click **OK**.

■ The files are transferred and the Synchronize dialog box is updated.

9 Click **Close**.

■ The local and remote sites are now synchronized.

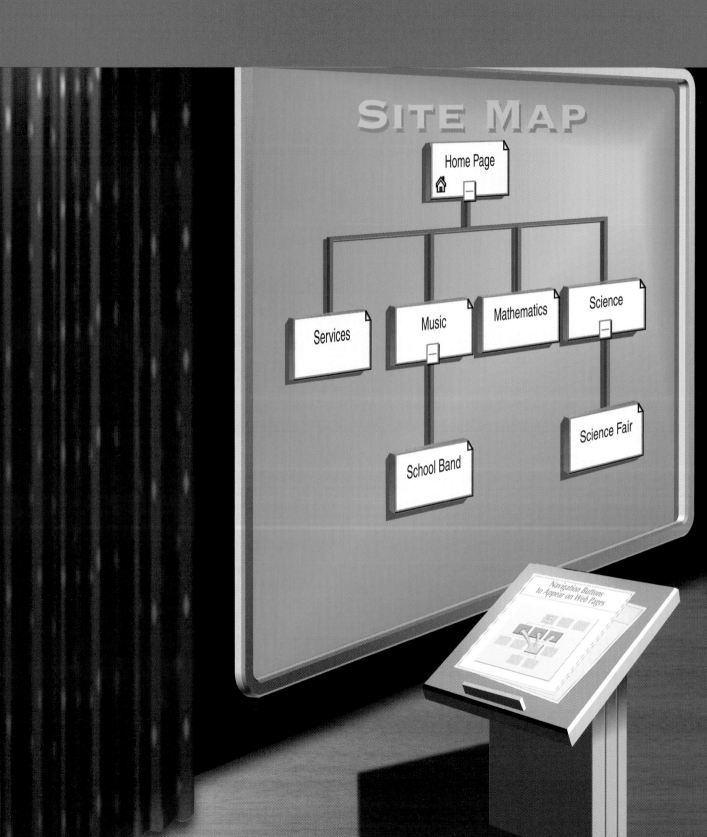

CHAPTER 15

Maintaining a Web Site

Keeping all the features of a Web site working and its content fresh can be as much work as creating the site. Dreamweaver's site collaboration tools make site maintenance faster and easier.

The Site Map View enables you to see your site in a flowchart form with lines, which represent links, connecting the document icons. This view highlights pages that have broken internal links, which can help you maintain your site.

USING THE SITE MAP

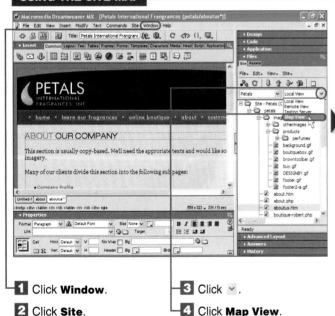

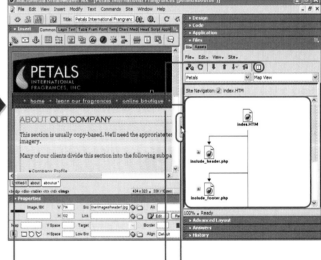

1 Click **Window**.

2 Click **Site**.

■ The Site panel opens.

Note: See Chapter 2 to set up a site and use the Site window. You must set up a site for the Site window features to function.

3 Click ⌄.

4 Click **Map View**.

■ A site map appears in the Site panel. By default, the site map displays the site structure two levels deep beginning from the home page.

5 Click and drag the side of the Site panel to expand it to fill the screen.

6 Click the Expand/Collapse button (□) in the Site panel to split the screen.

How do I fix a broken link in the site map?

A broken chain icon in the site map means the link to a page is broken. You can fix a broken link by right-clicking the destination page and clicking **Change Link** from the menu that appears. Links can break because a destination page is renamed or deleted.

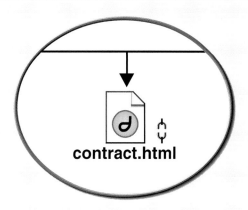

contract.html

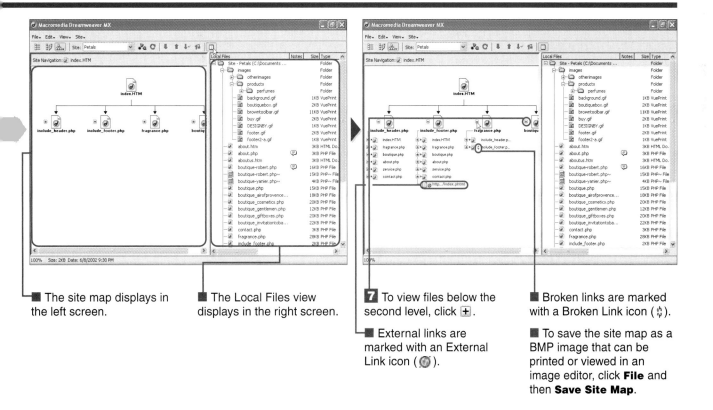

■ The site map displays in the left screen.

■ The Local Files view displays in the right screen.

7 To view files below the second level, click ⊞.

■ External links are marked with an External Link icon ( ).

■ Broken links are marked with a Broken Link icon ( ).

■ To save the site map as a BMP image that can be printed or viewed in an image editor, click **File** and then **Save Site Map**.

MANAGE SITE ASSETS

You can view and
manage important
elements that appear in
the pages of your site
with the Assets panel.

MANAGE SITE ASSETS

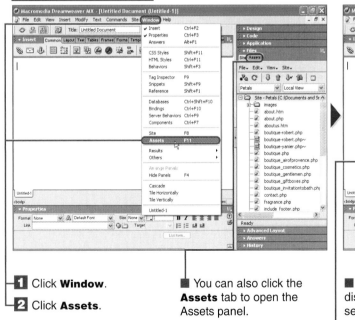

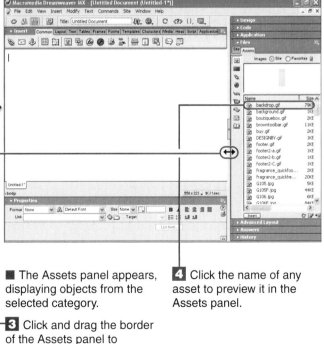

1 Click **Window**.

2 Click **Assets**.

■ You can also click the
Assets tab to open the
Assets panel.

■ The Assets panel appears,
displaying objects from the
selected category.

3 Click and drag the border
of the Assets panel to
expand it (⬚ changes to ↔).

4 Click the name of any
asset to preview it in the
Assets panel.

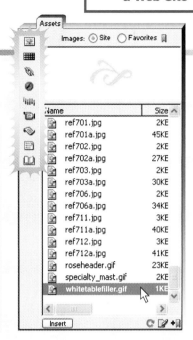

How are assets organized?

Items in the Assets panel are organized into the
following categories, top to bottom:

Images: GIF, JPG, and PNG images
Colors: Text, background, link colors, and style-sheet colors
URLs: External Web addresses that are accessible from your site
Flash: Flash-based multimedia
Shockwave: Shockwave-based multimedia
Movies: QuickTime and MPEG movies
Scripts: External JavaScript or VBScript files
Templates: Page layouts for your site
Library: Reusable page elements

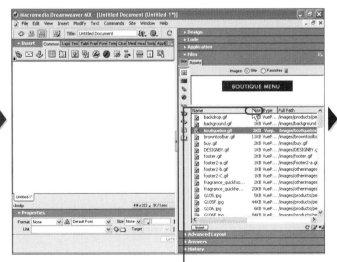

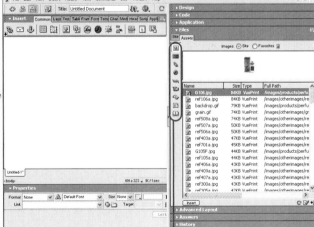

■ The panel assumes the
new dimensions and the
selected asset is previewed.

5 Click a column heading.

■ The assets are sorted by
the contents under the
selected column heading in
ascending order. You can
click the column again to
sort in descending order.

■ To view other assets, click
a different category button.

ADD CONTENT WITH THE ASSETS PANEL

You can add frequently used content to your site directly from the Assets panel. This technique can be more efficient than using a menu command or the Insert panel.

ADD CONTENT WITH THE ASSETS PANEL

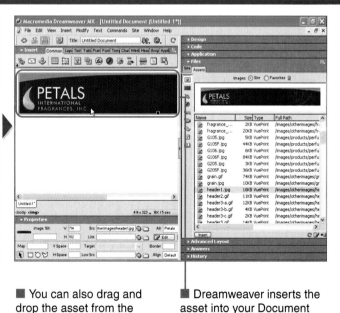

INSERT AN IMAGE OR OTHER FILE

1 Click inside the Document window where you want to insert the asset.

2 Click the **Assets** tab to open the Assets panel.

3 Click a category.

4 Click an asset.

5 Click **Insert**.

■ You can also drag and drop the asset from the panel to the Document window.

■ Dreamweaver inserts the asset into your Document window.

How do I copy assets from one site to another?

Click one or more items in the Assets panel, and then right-click the selected asset(s). Click **Copy to Site** from the menu that appears, and then click a site to which to copy. The assets appear in the Favorites list under the same category in the other site.

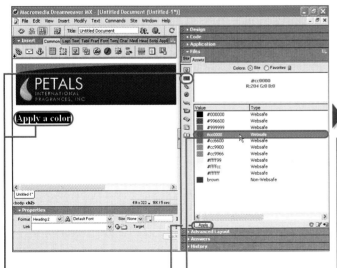

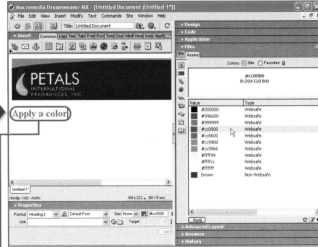

EDIT CONTENT USING THE ASSETS PANEL

1 Click the object that you want to apply the asset to in the Document window.

2 Click a category, in this example, Colors (▦).

3 Click an asset.

4 Click **Apply**.

■ You can also drag and drop the asset from the panel onto the selected object in the Document window.

■ Dreamweaver applies the asset in the Document window.

■ In this example, color is applied to the text.

SPECIFY FAVORITE ASSETS

To make your assets lists more manageable, you can organize assets that you use often into a Favorites list inside each asset category.

SPECIFY FAVORITE ASSETS

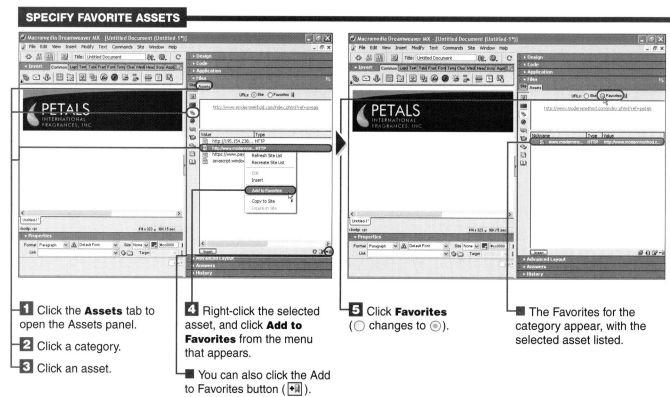

1 Click the **Assets** tab to open the Assets panel.

2 Click a category.

3 Click an asset.

4 Right-click the selected asset, and click **Add to Favorites** from the menu that appears.

■ You can also click the Add to Favorites button ( ).

5 Click **Favorites** (○ changes to ◉).

■ The Favorites for the category appear, with the selected asset listed.

How do I remove an item from the Assets panel entirely?

You need to delete the item from your local site folder. You can right-click (option + click) the item in the Site window and click **Delete** from the menu that appears. When you return to the Assets panel and click the Refresh button (), the asset is gone. See Chapter 14 for more information about the Site window.

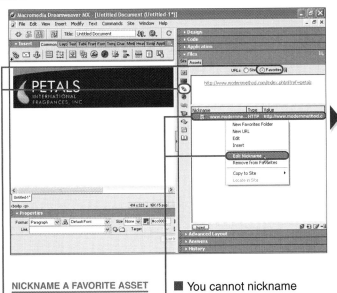

NICKNAME A FAVORITE ASSET

1 Click a category.

2 Click **Favorites** (○ changes to ◉).

■ You cannot nickname regular assets.

3 Right-click (option + click) an asset.

4 Click **Edit Nickname** from the menu that appears.

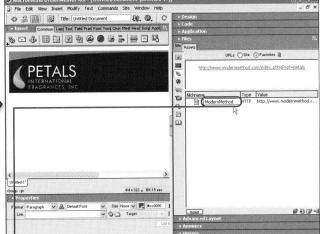

5 Type a nickname.

6 Press Enter (Return).

■ The nickname appears in the Favorites list.

CHECK A PAGE IN OR OUT

Dreamweaver provides a Check In/Check Out system that keeps track of files when a team is working on a Web site. When one person checks out a page from the Web server, others cannot access the same file.

When the Check In/Check Out system is off, multiple people can check out the same file at once.

CHECK A PAGE IN OR OUT

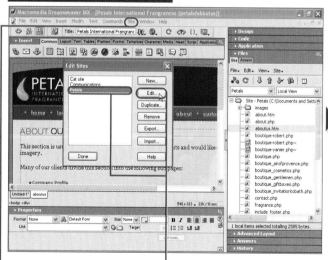

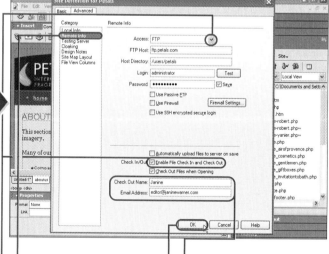

ENABLE CHECK IN/CHECK OUT

Note: You must specify the FTP settings for Check In/Out to function. See Chapter 14 to set up FTP options.

1 Click **Site**.

2 Click **Edit Sites**.

■ The Edit Sites dialog box appears.

3 Click to select the site on which you want to work.

4 Click **Edit**.

■ The Site Definition dialog box appears.

5 Click **Remote Info**.

6 Click ⌄ and select **FTP**.

7 Click **Enable File Check In and Check Out** (☐ changes to ☑).

■ The Check Out Name and Email Address areas appear.

8 Type your name and e-mail address.

9 Click **OK**.

10 Click **Done** in the Edit Sites dialog box.

■ Check In/Check Out is now enabled.

268

How is a file marked as checked out?

When you check out a file, Dreamweaver creates a temporary LCK file that is stored in the remote site folder while the page is checked out. The file contains information about who has checked the file out. Dreamweaver does not display the LCK files in the Site window, but you can see them if you access your remote site with an FTP client program.

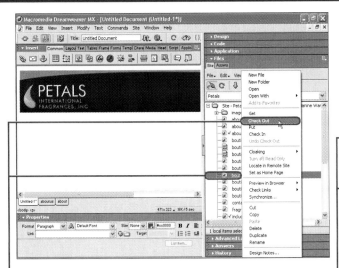

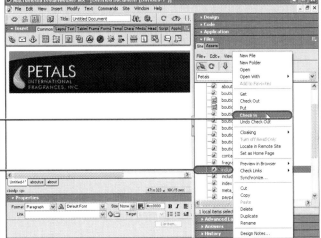

CHECK OUT A FILE

1 Click a file in the Site panel that is not checked out, and then right-click.

2 Click **Check Out**.

■ A check mark indicates files that are checked out.

■ Dreamweaver asks if you want to include dependent files. Click **Yes** to do so.

■ The page is marked as checked out.

■ You can also select a file in the Site panel and click 🔽.

CHECK IN A FILE

■ Files checked out by you have a ✓. Files checked out by others have a ✓.

1 Click a file that is checked out by you, and then right-click.

2 Click **Check In**.

■ The green check mark turns into a lock. To edit the file, check the file out again.

■ The page is marked as checked in.

■ You can also select a file in the Site panel and click 🔒.

MAKE DESIGN NOTES

You can attach accessory information, such as editing history and an author name, to your Web pages with Design Notes. Such notes can be useful if you are working on a site collaboratively because they let you add information about the development status of a file.

MAKE DESIGN NOTES

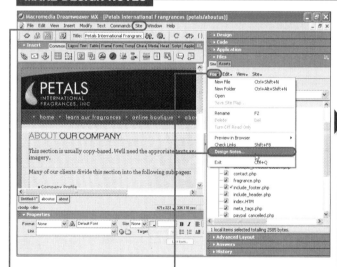

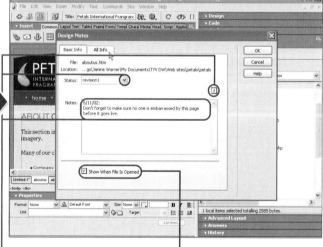

■ Design Notes are on by default when you create a site. You can turn them off in your site definition settings by clicking **Site** and then **Define Sites**.

1 Open the page to which you want to attach Design Notes.

2 Click **File**.

3 Click **Design Notes**.

■ The Design Notes dialog box appears.

4 Click ⌄ to select a status for the page.

5 Type any notes that are relevant to the development of the page.

■ You can click ▦ to enter the current date in the Notes field.

■ You can click **Show When File Is Opened** (☐ changes to ☑) to automatically show any Design Notes when a file is opened.

6 Click the **All Info** tab.

270

What are HTML comments?

Similar to Design Notes, HTML comments let you include text information in a page that does not display in a browser. HTML comments are bracketed by <!-- and --> characters and are stored in a page's HTML. Design Notes offer more security than HTML comments because they are stored separately from the HTML file. Design Notes are stored in a _notes folder inside the local site folder. To ensure that no one else can read your site notes, do not upload them to a public server.

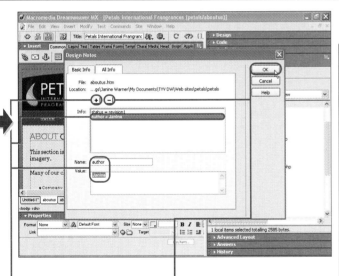

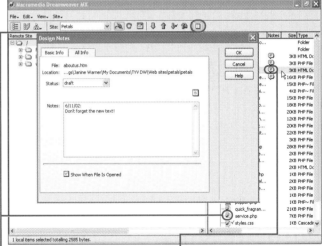

7 To enter new information into Design Notes, click ⊞.

8 Type a Name and Value pair in these fields.

■ The added information appears in the Info section.

■ You can delete information by clicking it in the Info section and then clicking ⊟.

9 Click **OK**.

■ Dreamweaver makes the Design Note.

VIEW DESIGN NOTES

1 Click the Expand/Collapse button (⊡) to expand the Site panel and split the screen.

■ The Design Notes icon (⋑) indicates files with associated notes.

2 Double-click ⋑.

■ The Design Note for that file opens.

■ In the Document window, you can view the notes of a page by clicking **File** and then **Design Notes**.

RUN A SITE REPORT

Running a site report can help you pinpoint problems in your site, such as redundant HTML code in your pages, and missing descriptive information such as image alt text and page titles. It is a good idea to test your site by running a report before you upload it to a Web server.

RUN A SITE REPORT

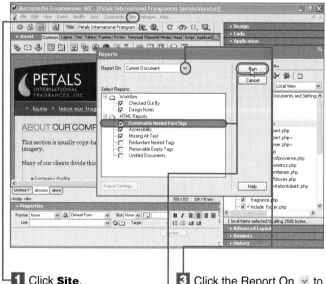

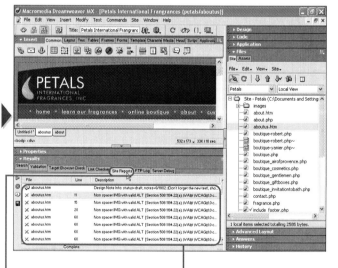

1 Click **Site**.

2 Click **Reports**.

■ The Reports dialog box opens.

3 Click the Report On ▾ to choose to run a report on the entire site or selected files.

4 Click the topics for which you want a report.

5 Click **Run**.

■ Dreamweaver creates a report and displays it in the Results panel.

6 Click any tab across the top of the Results panel to display the report.

■ Details appear in the Results panel.

You can search and
replace all the hyperlinks
on your site that point to
a specific address. This
is helpful when a page is
renamed or deleted and
hyperlinks to it need
updating.

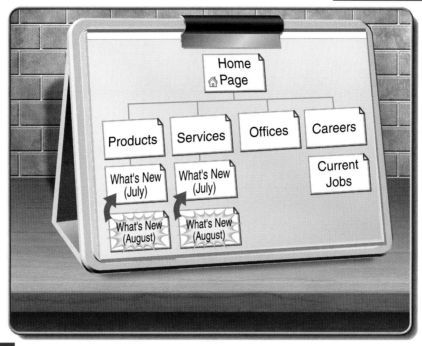

CHANGE A LINK SITEWIDE

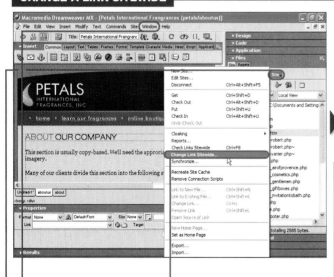

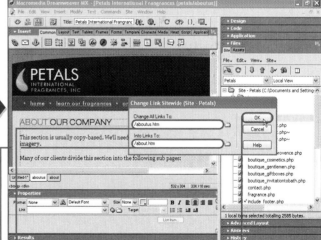

1 If the Site panel is not
already open, click **Window**
and then **Site** to open it.

2 Click **Site**.

3 Click **Change Link
Sitewide**.

■ The Change Link Sitewide
dialog box appears.

4 Type the old link
destination to be changed.

5 Type the new link
destination.

■ The links must start with
a /, mailto: for an e-mail
link, or a full URL.

6 Click **OK**.

■ Dreamweaver replaces
all instances of the old
destination. A dialog box
asks you to confirm the
changes.

FIND AND REPLACE TEXT

The Find and Replace feature is a powerful tool for making changes to text elements that repeat across many pages. You can find and replace text on your Web page, text in your source code, or specific HTML tags in your pages.

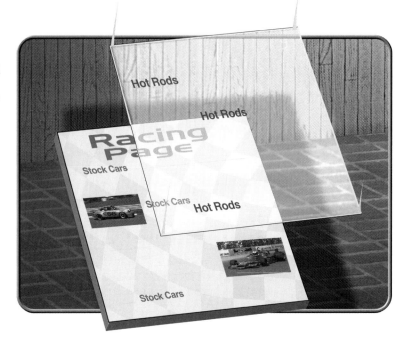

FIND AND REPLACE TEXT

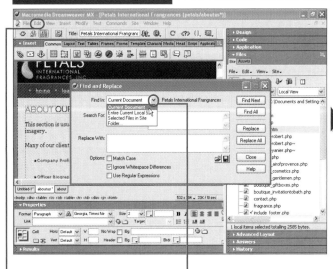

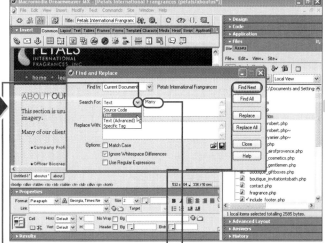

1 Click **Edit**.

2 Click **Find and Replace**.

■ The Find and Replace dialog box appears.

3 Click the Find in ✓ to specify a search of the entire site or only selected files.

■ You can select multiple files to search by Ctrl + clicking (Shift + clicking) the files in the Site window before step 1.

4 Click ✓ to select the type of text you want to search.

■ For example, you can select **Text (Advanced)** to find text that is inside a specific tag.

5 Type text you want to search for into the Search For box.

■ You can click **Find Next** to find instances of your query one at a time.

Can I use find and replace to alter an HTML attribute?

You can replace attributes to achieve many things. You can change the alignment of the contents of a table (change `align="center"` to `align="right"` in `<td>` tags), change the color of specific text in your page (change `color="green"` to `color="red"` in `<font>` tags), or change the page background color across your site (change `bgcolor="black"` to `bgcolor="white"` in `<body>` tags).

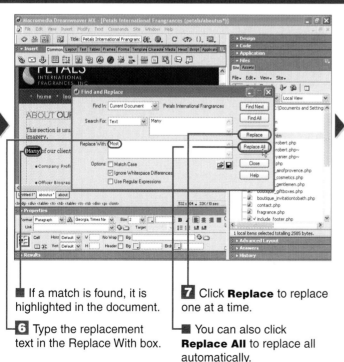

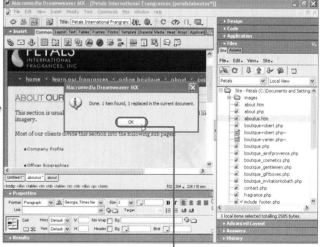

■ If a match is found, it is highlighted in the document.

6 Type the replacement text in the Replace With box.

7 Click **Replace** to replace one at a time.

■ You can also click **Replace All** to replace all automatically.

■ An alert box may appear asking if you want to replace text in documents that are not open. Click **Yes**.

■ Dreamweaver replaces the text. A dialog box with results appears. Click **OK**.

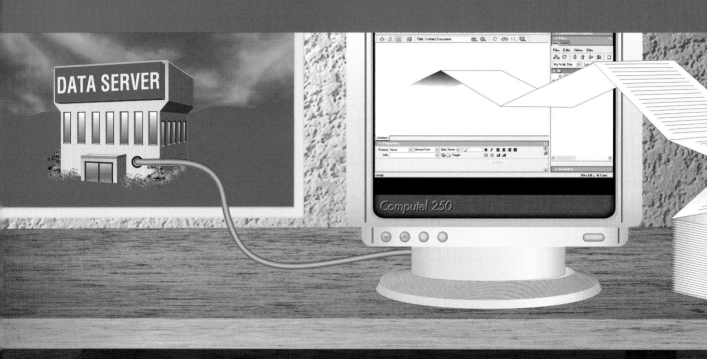

CHAPTER 16

Building a Database-Driven Web Site

If you are an advanced Dreamweaver user who understands databases, you can read this chapter to learn how to use server behaviors to create powerful dynamic Web sites.

THE POWER OF DYNAMIC WEB SITES

Dynamic Web sites use a database to store all kinds of information, and then make the data accessible in various ways. The Web sites that you visit for news, weather, e-mail, forums, and shopping are all examples of how powerful dynamic Web technologies can be.

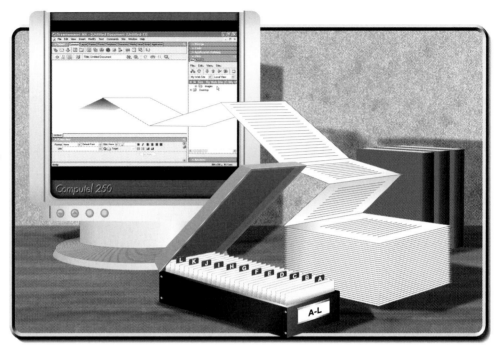

Database-Driven Web Sites

Dynamic Web pages communicate with a database to display and store content on demand. You can store thousands of pages of information and images in a database. You can then create a handful of dynamic Web pages that allow you to browse or search that content. This is much more efficient than creating a thousand individual HTML pages!

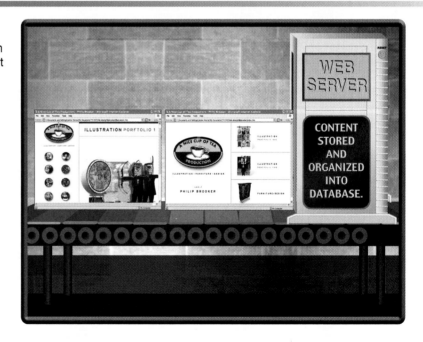

Growth- and Maintenance-Friendly

Dynamic Web sites are built to handle ever-changing content. For example, e-commerce sites typically consist of a few dynamic pages capable of displaying any item in a database. Why? Databases are easier to edit than Web pages. They are also more adaptable — you can sort, find, delete, and add information faster in a database than manually browsing through individual Web pages. With the help of dynamic Web pages, people visiting your site can perform those same tasks.

Get People Involved

Databases are not just about storing content. They can also collect and share data on demand. Web sites like eBay, Yahoo!, Amazon.com, and many others like them are powered by complex databases. Dynamic Web sites enable you to display and receive information from anyone who participates in dynamic areas of your site.

INSTALL A TESTING SERVER

A *testing server*, also called an *application server*, is software that enables a computer to receive connections from Web browsers. This software supports technologies such as ASP, PHP, and ColdFusion, which act as the liaison between your database and your Web pages.

This section assumes that you are running Windows XP Professional. You may need your Windows XP installation disk to install IIS. If IIS is not available for your version of Windows, you can download Personal Web Server from www.microsoft.com instead.

INSTALL A TESTING SERVER

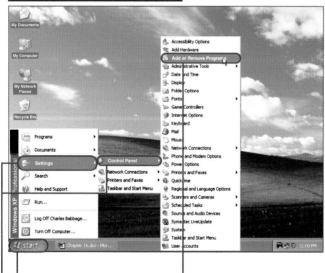

1 Click **Start**.

2 Click **Settings**.

3 Click **Control Panel**.

4 Click **Add or Remove Programs**.

■ The Add or Remove dialog box appears.

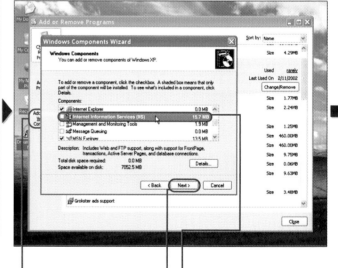

5 Click the **Add/Remove windows components** tab.

■ If Internet Information Services (IIS) is already checked, click **Cancel** and skip to step **13**.

6 Click **Internet Information Services (IIS)** (☐ changes to ☑).

7 Click **Next**.

■ The Windows Components Wizard guides you through the process of installation.

What is a server-side programming language? Are HTML or JavaScript server-side programming languages?

A server-side programming language is a technology that allows logic to be performed before a Web page loads. These technologies are commonly used to extract content from a data source or to perform mathematical logic, which in turn may appear as content between lines of HTML on the Web browser, or the client side. The most popular server-side languages are PHP, ASP, JSP, and Coldfusion.

HTML is a markup language, not a programming language. Its sole purpose is to provide the Web browser with instructions on how to display content on the page. JavaScript is a client-side programming language. It allows you to add brief programs between lines of HTML.

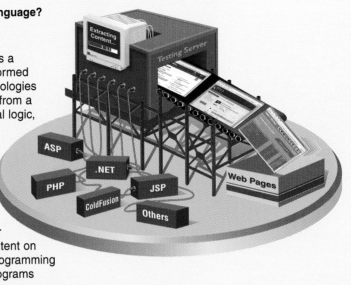

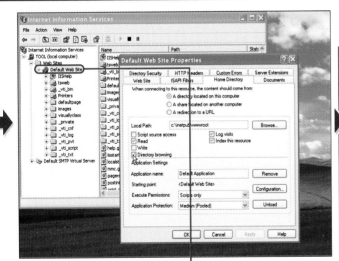

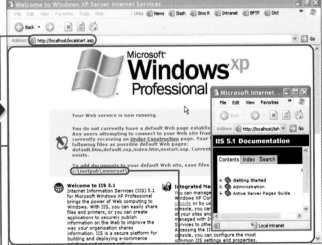

8 Click **Start**.

9 Click **Programs**.

10 Click **Administrative Tools**.

11 Click **Internet Information Services**.

12 In the IIS control panel, right-click and then click **Properties**.

■ IIS allows you to control various Web site settings, such as public folder browsing. For more information on IIS, visit www.microsoft.com.

13 Open your Web browser.

14 Type **http://localhost**.

■ The default testing server page displays, telling you the server was installed correctly.

■ This page also tells you where to move your Web site. The path is usually `c:\inetpub\wwwroot\`.

CREATE A DATABASE CONNECTION

A data source name, or DSN, is used to store database connection settings. Acting as a bookmark, it allows you to conveniently connect to your database from applications without defining a database's settings every time. You must first create a database before defining a DSN.

The task below uses a simple database created with Microsoft Access 2000, a popular database program for Windows.

CREATE A DATABASE CONNECTION

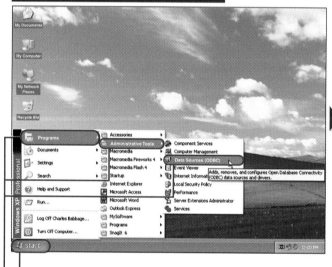

1 Click **Start**.

2 Click **Programs**.

3 Click **Administrative Tools**.

4 Click **Data Sources (ODBC)**.

Note: Windows XP hides folders that you do not regularly use. Click ⊗ to expand hidden items.

■ The ODBC Data Source Administrator dialog box appears.

5 Click the **System DSN** tab.

6 Click **Add**.

■ The Create New Data Source dialog box appears with a list of database drivers.

What is the difference between a System DSN, a User DSN, and a file DSN?

All three types of DSN store the same type of database connectivity information. A System DSN is used when you want every user on the PC to be able to access it. A User DSN only allows specific computer users to access it, usually the user that creates it. Both System and User DSN store the information inside the Registry. A File DSN creates a `.dsn` file, storing the information inside this text file instead of the registry.

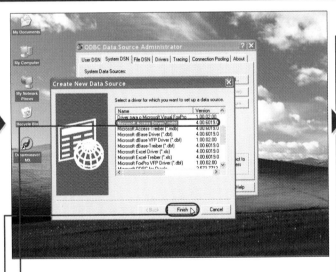

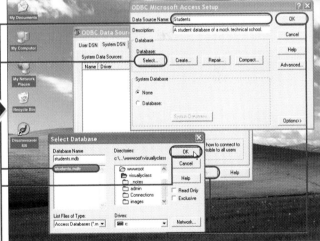

7 Click **Microsoft Access Drivers** from the list.

8 Click **Finish**.

■ The ODBC Microsoft Access Setup dialog box appears.

9 Type a unique, descriptive name for your database.

10 Click **Select**.

11 Click the desired MDB file.

12 Click **OK**.

13 Click **OK** to close the ODBC Microsoft Access Setup dialog box.

14 Click **OK** to close the ODBC Data Source Administrator dialog box.

■ The database connection is created.

283

CONFIGURE A DYNAMIC WEB SITE

Dynamic Web pages do not display database content when opened directly from the Web browser. Thus, you have to configure Dreamweaver to use your testing server. These features create a seamless authoring environment for you.

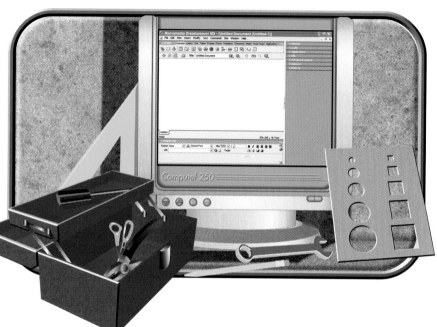

CONFIGURE A DYNAMIC WEB SITE

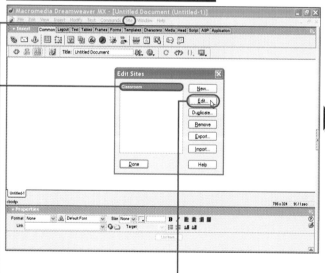

ASSOCIATE THE TESTING SERVER

1 Click **Site**.

2 Click **Edit Sites**.

■ The Edit Sites dialog box appears.

3 Click a site.

4 Click **Edit**.

Note: You must either move all the contents of your site into your testing server area (usually a folder inside c:\inetpub\wwwroot), or configure IIS to point to its current folder. For more about the testing server, see "Install a Testing Server."

5 Click **Testing Server**.

6 Click ⌄ and select **ASP VBScript**.

7 Click ⌄ and select **Local/Network**.

8 Click 📁 to select where your site is located on your computer.

9 Type the path to point to your local site folder. The URL prefix should begin with **http://localhost**.

10 Click **OK**.

Can I just open dynamic Web pages directly through my browser instead of installing a testing server?

No. Web browsers are not capable of understanding server-side programming languages without an application server. Instead of displaying a dynamic Web page, the Web browser displays the programming code that makes up such a page. Think of the testing server as a person that translates the results of this code into HTML, a language your Web browser understands.

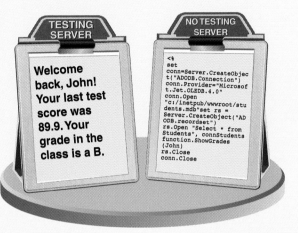

TESTING SERVER

Welcome back, John! Your last test score was 89.9. Your grade in the class is a B.

NO TESTING SERVER

```
<%
set
conn=Server.CreateObjec
t("ADODB.Connection")
conn.Provider="Microsof
t.Jet.OLEDB.4.0"
conn.Open
"c:/inetpub/wwwroot/stu
dents.mdb"set rs =
Server.CreateObject("AD
ODB.recordset")
rs.Open "Select * from
Students", connStudents
function.ShowGrades
(John)
rs.Close
conn.Close
```

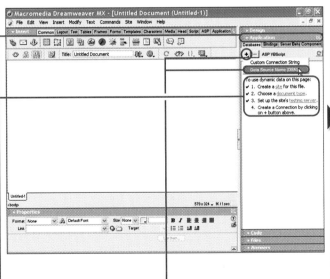

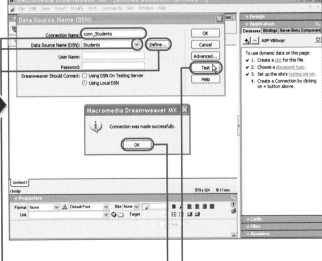

ASSOCIATE AND TEST YOUR CONNECTION

1 Click the **Application** panel.

■ Dreamweaver creates a checklist of items necessary to test your connection.

2 Click any unchecked links.

■ If testing server is not checked, verify that a testing server is associated with your site, and make sure IIS is running properly.

3 Click ➕ and select **Data Source Name (DSN)**.

■ The Data Source Name (DSN) dialog box appears.

4 Type a name for the connection.

5 Click ✔ to select your DSN.

■ You can click **Define** to create, edit, or troubleshoot your connections.

6 Click **Test**.

■ A dialog box appears confirming your connection.

7 Click **OK**.

■ Indicating a working connection, 🗐 appears in your Databases panel.

CREATE A RECORDSET

A *recordset* is a virtual group of items that you request to be retrieved from a database. This selection of data can then be manipulated and/or displayed on the Web page. A recordset can contain one or more items in it.

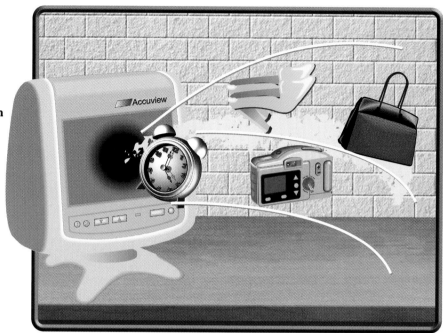

CREATE A RECORDSET

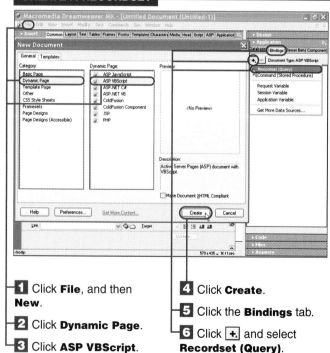

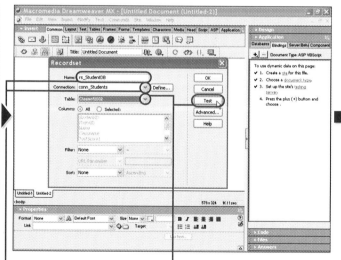

1 Click **File**, and then **New**.

2 Click **Dynamic Page**.

3 Click **ASP VBScript**.

4 Click **Create**.

5 Click the **Bindings** tab.

6 Click ➕ and select **Recordset (Query)**.

■ The Recordset dialog box appears.

7 Type a name for your recordset.

8 Click ⌄ and select your connection.

Note: Your connection is the DSN you assigned to this site. See "Configure a Dynamic Web Site."

9 Click ⌄ to select the table you want to use to create a recordset.

10 Click **Test** to view the recordset you have created.

How do I organize database content on a Web page?

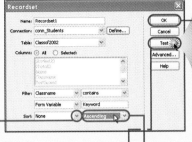

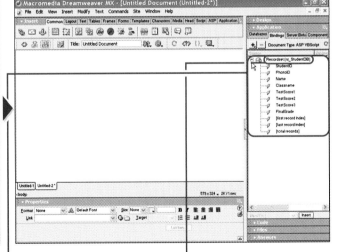

1 Create a recordset by following steps **1** to **9** below.

2 In the Recordset dialog box, click the Sort ⌄ and select the field to sort by.

3 Click the Sort Condition ⌄ and select either **Ascending** or **Descending**.

4 Click Test to preview the organized query.

■ The Test SQL Statement dialog box displays sorted results.

5 Click **OK**.

6 Click **OK** to save your sorted recordset.

■ For information on how to display a recordset on a Web page, see the sections "Work With Live Data" and "Repeat a Region."

■ The Test SQL Statement dialog box appears.

11 Click **OK** to close the test screen.

■ Filtering and sorting are optional. If you do not set either menu, your recordset will display everything in the table as it appears in the database.

12 Click **OK** to close the Recordset dialog box.

■ Dreamweaver creates a recordset within your Bindings panel.

■ You can click ⊞ to expand the column names of your recordset. Lightning bolts (⚡) represent the table columns in your recordset.

■ To modify a recordset, double-click its name from the Bindings panel.

WORK WITH LIVE DATA

With the live data feature in Dreamweaver MX, you can preview database content within the document window.

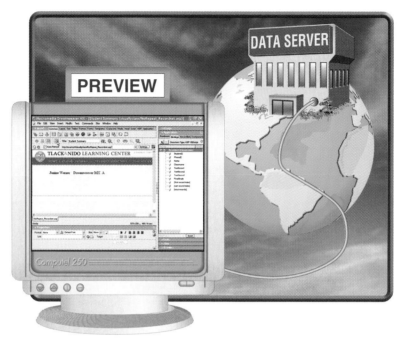

WORK WITH LIVE DATA

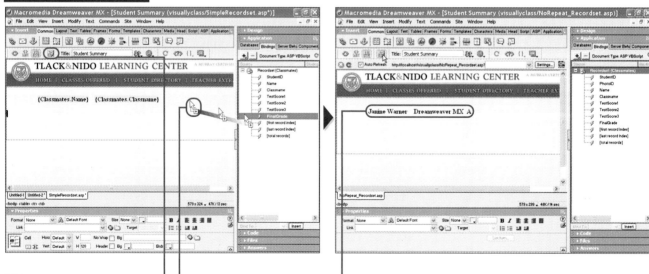

1 Create a recordset.

Note: See the previous section, "Create a Recordset" for more information.

2 Click and drag some items from your recordset onto your document body.

3 Click ▦.

■ Database content appears in place of your labels.

■ If an error dialog box appears, click **More Info** to read FAQs and fixes on Macromedia's technical support Web site.

A *region* is a selected area of a Web page that has been designated to receive a server behavior. Region server behaviors can determine how regions are displayed or repeated. Any selected area of a Web page can become a region; however, some region behaviors have recordset prerequisites. See "Create a Recordset" for more about recordsets.

REPEAT A REGION

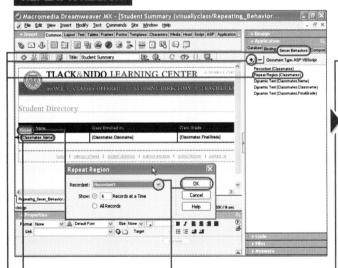
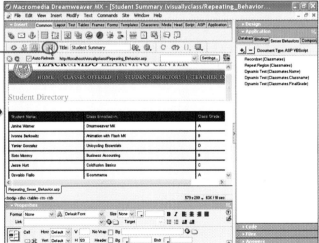

1 Select the region of the page that you want to repeat.

Note: The region you select must contain items from your recordset.

2 Click the **Server Behaviors** tab.

3 Click ➕ and select **Repeat Region**.

■ The Repeat Region dialog box appears.

4 Click ⤵ and select a recordset.

5 Click **OK**.

■ A Repeat tab appears around the region you specified.

6 Repeat steps 1 to 5 for any other regions you want to repeat.

7 Click the LiveData button (▦).

Note: You can also open a Web browser to preview the recordset. See Chapter 2 for more information.

■ The recordset appears in the repeat region areas you specified.

ADD DYNAMIC IMAGES

You can store the path (or URL) of an image file in your database to display images dynamically. The Dynamic Image server behavior will populate the SRC of the IMG tag with the path specified in your database.

ADD DYNAMIC IMAGES

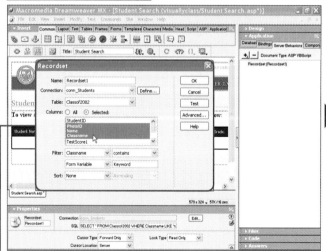

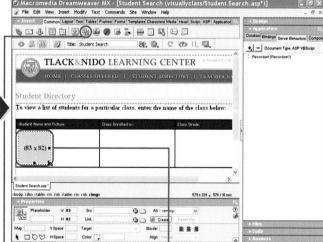

1 Create a recordset, including fields that specify your image paths.

■ When you write the image paths in your database, make them relative to your Web page, not your database file.

■ Do not use absolute paths, for example, `c:\photos\student.jpg`. While this will appear to work on your computer, other PCs will see broken images.

2 Click in the table to indicate the image's placement.

3 Click the Insert Image Placeholder button (📷).

4 In the dialog box, type in values that best fit the images, and click **OK**.

■ If your images are different sizes, delete the values for height and width in the Property inspector or the browser will stretch your images.

■ A placeholder appears.

How do I get pictures into my database?

The most practical way to display images dynamically is to store *where* each image is located, expressed as a directory path and image name. For example, you can create an entry in your database for the graphical file `images\maps\usa\florida\miami.jpg`. Clicking the Insert Image Placeholder button (⊞) inserts an IMG tag with no SRC value. (SRC appears in your Property inspector when an image is selected.) The dynamic image behavior inserts the IMG's SRC value, which tells the Web browser the image location.

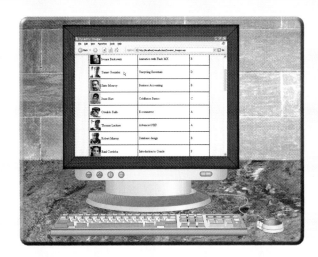

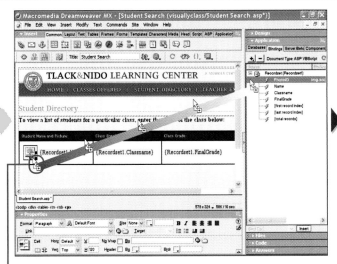

5 Click and drag the image path field from the Bindings panel onto the image placeholder.

■ A lightning bolt (⚡) appears on the image placeholder.

6 Click and drag any other fields from the bindings panel you wish to display onto your page.

7 Preview the page in a Web browser or click ⊞ to test results.

■ The images and selected database content appear on your page.

■ If you encounter broken images, your file names or paths are incorrect. Right-click on the image and choose **Properties** to view the bad URL, and then correct it in your database.

ADD A RECORD

Your new records have been added to the database.

Instead of entering information into your database with desktop software, you can create your own Web page forms that enable you to input content into your database using a Web browser.

ADD A RECORD

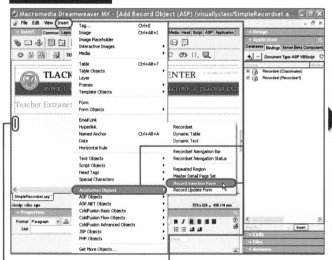

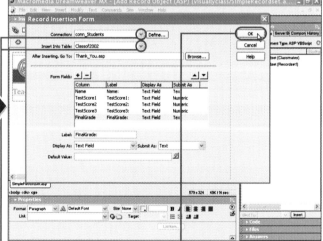

1 Create a recordset containing the tables to which you want to add a record.

Note: See the section "Create a Recordset."

2 Click on the page to indicate the form's placement.

3 Click **Insert**.

4 Click **Application Objects**.

5 Click **Record Insertion Form**.

■ The Record Insertion Form dialog box appears.

6 Click ☑ and select your connection.

7 Click ☑ and select your table.

■ You can click ➕ or ➖ to add or remove items, and ▲ and ▼ to sort the order of the items.

8 Click **OK**.

■ A completed form with highlighted fields and server behaviors already assigned appears.

9 Preview the page in a Web browser.

■ The first record to be added loads.

Similar to the Record
Insertion Form object,
this server object creates
a form that lets you view
content from a database
in form fields, modify
them on the page, and
submit your changes
back to the database.

UPDATE A RECORD

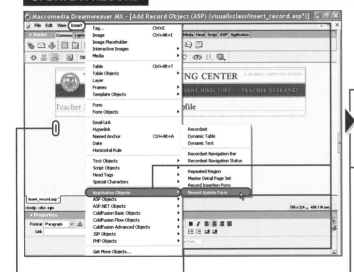

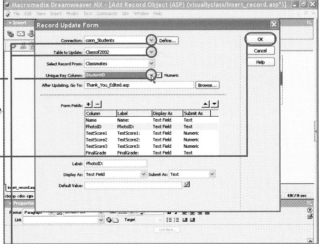

1 Create a recordset
containing the tables to which
you want to update a record.

*Note: See the section "Create a
Recordset."*

2 Click on the page to
indicate the form's
placement.

3 Click **Insert**.

4 Click **Application
Objects**.

5 Click **Record Update
Form**.

■ The Record Update Form
dialog box appears.

6 Click ⌄ and select a
connection and table.

7 Click ⌄ and select a
unique key for the table.

■ You can use a database
program such as Access to
create a unique key.

8 Click **OK**.

■ A highlighted form and
submit button appear.

9 Preview the page in a
Web browser.

■ The first record to be
updated loads.

*Note: See "Add Recordset Paging" to
navigate to other records.*

ADD RECORDSET PAGING

You can display a desired amount of information per page with the server behavior Recordset Paging. Most search engines, for example, limit their pages to twenty results per page. Navigation to the rest of the content is made possible by dynamic links or buttons.

Recordset Paging

ADD RECORDSET PAGING

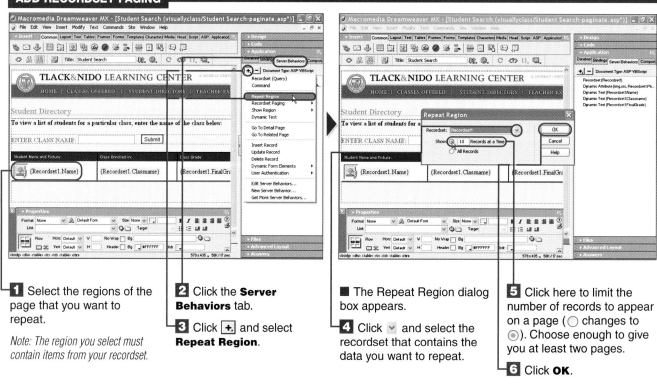

1 Select the regions of the page that you want to repeat.

Note: The region you select must contain items from your recordset.

2 Click the **Server Behaviors** tab.

3 Click ➕ and select **Repeat Region**.

■ The Repeat Region dialog box appears.

4 Click ✓ and select the recordset that contains the data you want to repeat.

5 Click here to limit the number of records to appear on a page (○ changes to ⊙). Choose enough to give you at least two pages.

6 Click **OK**.

How can I protect my add/update record forms from being discovered by hackers?

First, save all the data-entry screens in an obscurely named area of your Web site. For example, avoid storing these files in a folder called "Admin" or anything guessable. Next, utilize simple password authentication. IIS lets you modify a folder's properties to have directory security. Finally, install an SSL certificate so that passwords sent to unlock this directory cannot be intercepted. To purchase a certificate and learn more about SSL, visit www.thawte.com and www.verisign.com.

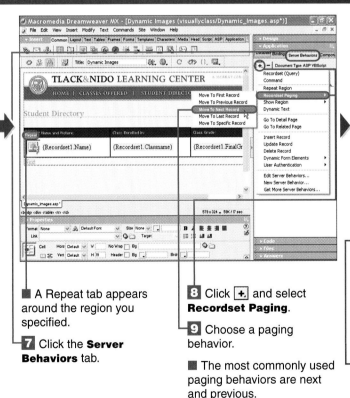

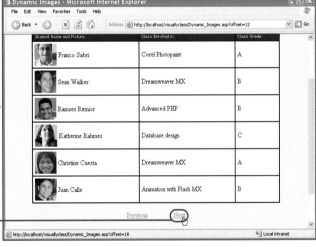

■ A Repeat tab appears around the region you specified.

7 Click the **Server Behaviors** tab.

8 Click ＋ and select **Recordset Paging**.

9 Choose a paging behavior.

■ The most commonly used paging behaviors are next and previous.

■ A highlighted text link appears on your page.

10 Preview the page in a Web browser.

11 Click the links you created to browse your database.

■ Show Region allows you to hide your navigational links when they are not needed. Select your Next button or link, click **Show Region** from the Server Behaviors panel, and then click **Show If Not Last Record**. Click **Show if Not First Record** to hide the previous button.

CREATE A SITE SEARCH

You can create a *site search* to quickly and easily enable Web site visitors to locate records in a database. Creating a site search essentially combines several sections of this chapter. You must create the search form, define the search parameters in a recordset, and then lay out where the search results will appear with the Repeated Region server behavior.

CREATE A SITE SEARCH

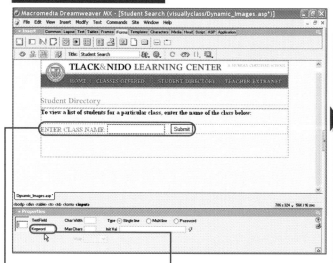

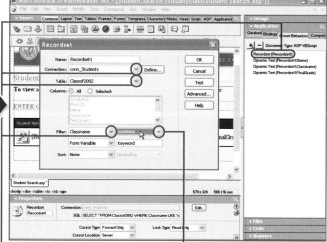

1 Create a new dynamic page using ASP VBScript technology.

Note: See the section "Create a Recordset."

2 Create a form with a text field and a Submit button.

■ The form method should be post by default.

Note: See Chapter 10 for more about creating forms.

3 Type a name for your text field.

4 Click **Recordset**.

5 Click ⌄ and select the table and connection for your site search.

6 Click the **Filter** ⌄ and select the column in the database that matches the field with which you will search.

7 Click ⌄ and select how the filter should behave.

■ Click **contains** for flexible searching. Click **choose** when you only want exact matches.

**How do I create a site search that
indexes my site's Web pages like a
search engine?**

There are no page indexing features
packaged with Dreamweaver MX.
However, there are third party
extensions you can install, plus manual
indexing methods. Visit http://exchange.
macromedia.com and search on the
term "search". Atomz Search and Deva
Tools are among the best third party
indexing extensions. To create your own
index, add a table in your database that
contains URLs and keywords about
your pages, and then create a site
search that looks at those
keywords. Your repeated region can
then display the URLs to those
relevant pages in your database just
like a search engine would.

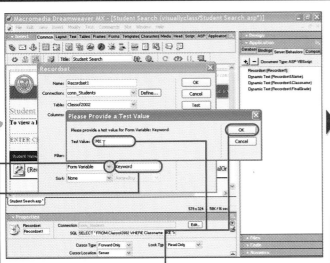

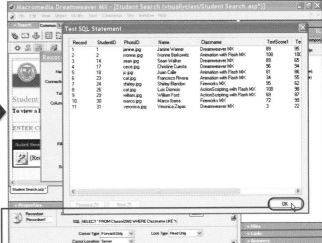

-8 Click 🔽 and select **Form
Variable** as your filter style.

-9 Type the name of your
text field as the filter style
variable, using the name
of the field you created in
step **3**.

10 Click **Test**.

■ The Please Provide a Test
Value dialog box appears.

11 Type in a search term
you know is in the specified
area of your database.

12 Click **OK**.

■ The Test SQL Statement
dialog box displays filtered
results. In this example, the
test value was the word MX.

13 Click **OK** to close the
Test SQL Statement
dialog box.

14 Click **OK** in the
Recordset dialog box to save
your filtered recordset.

CONTINUED

CREATE A SITE SEARCH

A site search is made possible by formulating a recordset with a dynamic value set by a site user. The form allows the Web site visitor to input what the recordset filters. The user submits the form, the server behaviors perform the filter script, and the filtered data is returned as a recordset to display on the Web page.

CREATE A SITE SEARCH (CONTINUED)

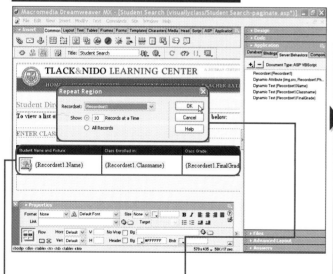

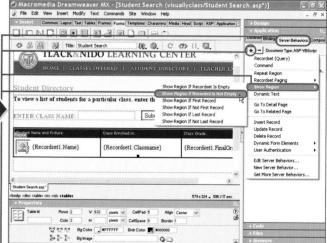

15 Create a table with the fields from the recordset that you want to display as search results.

16 Apply the Repeat Region server behavior to your table.

Note: See the section "Repeat a Region" for more information.

17 Select your repeat region table.

18 Click the **Server Behaviors** tab.

19 Click ➕ and select **Show Region**.

20 Click **Show Region If Recordset Is Not Empty**.

■ This step hides the empty table when the first page loads and prevents empty recordset errors.

■ A dialog box appears. Confirm your recordset by selecting it from the menu.

21 Click **OK**.

How can I create a site search for a photo gallery?

A photo gallery site search relies on keywords associated with a photo, which must be entered into a database along with the path to the image. First, set up a column in the database and enter keywords associated with each image. Next, follow the steps from "Add Dynamic Images" to set your gallery search results region. Lastly, follow the concepts in the Site Search task, setting the recordset filter to search your keyword column in your database.

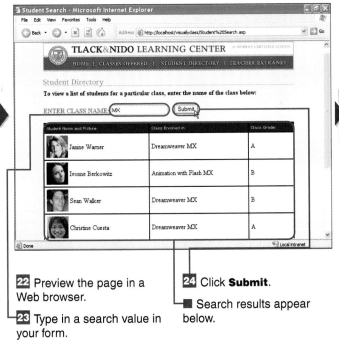

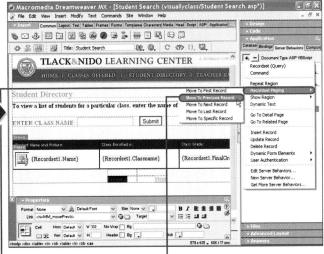

22 Preview the page in a Web browser.

23 Type in a search value in your form.

24 Click **Submit**.

■ Search results appear below.

■ You can apply the Recordset Paging server behavior to aid in navigating through a long list of search results. See the section "Add Recordset Paging."

■ Remember to apply the appropriate **Show Region** behaviors to your Next and Previous links. Otherwise, both these links will show up before a search is performed.

INDEX

INDEX